THE POLITICS OF CODIFICATION

The Lower Canadian Civil Code of 1866

Patrons of the Society

Aird & Berlis
Blake, Cassels & Graydon
Davies, Ward & Beck
Holden Day Wilson
McCarthy Tétrault
Osler, Hoskin & Harcourt
The Harweg Foundation
Tory Tory DesLauriers & Binnington
Weir & Foulds

The Society also thanks
The Law Foundation of Ontario
and the Law Society of Upper Canada
for their continuing support.

The Politics
of Codification

The Lower Canadian
Civil Code of 1866

BRIAN YOUNG

The Osgoode Society for Canadian Legal History

To Lee, Cameron, and Gregory

© McGill-Queen's University Press 1994
ISBN 0-7735-1235-7
Legal deposit fourth quarter 1994
Bibliothèque nationale du Québec

Printed in Canada on acid-free paper

This book has been published with the help of a grant
from the Social Science Federation of Canada, using funds provided by the Social
Sciences and Humanities Research Council of Canada.

McGill-Queen's University Press is grateful to the Canada Council
for support of its publishing program.

Canadian Cataloguing in Publication Data

Young, Brian J., 1940–
The politics of codification: the lower Canadian civil code of 1866
(Studies in the history of Quebec = Études d'histoire du Québec)
Includes bibliographical references and index.
ISBN 0-7735-1235-7
1. Civil law – Political aspects – Quebec (Province). 2. Civil law – Quebec (Province) –
History. 3. Quebec (Province). Civil code of Lower Canada.
I. Osgoode Society for Canadian Legal History. II. Title.
III. Series: Studies in the history of Quebec.
KEQ214.52.Y69 1994   346.714'009   C94-900701-3

Contents

Tables

Illustrations

Foreword

THE OSGOODE SOCIETY
FOR CANADIAN LEGAL HISTORY

The purpose of The Osgoode Society for Canadian Legal History is to encourage research and writing in the history of Canadian law. The Society, which was incorporated in 1979 and is registered as a charity, was founded at the initiative of the Honourable R. Roy McMurtry, former attorney-general for Ontario, and officials of the Law Society of Upper Canada. Its efforts to stimulate the study of legal history in Canada include a research support program, a graduate student research assistance program, and work in the fields of oral history and legal archives. The Society publishes (at the rate of about one a year) volumes of interest to the Society's members that contribute to legal-historical scholarship in Canada, including studies of the courts, the judiciary, and the legal profession, biographies, collections of documents, studies in criminology and penology, accounts of great trials, and work in the social and economic history of the law.

Current directors of The Osgoode Society for Canadian Legal History are Jane Banfield, Marion Boyd, Brian Bucknall, Archie Campbell, J. Douglas Ewart, Martin Friedland, John Honsberger, Kenneth Jarvis, Paul Lamek, Allen Linden, Colin McKinnon, Roy McMurtry, Brendan O'Brien, Peter Oliver, James Spence, and Richard Tinsley. The annual report and information about membership may be obtained by writing The Osgoode Society for Canadian Legal History, Osgoode Hall, 130 Queen Street West, Toronto, Ontario, Canada M5H 2N6. Members receive the annual volume published by the Society.

The Osgoode Society for Canadian Legal History is delighted to be join-ing McGill-Queen's University Press in publishing this important study of the origins of Quebec's Civil Code. Its author, Brian Young, has pub-lished extensively on the history of nineteenth-century Quebec. Timed to coincide with the implementation of Quebec's revised Civil Code, *The Politics of Codification: The Lower Canadian Civil Code of 1866* emphasizes the political compromises embodied in the code between traditional cul-ture and society and pressures from mercantile and industrial élites. It is a timely study of how a society's legal culture becomes an essential part of the politics of accommodation, contributing to the entrenchment of pluralism in nineteenth-century Quebec. As such, it makes a significant contribution to our understanding of the current Canadian condition.

R. Roy McMurtry
President

Peter N. Oliver
Editor-in-Chief

Preface

This work is intended to provide an entry for the generalist into the study of nineteenth-century Quebec legal history, thus breaking down the insularity of that discipline. And although materialist history has fallen on rocky times, I strongly support the view that legal historians must recognize the centrality of law to class relations. Nor is the history of a codification that took place more than a century ago somehow foreign to contemporary concerns in Quebec over individual rights, gender, and language. The process of codification itself is entirely relevant given Quebec's new Civil Code, which came into effect in January 1994 after several decades of recodification.

Why the 'politics' of codification? I came to this study, not as a specialist in legal history, but as someone interested in institutions, the bourgeoisie, business and political history, and the development of the state in Quebec. Codification and the circumstances surrounding it confirm my own sense of history as a complex process involving personality, gender, and economic and social condition. From this perspective, the Lower Canadian Civil Code of 1866 was a political act – part of a larger process that included responsible government, Confederation, and the dismantling of seigneurial tenure – marking the transition in Lower Canada from a pre-industrial condition in the late eighteenth century to one dominated by capitalist relations a century later. As such, it was integral to a fundamental transformation of Lower Canadian society in which the autonomy, custom, and privilege of feudal relations gave way to strong central government, universal institutions, and a bilingual legal system that buttressed individual rights, freedom of contract, and equality before the law.

The codification process – which culminated in the Civil Code of 1866 and the Code of Civil Procedure (1867) – was never simple. The emphasis given to contract law was a natural companion to the dismantling of the feudal property relations of seigneurialism. At the same time, codification affected the family, marriage, inheritance, and the legal position of women – intensely sensitive areas in which old French law, and particularly the Custom of Paris, had assured coherence, social stability, and the maintenance of traditional forms of power. The successful harmonization of legal cultures rooted in feudal and capitalist conceptions of society was the essential political achievement of the codifiers.

In the dynamic of codification, I reject the view of the Civil law of Quebec as somehow feudal, reactionary, and alien to Canadian liberal democracy, what Arthur Lower, describing Quebec law in the post-conquest period, called a 'legal cesspool.' Jean-Gabriel Castel gave credence to this interpretation when he described the Civil Code as having given 'a legal expression to the spirit of conservatism of the French Canadian people ... In the Code, the French Canadians found a new basis for self-expression, a new pride, a monument to keep alive the spirit of their ancestors ...'[1] More recently, David Bercuson and Barry Cooper argue that Quebec nationalists have, historically, not respected the politics 'of bargaining and mutual accommodation.'[2] The Civil law tradition, as interpreted herein, is seen rather as an inherent and original part of Canadian federalism. And, far from being an anachronism, the codification process in Lower Canada had important counterparts in the codification movements of Germany, France, and the United States.

Codification was the result of two decades of collaboration between important elements in the anglophone and francophone élites in Lower Canada, and it helps us resituate the legal power of the anglophone bourgeoisie in nineteenth-century Quebec. The code's central ideological parts were written in English by an American-born judge whose political and intellectual stature in the anglophone community was epitomized by his position as the first chancellor of McGill University. Codification, to the disappointment of promoters among moderate French Canadian nationalists in the pre-rebellion period, did not emerge as a monument to the scientific and legal accuracy of the French language; instead, the Civil Code became a symbol of Lower Canadian bilingualism.

With its compromises between customary and Civil law authorities, languages, and the legal traditions of the ethnic minority, the merchant community, and canon law, and with its definitions of civil status and family relations, the Civil Code of Lower Canada was an important part of state formation. Codification and its enveloping legal culture was also, as Max Weber reminded us, an important element in legal bureaucratization, a process that included professionalization of the bar, the establishment of two law faculties, the growth of the law as a 'science,' and the establishment of a centralized and universal legal system across Lower Canada's diverse regional and ethnic precincts.[3]

The first chapters of the book establish the legal landscape, particularly the incoherence and polyjuralism of both property and commercial law. Particular attention is paid to the origins of the codification movement before 1837–8 among moderate French Canadian nationalists who linked Civil law reform to their professional, linguistic, national, and capitalist aspirations.

Acceptable in pre-industrial society, Lower Canada's private law system – essentially unorganized since the conquest – was an increasing liability in a modernizing state with an evolving capitalistic economy characterized by corporations, industrial worksites, wage labour, and fundamental changes in attitudes to both property and the individual.

Chapter 3 sets codification in the political conjuncture of the 1840s and 1850s – decades characterized by the autocratic measures of the Special Council and by the bureaucratization and rationalization of the state, the successful implementation of bourgeois democracy, and the negotiations that led to Canadian federation. A critical result of the changing political scene was the dismantling of seigneurial tenure. Its breakdown as a system of landed and social relations and its subordination to the ideology surrounding freehold tenure is interpreted here as an essential precursor to codification, since it removed feudal impediments to reform and emphasized social relationships that gave priority to exchange and individual property rights.

Alongside these larger political and structural considerations is an examination in chapters 3 and 4 of the key individuals of codification: Attorney General George-Étienne Cartier and the three members of the codification commission, René-Édouard Caron, Augustin-Norbert Morin, and Charles Dewey Day. Of particular importance is their training in the Civil law, their class affiliations, and their professional relationships in the urban, institutional, and legal communities of Montreal and Quebec.

Also of critical importance is the close links between the codifiers' public careers and their family, home, health, and social life.

Chapters 5 and 6 treat the politics of codification during the years 1857–66, including formation of the commission, the actual work of the codifiers, and approval of their draft code by the legislature. Here, ideology and the role of the official opposition, of the Roman Catholic élite, and of the Protestant community were important as the codifiers prepared a code that might harmonize with Lower Canada's institutional, social, and economic realities. Legal authorities for the Civil Code were of course crucial, and the commission avoided liberal French thinkers like Cambacérès in favour of pre-revolutionary legal intellectuals like Jean Domat and Robert-Joseph Pothier. Their focus on Roman and customary French law was important in the complicated legal task of merging traditional social attitudes with an evolving capitalist society.

The essential theme of this work is the codifiers' use of the past to formulate a code that gave centrality to freedom of contract through the law of Obligations and new definitions of delivery while reinforcing historic concepts of social organization which included inheritance, patriarchy, marital authority, and female access to public space. The case study of female public traders in chapter 7 is one example of how Quebec remained a distinct legal constituency in Confederation. Only in our lifetimes – women's suffrage in Quebec (1940), the right of married women to administer and dispose of their own property (1964), the Quebec Charter of Human Rights and Freedoms (1975) which recognized the equality of spouses in marriage, and important amendments to the Civil Code in 1977 and 1989 that reformed concepts of paternal authority and family patrimony – have these fundamental relationships been challenged. The massacre of fourteen women at Montreal's École Polytechnique in December 1989 reminds us of the social trauma of this process.

The chronology, placed at the end of the text, is arranged to show a broader periodization. It is intended to give a sense of the physical, of time and place, a broader glimpse of the relationship between the intellectual work of codifying the law and the codifiers' world of family, home, profession, class, and community. Raymond Williams describes this aptly as a 'wider system' in which 'the relations are not only of ideas and experiences, but of rent and interest, of situation and power.'[4] The chronology emphasizes the code's antecedents in Roman law, French customary law, royal decrees, commercial usage, and canon law. The chronology also illustrates the conjuncture of codification with the collapse of seigneurial relations in favour of liberal ideology centred on freedom of contract.

A NOTE ON LANGUAGE

Passages in French have been systematically translated into English. Some of the terms used are specific to Quebec. Indeed, anglophones in the francophone environment of Quebec have developed a distinct Civil law language, and terms (such as *substitution*, Obligations, *tradition*) are explained in brief in the text when they first occur. I have largely relied on the *Private Law Dictionary and Bilingual Lexicons*, by Robert P. Kouri et al., or on the Civil Code for the definitions. When I refer to 'Civil law,' I am using the careful definitions of John Brierley. He uses 'Civil law' to separate the Romano-Germanic system on which Quebec's code is based from 'civil law' which refers to any body of private law rules. He uses the same distinction between 'Common law,' a legal tradition based on English law, and a broader 'common law' referring to laws common to the whole area of the state (including those with Civil law systems) as opposed to local customs.[5]

ACKNOWLEDGMENTS

The research and writing of this book was facilitated by a sabbatical leave from McGill University, by funds provided by a team grant from the Fonds pour la formation de chercheurs et l'aide à la recherche (FCAR), and by a research grant – including a research-leave stipend – from the Social Sciences and Humanities Research Council of Canada. Given on-going cutbacks to Canadian funding bodies like SSHRC, I must emphasize the importance of this research aid in providing the time and means for historians to research and write: books and major research projects cannot be accomplished on weekends or in evenings after teaching.

Librarians at the Law Library of McGill University, particularly Louise Robertson, were very helpful in making the superb rare book collection available to me. Two important collections of codification papers are in the Séminaire de Québec and the Séminaire de Saint-Hyacinthe. In the archives of the latter, Jean-Nöel Dion was particularly gracious. Michel Morin of the Université d'Ottawa law faculty directed me to judges' reports in the National Archives of Canada.

As so often before, friends in the Montreal History Group – Bettina Bradbury, Colin Coates, Don Fyson, Peter Gossage, Katherine Harvey, Evelyn Kolish, Tamara Myers, Mary Anne Poutanen, Alan Stewart, and Eric Whan – read parts of the manuscript, commented, cajoled, pushed, and generally helped me over the finish line. At McGill-Queen's, Philip

Cercone and Joan McGilvray ride herd, bringing order to a creative press and obstinate authors; the strong support for this project – and for their larger contribution to the study of Canadian legal history – from Peter Oliver, Marilyn MacFarlane, and The Osgoode Society for Canadian Legal History is much appreciated. It is worth waiting in line to have Mary McDougall Maude as one's editor; this is not the first of my manuscripts to benefit enormously from her skills, experience, and wisdom.

John Dickinson offered friendship and cryptic criticism. Blaine Baker first showed me the legal history treasures buried in the McGill Law Library; his interest in intellectual elements of the law and his patience as a teacher make him a unique colleague. In various corners of the McGill campus, John Brierley regularly sat down with me, pointing out the obvious to him and revelatory to me. His own multiple works form essential reading on codification and Quebec legal culture; his fastidiousness and broad understanding – along with his tolerance for competing views – permitted me to improve my text greatly.

Despite the efforts of these friends, errors and interpretative 'snafus' remain entirely my responsibility.

The Politics of Codification

The feudal system like many other things, has outlived its age;
   for there is a decreptitude in human institutions as in the human frame.
   Each fulfills a mission, and when, its purpose is accomplished, must give
   way to the new ideas, and the new men which time and social progress,
   or at least social change require.
Judge Day to Seigneurial Commission (1856)[1]

As a means of always being natural and to capture tone in the writing of
   la Chartreuse, I read two or three pages of the Civil Code every morning.
Stendhal to H. de Balzac (1840)[2]

1

The Legal Landscape

The function of the law is to establish general maxims in a large framework –
to establish principles fertile in consequence without going into the details
that each issue can engender.

French codifier Jean-Étienne-Marie Portalis[1]

The laws are very closely related to the way that various peoples procure their
subsistence. There must be a more extensive code of laws for a people
attached to commerce and the sea than for a people satisfied to cultivate
their lands. There must be a greater one for the latter than for a people who
live by their herds. There must be a greater one for these last than for a
people who live by hunting.

Montesquieu, *Spirit of the Laws* (1748)[2]

In 1859 – the year that the new Victoria Bridge permitted rail transportation from the Atlantic coast at Maine, through Lower Canada, and
across Upper Canada to the Michigan border – three middle-aged men
began meeting in Quebec City to codify the Civil law of Lower Canada.
Although of different ethnic backgrounds, René-Édouard Caron,
Augustin-Norbert Morin, and Charles Dewey Day shared a common
social class, profession, and position on the bench. Freed by the state
from their judicial duties and setting their own timetable, they continued to meet over five years; they had their own clerks, library, and
budget. And although codification was closely linked to legislative

power, the actual process was distanced from politicians, journalists, and the public.

Once drafts of law titles had been prepared, the codifiers convened, spreading large, lined sheets in front of them. The columns they filled in corresponded roughly to past, present, and future. Their discussions ranged from the lofty to the picayune, from the technical to the spiritual. On inspired days they would have agreed with French codifier Jean-Étienne-Marie Portalis that 'laws are not pure expressions of power,' but rather 'they are acts of wisdom, justice and reason' in which the lawmaker exercises less an authority than 'a sacrament.' On days of arthritis and fatigue, their offices rang with rancour and minority reports.[3]

In consolidating the old and in writing new law, the codifiers' source materials ranged across Roman, customary, and statutory jurisprudence; as is always the case, their own life experience, economic interests, social class, ethnicity, and gender formed vital ingredients of their work. None of the three was from the landed or bureaucratic ranks that had dominated Lower Canada before 1837. Nor, although one was a law school dean and another a university chancellor, were they legal intellectuals in the tradition of Portalis of France, Germany's Friedrich Carl von Savigny, or the Americans John Marshall or Joseph Story. Before becoming judges, the Lower Canadian codifiers had been practitioners of commercial rather than academic law. Far from esoteric, their ideology fitted easily into the political and intellectual consensus that characterized the dominant faction of the Lower Canadian élite after the collapse of the Rebellions of 1837–8. Its legal essence was double-barrelled: a social conservatism centred on the family, and an economic liberalism that gave priority to the individual and to the rights of contract and property.

It followed from this, and not at all paradoxically, that their discourse and authorities were both patriarchal and capitalist. Starting with contract law, they codified across the spectrum of civil relations: persons, property, succession, and marriage. They spliced discussions of vibrant social import like civil status and paternal authority into technical debates over mortgages and bottomry. In 1865, the legislature, with only minor modifications, enacted their draft as the *Civil Code of Lower Canada*, and a year later, with even fewer changes, their draft code of civil procedure was passed.

A code is a comprehensive, systematic, and written statement of a legal corpus, such as civil relations, criminality, commerce, or slavery.[4] Invariably part of a larger process of universalizing and centralizing law, a code normally abrogates customs, case law, statutes, and other existing laws.

Codes of law have a long history, with the Theodosian (438 AD) and Justinian codes (529–34) forming essential lodes for European intellectuals. In the modern world, codes have frequently been associated with the development of the centralized and unified nation-state. The five codes of Napoleonic France (1804–11) are the best-known examples of European codification; the Louisiana Civil Code of 1808 (amended in 1824) became the flagship of American codification. The German Civil Code, so important not only for the newly formed Germany but for other central European states, was enacted in 1896.

By its very nature, codification is a highly sensitive process, touching the quick of a society's definition of self and, in the case of a civil code, of authority in private relations. It is this ordering, this defining, this inevitable trespass into the intimacy of normally private family, marriage, and property relations that makes Civil law of particular interest to the social and economic historian. In Quebec, competing Civil and Common law traditions inherited from France and England, coexisting feudal and free-and-common-socage landholding systems with their accompanying social values, and the political imperative to create a modern, unified, and capitalist state provided fertile soil for codification schemes that promised order and authority across diverse ethnic, class, and regional constituencies. Within years of the British conquest, Attorney General Francis Maseres provoked a crisis with his recommendaton of a civil code (1768) which, while apparently respecting New France's landholding and succession practices, would have united French and British legal traditions; for its part, the Seminary of Montreal proposed a codification that would not involve significant change.[5] Joseph-François Perrault's *Rural Code* (1832) was part of the attempt by French Canadian intellectuals in the pre-rebellion period to instruct the populace – in this case the rural anglophone and francophone population – through application of a code of religious and civic duties. In 1870, the *Code des curés* provided guidelines for priests; in the same decade the Quebec legislature initiated a codification of its provincial statutes. The Criminal Code of 1892 reformed criminal law on a pan-Canadian basis.

The Civil Code of Lower Canada (1866) and the accompanying Code of Civil Procedure (1867) resulted from the particular political dynamic of the Union period, 1840–67. The colony's system of private law was essentially a legacy from imperial authorities in Paris and London; its consolidation – the resolution of inconsistencies and the incorporation of new law into a written code applicable across Lower Canada – was engineered by the local political élite, which took power in the late 1840s.

Like responsible government, creation of a federal structure, and the establishment of state bureaucracies, codification was a building-block of state formation. It was therefore not at all coincidental that preparation of a simple, written code, theoretically accessible and understandable by all citizens, coincided with the implementation of universal education.

PERIODIZATION

These changing perspectives on codification emphasize that periodization – the time framework given to historical explanation – is of decisive importance to the legal historian.[6] This work insists on a longer view of codification in a changing ideological horizon that includes struggles over feudalism, historic concepts of property, the meaning of the French Revolution, and the rise of the bourgeois state. While Canadian legal intellectuals undoubtedly did not join Stendhal in beginning their workday with readings from the Napoleonic Code, they understood the implications of being heirs and arbiters of legal cultures stretching from Rome, to natural law philosophy, the Custom of Paris, Napoleon, and the New World. Alongside their daily round of caucus and courts, of defending their patriarchal, trading, and property interests as fathers, jurists, and heirs, Attorney General George-Étienne Cartier and the codifiers belonged to an international world of legal ideas. That world saw French codifier Jean-Étienne-Marie Portalis buried in the Pantheon, and included libraries where Justinian was read in Latin and where eighteenth-century legal intellectuals Sir William Blackstone and Robert-Joseph Pothier were common coin, where Montesquieu and Bentham constituted familiar weekend reading, and where the legal élite sought to impress their peers by contributing European legal tomes to the Advocates' Library in Montreal.[7] And during the early Victorian period, when codification was actually accomplished, Lower Canada was marked by changing views of nature and society. Science, education, and law, for example, were profoundly influenced by a rationalism that expressed itself in a willingness to collect, to codify and inventory, and to build new systems.[8]

Codification, in its Lower Canadian form, resulted from a particular mid-century conjuncture of politics, jurisprudence, and human agency. Each of the codifiers, as well as sitting on the bench, had important legislative and executive credentials. Representing the anglophone élite, Charles Dewey Day had roots in the Montreal merchant community; his power emanated from McGill University, the bench, and the Montreal bar. After Chief Justice Louis-Hippolyte LaFontaine had refused a place on the commission, Day became the central figure in codification, writing Obligations and most of the commercial sections. A prominent commercial lawyer, René-Édouard Caron acted as chair of the Codification Commission preparing important sections such as Persons and Successions. A skilled arbiter, Caron appears to have moderated social and ideological differences separating Day and Augustin-Norbert Morin. A sensitive individual, committed Catholic, and veteran of political wars stretching back to the 1820s, Morin was happiest in the village of Sainte-Adèle which he had founded and where he would die. By the time the Codification Commission was established, his body was prey to arthritis and his spirit blunted by political wars over clergy reserves and seigneurial reform. Further, his sharp mind, which had enlivened nationalist newspapers and government benches for three decades, had been little directed towards the labyrinth of contract and commercial law.

A periodization shading back across the six decades to the Napoleonic Civil Code of 1804, and even further to the Quebec Act, the conquest, and the society of New France, also permits a strong sense of the gradualism that characterized legal change, of the relation between law reform and economic process, and of the careful compromise between respect for tradition and connection to present.[9] Alongside new social, educational, workplace, and political structures, there persisted the traditional merchant, religious, and legal élites. Pre-industrial institutions and ideology – the church, seigneurial tenure, and traditional gender and class relations, such as those of master and servant – were not swept away but were blended into new social contracts. Old law, with its roots in sources such as the Custom of Paris or canon law, remained important in ensuring hierarchy and social stability by assisting in the persistence of family and larger social relations based on natural law, particularly patriarchy; at the same time, contract law was of increasing importance in a society with expanding capitalist activities.

This longer periodization also emphasizes that codification was a process whose potential was perceived differently by competing social groups at particular historical moments. In the first decade after the British conquest, codification was proposed by an anti-papist and Cambridge-educated attorney general who had read law in the Inner Temple. Early in the nineteenth century, codification was promoted by moderate French Canadian nationalists who saw it as a defence of seigneurialism, church, and language. After the Rebellions of 1837–8, it was co-opted by a younger élite, less equivocal in their commitment to capitalist values. From this perspective, the Lower Canadian Civil Code of 1866 did not represent a rupture between a golden pre-industrial Custom of Paris and a post-Confederation legal environment in which French civil jurisprudence was chronically assaulted by Anglo-Saxon traditions. Rather, codification formed part of a longer dialectic over class, ethnicity, and power in Quebec.[10] While this does not deny a certain autonomy to the law or the possibility that reform might emanate from practical, on-site problems faced by practitioners, it does insist on the historicity of codification, its symbolic value, and its weight, as John Brierley described it, as 'the fundamental reference point from which other legislation proceeds.'[11]

While no such scheme is perfect, I divide the century before codification into three major periods. Law in the pre-Napoleonic period was characterized by the persistence of customary law alongside expanding regional and national legal traditions. The second period, four decades from the Napoleonic Code in 1804 to the 1840s, saw increasing ethnic and social hostilities. It was marked by the rapid expansion of the francophone professional bourgeoisie, by British immigration, and by the impotence of seigneurial and clerical ideologies to resist accelerating capitalist relationships in city, town, and countryside. Codification occurred in the third period, the two decades before Confederation. Politically, Lower Canada, its bourgeois democracy entrenched in the 1840s, was on the threshold of integration into a larger federal system in which francophones would form a cultural minority. At the same time, the collapse of seigneurialism, the expansion of canals, railways, and large worksites, and the chartering of financial institutions, like banks and insurance corporations seeking legal protection for their capital, bore witness to the St Lawrence Valley's engagement in the transition to industrial capitalism. Finally, the codification period was characterized by evolving state, institutional, and professional structures, all of which aggravated Lower Canada's social tensions.

In the first period – from the Conquest to the Napoleonic Wars – the anglophone élite, particularly the merchants, pressed for the imposition of English law in matters affecting commerce and succession practices. Chief Justice William Hey, for example, opposed Governor Carleton's plan for the general use of French Civil law urging in 1775 that it be restricted to family matters.[12] Changes in the rules of inheritance under the Quebec Act of 1774 permitting individuals to bequeath alienable property by Canadian or English law (freedom of testation), and the application in 1777 of English rules of evidence in commercial cases were perceived by English merchants as only partial victories, since the main thrust of the Quebec Act was to respect French religious and customary

This British political cartoon, 'the Contrast, 1793,' by Thomas Rowlandson illustrates effectively attitudes during the French Revolution of the anglophone intellectual and merchant élite in Lower Canada. The emphasis on English inheritance laws, property rights, and individual autonomy were persistent themes.

institutions. A 1775 merchant petition called for the preservation of English law in 'matters of navigation, commerce, and personal contracts,' and in 1784 merchant James McGill complained that commerce was being destroyed by 'anarchy and confusion' in the Civil law. By the 1790s the anglophone élite was digging in its heels with what Murray Greenwood describes as a 'garrison mentality.'[13]

The period from codification in Napoleonic France to that in Lower Canada several decades later coincided with the establishment of large land companies, such as the British American Land Company (1832) in the Eastern Townships, of financial institutions like the Bank of Montreal (1817) and the Quebec office of the Standard Life Assurance Company (1833), of steamships on the St Lawrence (1809), of completion of the Lachine Canal in the 1820s, and of Canada's first railway, the Champlain and St Lawrence (1836).

This development fostered a broad coalition of urban land speculators, industrial producers, timber entrepreneurs, commercial lawyers, millers, financiers, large employers, and development-minded seigneurs, who protested against the system of general and secret hypothecs, the confusion engendered by the colony's motley legal forms, and the absence of judicial authority in the Gaspé, Ottawa Valley, and Eastern Townships. Francophone professionals, seigneurs, and entrepreneurs, whose careers, seigneuries, and capital were endangered by this legal incoherence, were among these critics. Legal intellectuals like Denis-Benjamin Viger, for example, called for Civil law reform early in the century.

Anglophones were particularly vehement in their complaints about the patchwork nature of Civil law, particularly those ensuring property titles, and the lack of an English version of the Custom of Paris. Although some seigneurs were active in industrial production and although many seigneuries were bought by anglophones, seigneurialism and Civil law were often lumped together as feudal phenomena obstructing progress. Milling monopolies, mutation levies on land improvements, and seigneurial control over waterways and power sites offended many capitalists. Some emphasized that maintaining the seigneurial system would inevitably mean reinforcement of French marriage, succession, and mortgage practices.[14] The expanding anglophone population in the Eastern Townships (in which lands were held in free and common socage) was another important source of vociferous dissent against French customary law.

Although abortive, the Union bill (1822) and the Canada Tenures Act (1825) represented bold attempts by the imperial parliament to overturn the Civil law system through the union of Upper and Lower Canada, the dismantling of seigneurialism, and the subordination of the French language. The Canada Tenures Act was particularly threatening in its provision that freehold lands would be governed by 'the Law of England' in matters of alienation, inheritance, and dower.[15]

This campaign to expand English law and the legal pluralism of Lower Canada provoked a sharpening nationalist response, one wing of which called for codification of the Civil law. By the late 1820s and particularly in the 1830s, there was consensus among French Canadian legal intellectuals in favour of a strengthening of the Civil law, of the need for immigrants and peasants to be instructed on the responsibilities of the citizen, and of the necessity to unify the law so that inheritance, notarial, and landholding practices became uniform across Lower Canada.

In the pre-rebellion period, nationalists drew a strong link between Civil law and language. During the Revolution, the French had fastened on the relationship between language and law. A decree of Thermidor II (20 July 1794) enforced monolingualism in Republican law: all public acts and private contracts were, under pain of imprisonment, to be written in French.[16] This process was reinforced a decade later as the Civil Code became a centre-piece in the Napoleonic process of rationalization: it was a mighty occasion to rid Civil law of its ambiguity, to refine technical vocabulary and definitions, and, by clear and simple language, to open the law to the general citizenry. The Napoleonic Code was a celebration of the scientific accuracy of French and of its finesse as a judicial language.[17] This common front of language and Civil law was central to the arguments of Lower Canadian nationalists like Denis-Benjamin Viger and Louis-Joseph Papineau.

Our third period was initiated with the dramatic change in the relations of power and in concepts of the state which followed the Rebellions of 1837–8. Their collapse was a blow to French Canadian nationalists' plans for political autonomy and vision of an increased role for the French language and the defence of French and Catholic institutions. This defeat was marked by significant change in the tone, personnel, and ideology of the Lower Canadian codification movement in the 1840s and 1850s. Suspension of the legislature, Lord Durham's chastisements, the Special Council's rush of ordinances, the distancing of the Colonial Office from Canadian internal affairs, and the growth of party government and responsible government in the 1840s signalled the changing institutional dynamic of law reform.

With the dramatic reshuffling of personalities and power in the post-rebellion years, a new consensus was established among the élite of the Lower Canadian bar. Younger anglophone commercial lawyers – trained in the Civil law, aware of the effectiveness of the law of Obligations, impressed with natural law, and conscious of the Civil law's prestige in both Europe and the United States – were increasingly receptive to French Civil law. Influential anglophone legal intellectuals like Thomas McCord and T.K. Ramsay – trained in the French classical college tradition and comfortable in the French language – spoke of their 'enchantment' with French legal intellectuals like Pothier and 'his perfectly clear explanation' of the law. In the same period, anglophone lawyers active in politics were forming Reform party alliances with peers from the francophone bar.

During these years, a younger generation took control of the political apparatus and the francophone bar. Less wealthy and seigneurial than nationalists like Viger, younger lawyers like LaFontaine and Cartier moved in a legal milieu that flourished with work from clients active in urban capitalist activities: land speculation, manufacturing, and trade. This élite – both anglophone and francophone – monopolized the attorney general's office and legal patronage, the law faculties, legal journals, and bar associations and moved to power on corporate boards and party caucuses. They accepted the tenets of British liberalism as a means of protecting the class, religious, and ethnic interests of clients and constituents. It was this group of professionals who took the initiative in Lower Canada's integration into an expanding capitalist economy through reforms such as the Civil Code, the scuttling of the seigneurial system, the new primacy given to contract and individual rights, the extension of a legal bureaucracy across Lower Canada, and the imposition of civic bilingualism.

THE IDEOLOGY OF CODIFICATION

Lawrence Friedman has described the nineteenth century as 'the golden age of the law of contract.' In both England and the United States, contract law rapidly expanded to meet the needs of changing market economies.[18] In giving a central position to the law of Obligations – to principles of contract – the Lower Canadian codifiers emphasized individual rights and equality over certain values inherent in customary law. The significance of the primacy given to the law of Obligations in the civil codes of both Lower Canada and France has been emphasized by subsequent commentators. 'With the triumph of liberalism in the eighteenth century,' Colin and Capitant wrote in their *Traité de droit civil*, 'contract – the agreement of two free and equal wills – was, along with property, one of the essential bases of civil society.' In a contemporary French textbook, Gabriel Marty and Pierre Raynaud emphasize the theory of Obligations as 'constituting the base of both commercial law and of the daily juridical life of every legal person.' In Quebec, Jean-Louis Baudouin's standard text describes Obligations as the 'touchstone' of the entire Civil law system.[19]

Behind these changing contract relationships was the increasing ubiquity of capitalist activities. Rapidly expanding life insurance and mortgage institutions provide useful examples. In 1860, the Life Association asked its lawyers if the Custom of Paris – in which Article 282 prohibited husband and wife from benefiting each other by *donations inter vivos* or any other means – did not make it impossible for a husband to name his wife beneficiary of his policy. Lawyers Torrance and Morris replied urging the company to ignore the terms of the Custom even though a policy was

manifestly an advantage granted by the husband to wife. But can anyone but the Company call it in question? Their contract was to pay to the wife and if they pay her is not the payment a good one discharging their obligations under the policy?

For its part, the Permanent Building Society consulted its lawyers to determine if the Custom of Paris and Registry Ordinance of 1841 permitted a wife to mortgage her own land.[20]

Individual rights, although trumpeted by legislators and jurists, were another area of shifting sands. In fact, the period was characterized by increasing circumscription and definition of the citizen and legal person. In defining 'Indian' for example, an 1850 act, applicable to Lower Canada, differentiated between 'status' and 'non-status' Indians. In 1857, a Canadian act 'to encourage the gradual civilization of the Indian tribes' enfranchised adult male natives who renounced their share of tribal lands and moneys. Since only one Amerindian accepted enfranchisement in the decade following its enactment, the law, purportedly passed to reduce legal distinctions, 'actually established them,' as John Tobias aptly put it.[21] Women, particularly wives, also saw their rights as persons deteriorate in a period which, theoretically, saw an expansion of individual rights. The voting rights of Lower Canadian women, permitted under the Constitutional Act of 1791, were challenged first in 1834 and finally removed in 1849. Other laws, such as the Registry Ordinance (1841), increased wives' dependence on their husbands for the protection of their property.

This slippage formed part of a larger conservative and patriarchal framework that left little place for public debate of these issues.[22] The Civil Code emerged from this consensus, drawing support from nationalist, clerical, capitalist, and professional quarters – even the opposition Rouges promoted the principle of codification. Professional organizations might have been expected to play a vocal part, but the Chamber of Notaries and the bar associations were youthful corporations and were timid about approaching the attorney general's office with its control of legal patronage. The hierarachy of the Roman Catholic Church – or at least its dominant moderate wing – was brought onside by family connection, closed-door negotiations, respect for clerical jurisdictions, and, above all, by the code's careful reiteration of the patriarchal and religious powers entrenched in the Custom of Paris. Unlike the implementation of taxation and universal education, which were greeted with riots and civil disobedience, there was no apparent popular resistance to codification by farmers, workers, women, or the young.

Restoration of the assembly in 1841 and achievement of responsible government delivered power – and the accompanying problems of establishing authority – to the local élite. The anglophone bourgeoisie of Montreal, so distrusted by the generation of Louis-Joseph Papineau, moved into new party alliances with younger francophones like LaFontaine and Cartier. Anglophones like Alexander Galt, Lewis Drummond, and John Young became central figures in establishing new state structures and institutions in the 1840s and 1850s. They were comfortable with the dominant francophone bourgeoisie, which emerged from the rebellions and Special Council period. And with reason. The francophone professionals in the LaFontaine and Cartier camp believed in modernization, an end to the seigneurial system, free market principles, ethnic harmony, and alliances with the great landowners and industrial capitalists. Distancing themselves from the *angst* of Papineau, they subordinated – albeit with handsome recompense and privileges – the pre-industrial élite, particularly the seigneurs and Roman Catholic clergy.

This maturing of bourgeois democracy, epitomized by responsible government and its changed concept of sovereignty, posed contradictions of legitimacy and power for Cartier and his conservative allies on the bench, bar associations, and new law faculties. Yes, they would have agreed, law resulted from a rational, legislative process.[23] But along with this instrumentalist belief in the sovereignty of the legislature, they remained troubled by the potential of radicalism evident in the second round of rebellions in 1838 and in the sacking of the Parliament in Montreal in 1849. Through the 1850s and 1860s, Cartier, for example, feared the popular classes and supported the transfer of the capital from Montreal to Bytown (Ottawa), the principle of an appointed upper house, and strict limitations on an enlarged franchise. In contrast to the experience in the German states in the nineteenth century, the process of codification was isolated from legislators and interest groups and was entrusted to a coterie of conservative judges. Hammered out by the three judges and their secretaries in closed sessions, the published reports of the commission received minimal circulation. In 1865, the draft Civil Code came before the legislature for perfunctory committee hearings and assembly debate. There was little public debate over codification. Only under pressure and with several reminders, did a few judges forward short commentaries; during debate in the Legislative Assembly, only one public body, the Quebec Board of Trade, tried to intervene.

Language formed a fundamental part of the codification gristle. Napoleonic codifiers had portrayed language, law, and national culture as inextricably entwined, a point of view reiterated forcefully by Papineau and the Patriotes. After the collapse of Patriote nationalism in the rebellions of 1837–8, civic bilingualism – English and French 'standing side by side' in the code – became a fundamental principle of codification. Much more than a legal technicality, it was part of a broader political and cultural recognition of the anglophone minority of Lower Canada. In the same period, McGill set up its law faculty – and of course, English was the dominant language of instruction. Shortly after the opening of the McGill faculty, the other law school in Montreal – François-Maximilien Bibaud's law program in French at the Jesuit's Collège Sainte-Marie – was dismantled. The emphasis on anglicization was evident in the codification process: the central and most innovative parts of the code were conceived and written in English by an anglophone judge whose abilities in French were suspect.

Codification in Lower Canada was a seven-year process. The Codification Commission was named in February 1859 and prepared the Civil Code in the period from the spring of 1859 to December 1864; it was enacted in 1865 and, significantly, came into effect in August 1866, just months before the Confederation of Canada. The commission also prepared the Code of Civil Procedure which was approved in June 1866 and came into effect a year later.

As we shall see, the commission's task was delicate. It would confirm fundamental institutions and practices concerning the family, transmission of property, and marriage while giving new centrality to a capitalist society's need for legal equality, universality in law, and the place of the individual. This dualism characterized its entire work.

A sense of historicity – more simply, harmonizing law with the past – remained a central priority of the codifiers. Portalis – the intellectual force behind the Napoleonic Code – told the French commission that codification would be beyond human capacity if one tried to impose an absolutely 'new institutution,' if one 'ignored the experience of the past, the tradition of good sense, and the rules and maxims which have come down to us, and which form the spirit of the centuries.'[24] It was this sense of the past, this marriage of law and a particular history, this understanding that the law's fundamentality had to be rooted in a perception of its persistence and timelessness, that led the attorney general to present codification to the assembly as 'only a repetition in a more methodical form of the law already existing in Lower Canada.'[25]

This assurance of continuity and social stability became increasingly important to nationalists in the decades after 1866. With the execution of

Louis Riel and the development of monopoly capitalism in late nine-teenth-century Quebec, socially conservative and nationalist intellectuals such as Thomas-Jean-Jacques Loranger and B.-A. Testard de Montigny dug in their heels on particular legal issues, such as divorce and provincial rights. These authors often subordinated the code's intended universality and scientific basis to specific, French Canadian, and Catholic interpretations. Lawyer and later judge Charles-Chamilly de Lorimier, for example, tied the 'noble and patriotic' Civil Code to 'the great French-Canadian family' which was 'tightened by the unity and homogeneity of its laws': the code represented 'a new link in the chain which must always ally our destinies to those of the ancient mother country.'[26]

Commercial lawyers and the anglophone élite interpreted the code in very different fashion, emphasizing its importance as a vehicle of fundamental change. The secretary of the Codification Commission, Thomas McCord, for example, explained the code's role in the 'adaptation' of 'the old law,' 'the ancient law,' 'the conservative spirit of the law' to what he called 'the new state of society.' In place of 'landed property' and 'things' defining place and social order, the code, by emphasizing the individual, would 'furnish elements of stability' and would 'facilitate the free exercise of man's dominion over property.' From McCord's perspective, the code, by the centrality it gave to Obligations and particularly by making contracts 'definitive and reliable,' recognized the dominance of capitalist relationships in Lower Canada's legal culture.[27]

The Lower Canadian Civil Code, as finally passed, consisted of 2615 articles divided into a 'Preliminary Title' (articles 1–17), four parts or 'Books': Book First – Persons (18–373); Book Second – Of Property, of Ownership and of Its Different Modifications (374–582); Book Third – Of the Acquisition and Exercise of Rights of Property (583–2277); and Book Fourth – Commercial Law (2278–2612), and Final Provisions (2613–2615). Each book was subdivided into titles or subjects, such as 'marriage,' 'paternal authority,' 'ownership,' 'successions,' 'obligations,' and 'merchant shipping.'

Confederation and codification were bedfellows in the crucial juncture of the 1860s when the form of Canadian federalism was being negotiated. In the process by which Quebec became one province among others and in which French Canadians became a minority element in a federal state in which English would be the dominant language, codification institutionalized and reconfirmed Lower Canada's separate legal culture. This anchor remains firm a century and a half later. The ultimately rejected Charlottetown accord of 1992 identified Civil law as one of the three fundamental elements of Quebec's 'distinct society' (along with language and culture), and in January 1994 Quebec's recodified Civil Code came into effect.[28]

Applied universally across Quebec, the Civil Code of 1866 brought legal coherence to the province's diverse and competing constituencies. It fit into a political arrangement that included the expansion of bourgeois democracy through responsible government and party rule, the development of state institutions and measures such as universal education of the citizenry. It followed the dismantling of seigneurialism, and became Quebec's legal bedrock for a compromise between a conservative social vision and the principles of individual rights and freedom of property inherent in the modern capitalist state.

2

Attitudes to Codification
before the Rebellions

Our law is simple and well-defined.
Denis-Benjamin Viger (1828)[1]

We have a systematic and wise Code of laws; we are seeing it distorted.
Louis-Joseph Papineau (1831)[2]

The Custom of Paris was the central element in the Civil law of New France. Edited in 1510 and 1580, the Custom of Paris was introduced into the colony around 1640 but there was a diversity of customary law until a 1664 edict imposed it as the only one permitted.[3] The Custom of Paris consisted of sixteen titles containing 362 articles. Six titles dealt with family and inheritance, five with property, and four with debt recovery. Certain articles, including all of Title XII, 'Of the Noble Guardianship and Bourgeoisie,' were not established in the colony.[4]

The Custom emphasized seigneurial tenure, the privileged classes, and the patriarchal family as the anchors of social order. The first title of the Custom treated fiefs, the second seigneurial rights. Largely inspired by Louise Dechêne, much recent scholarship has emphasized the rigour of the seigneurial system in Canada, the reinforcement of customary laws concerning seigneurialism by the ordinances of intendants, and the persistence and strengthening of the system after the British conquest. In her study of Île Jésus, for example, Sylvie Dépatie demonstrates the multiple levels of seigneurial power, not just as holder of a fief, but as judge in seigneurial courts, and as a privileged creditor.[5]

Title XV, 'Successions,' gives a strong sense of the Custom's emphasis on social class. While the eldest sons of seigneurs benefited from a system of seniority of birth under which they inherited the manor house and half the fief, all children not of the aristocracy theoretically 'came equally to the succession' (article 302).[6] However, Dechêne, Dépatie, Pauline Desjardins, Allan Greer, Louis Lavallée, and Gérard Bouchard all insist on important differences between the letter of the Custom and the actual inheritance practices of the colonists – whether peasant, merchant, or seigneur.[7]

Also significant for the later process of codification was the fact that the Custom was not a complete legal system; for example, Roman jurisprudence concerning obligations and male authority were of central importance in the colony's law. In 1828, appearing before a parliamentary committee at Westminster, Denis-Benjamin Viger explained the relationship between the Custom, ordinances, and other elements of the Civil law:

When I speak of civil law, it is to be observed that though we speak very much of the *coutume de Paris* and the ordinances of the King of France, it is but a small part of our law. The common law of Canada may be called the common law, as it was interpreted, and as it was practised in the Parliament of Paris. Where the *coutume de Paris*, or the ordinances of the kings are silent, then we take the general principles of the civil law as the *raison écrite*; in this sense it may be looked upon as the civil law of Canada.[8]

The Custom did not deal with procedure (encompassed in the Civil Ordinance of 1667) or crime (the Criminal Ordinance of 1670). Commentaries were crucial in fleshing out and interpreting the Custom, particularly those of jurist Charles Dumoulin and, in the eighteenth century, the works of Robert-Joseph Pothier and Claude de Ferrière.[9] The century from the imposition of the Custom of Paris in New France in 1664 to the British conquest was an extended period of law reform in France, activity characterized by the strengthening of royal power, of the French language, and of the standardization of law across France. Of particular importance to the development of the colony's corpus of Civil law, and to the later history of codification, was the commercial law of 1673 (the Merchant Code), the maritime law of 1681 (the Marine Ordinance), and important ordinances covering donations (1731), wills (1735), and substitutions* (1745). In addition, the Custom of Paris in New France was supplemented by royal edicts and ordinances as well as by local ordinances.[10] After the conquest, law was further changed by statutes enacted by the British parliament for Canada or in which Canada was specifically named, laws promulgated by the military government from the conquest until 1774, laws and ordinances passed by the Legislative Council from 1774 to 1791, provincial statutes enacted after 1791, along with the ordinances of the Special Council named in 1840.[11]

Another characteristic of the Custom – and a factor central in codification – was the absence in the Custom of a law of obligations. As we will see in chapter 8, customary regions of France had by the fifteenth century largely adopted the Roman law of obligations. In the sixteenth century when customs such as that of Paris were reduced to writing and published, few dispositions concerning obligations were included, 'the practice of the Roman law [of obligations] having already triumphed.'[12] This was clearly reflected in Canada. For example, to remind himself of the law of obligations, lawyer Stephen Sewell, writing about 1800, could ignore the Custom, copying by hand instead 102 pages of Pothier's classic work on obligations.[13]

A final characteristic – treated in chapter 7 – was the Custom's insistence on the dependence and legal inferiority of women. The law of fiefs in the Custom was succinct in its treatment of women in the seigneurial class. They ceded their place to males in the same line of descent: brothers, for example, excluded sisters from inheriting fiefs and it was the eldest son who swore vassalage, the *foi et hommage*. In a seigneurial family without male heirs, a woman might swear *foi et hommage*; however, if she was married, her husband took the oath on her behalf.[14]

Customary law on matrimonial property regimes was at the core of the legal dependence of women. The husband administered family property, including his wife's assets. A wife's ability to enter into contracts, even concerning her own property, essentially depended on the permission of her husband; this fact, as we shall see, sharply restricted the capacity of wives to participate independently in trade or in other business or public activities dependent on contract. Article 225 of the Custom described the husband's power as that of 'seignior':

---

* In *substitutions*, a person receives property subject to the duty of handing it over, at death or another time, to another person.

The husband is Seignior of the moveable and conquests immoveables acquired by him during the marriage of him and his wife in such manner that he can sell, alienate or mortgage them and make use of and dispose of them by donation or other disposition *entre vifs* at his pleasure and will them without the consent of his said wife to a person capable of receiving and without fraud [*sic*].[15]

These restrictions in the Custom were only elements in a larger pattern of patriarchy in pre-industrial society. To thwart the Custom's emphasis on equality in succession, for example, there are instances of the peasantry – at least on Île Jésus in the mid-eighteenth century – using *donations* to favour sons and to keep landed property out of the hands of daughters.[16]

BRITISH ADMINISTRATION, ANGLOPHONES, AND CIVIL LAW

Much of the recent historiography of Quebec has minimized the effects of the conquest on economic and class structures, emphasizing instead the persistence of seigneurial and religious institutions across the eighteenth century.[17] The effect of the change of empire on the legal system of the conquered colony, however, must – as Evelyn Kolish and Murray Greenwood have forcefully reminded us – give us serious pause. The imposition of the English criminal law system at the end of the British military regime in 1764 is, of course, of major importance. And although the Custom of Paris and other elements of New France's civil law system ultimately survived, the conquest did bring two historic systems of private law face to face: the French Civil law, strongly influenced by Roman and customary law and by legislation; and English Common law, with its preference for individual remedies.[18] The Custom's recognition of seigneurialism and the privilege of class clashed with Blackstonian tenets of individual liberty and absolute rights of private property.

The decade between 1763 and the passage of the Quebec Act in 1774 was one in which judicial and political authorities sought a legal *modus vivendi*. Widely heralded as a significant concession to the French majority's Catholic, seigneurial, and Civil law traditions, the Quebec Act did not in fact settle the issue of private law. Powerful elements in the colony's English and Scottish élite refused to accept the settlement of 1774 and, important spokes in the judiciary and bureaucracy, they were well placed to obstruct and undermine.

Commercial law presented other difficulties. While commercial cases were governed under Civil law, relying heavily on French authorities like

Pothier, Lower Canadian judgments frequently cited English, Scottish (George Joseph Bell and Charles Abbott), and, with industrialization, American commercial sources (especially Joseph Story).

Old commercial law was often based on the legal status of the trader. However, as markets, capitalist relationships, and industrial production expanded, special rights such as those of the trader were increasingly downplayed in favour of contract relations based on principles of universality and equality. This was particularly evident in railway judgments, which often relied on American or British law. In the important master-servant issue, of whether the Grand Trunk was responsible for injuries caused to an employee by the negligence of a fellow employee, for example, Justice William Badgley turned to English precedents and, emphasizing the worker's contract with the employer, he found in the company's favour:

The plaintiff in this case was the servant of the Company. He undertook by the fact of his engagement in their service to guarantee himself from all the consequences of his engagement. The road belonged to the Company, but it was in evidence that there were persons of competent skill who had charge of the road … They were equally servants with the plaintiff, and if there was anything wrong, the blame must be on the servants, because they were in charge of the road.[19]

As well, the Quebec Act's application of English rules of evidence regarding commercial facts introduced confusion over issues of prescription, evidence, the definition of artisans as merchants, and jury trials in commercial cases. The applicability of French maritime law was only settled in 1813 when Chief Justice Sewell, in *Baldwin v. Gibbon and McCallum*, held that the Marine Ordinance of 1681, although registered by the Conseil souverain, had been superseded by British admiralty law through the conquest.[20] Before the 1840s merchants were hindered by the lack of an effective bankruptcy law. And, prior to the Registry Ordinance of 1841, merchants – and others with capital – complained of the general hypothec conferred by notarized debt contracts upon the whole of a person's estate.[21]

The Eastern Townships, where English tenure (free and common socage) was provided for under the Quebec Act, were a particular source of legal confusion. Settled by waves of immigration from the United States, Britain, and francophones from the seigneuries, the population of the Eastern Townships grew from some 20,000 in 1815 to over 140,000 in 1861; by the 1860s French Canadians represented 47 per cent of the region's population.[22] The system of property law which was to apply in the Townships remained disputed. John Brierley gives a strong sense of the Quebec Act's ambiguity:

Did it [section 9 of the Quebec Act] intend to exclude the operation of the 'laws of Canada' (established in section 8) in the free and common socage lands, thereby opening the way for English private law, or some part of it … Or was it intended to do no more than to exclude from such lands the operation of the French seigneurial system in favour of the English tenure, thereby leaving in full operation in socage lands the 'ancient laws' in Canada.[23]

The situation was complicated by the Constitutional Act of 1791, which authorized the newly established provincial legislature to alter the laws affecting lands held in free and common socage.

Isolated by geography, language, and ethnicity from the seigneuries and their customary law and used to New England or New York legal practices, anglophones from older counties like Brome, Mississquoi, and Stanstead persistently protested application of Custom of Paris provisions concerning matters like succession, dower, or alienation. An 1819 petition called for a registry office; another in 1823 – signed by 10,000 'inhabitants of British birth and descent' – complained of the legal system, the system of land titles, the language of the laws, and the lack of local courts.[24] In 1828, some 40,000 inhabitants from the communities of Stanbridge, Dunham, and Saint-Armand petitioned that French law 'not be constructed to extend to lands granted in free and common soccage.' In 1849, John McConnell, member of the Legislative Assembly for Stanstead, used almost the same language in warning the government not to extend customary law concerning the franchise of leaseholders onto free and common soccage lands.[25]

Other petitioners in Missisquoi forwarded their list of legal grievances, including demands for security against the 'imposition and fraud to which the present Notarial system of conveyances is liable.' Part of the large judicial district of Montreal, they complained of the expense and delay occasioned by the some sixty-mile distance from Missisquoi to the Montreal courts. Another objection was the French system of administering roads. Instead of the appointed *grand voyer* – the local official in charge of roads – they called for 'English Road Law' with inspection by local elected officials.[26] Nor did the establishment after 1830 of registry offices in five counties of the Eastern Townships appease demands for a colony-wide system of public registry to replace the customary practice of private registry by notaries.

Over the decades, authorities debated solutions. While observers such as Denis-Benjamin Viger and a special committee of the assembly (1826) argued that the Townships remained subject to French law, influential lawyers like Samuel Gale insisted that 'the Townships are entitled to English laws as a right, and must have them ...' Seigneur Edward Ellice expressed this confusion, noting that, before 1825, 'I do not believe any person holding real property in free and common soccage in Canada knew very well by what law his property was regulated.' Auctioneer Augustin Cuvillier also told the same parliamentary committee that

in the Townships neither the law of England nor any other law is known: they have been in great measure without law in that country since their establishment. The laws, I believe, that are now prevalent in the United States of America are the laws which they understand best.[27]

The attempt by British authorities to confirm English law in alienations, inheritance, and dower in the Canada Tenures Act (1825) was sharply contested, and the issue remained unresolved by a poorly drafted bill enacted by the legislature in 1831, permitting both English and French property law in the Townships. This pluralism – what John Brierley calls 'a "co-existence" of legal systems' – resulted in confusion, fraud, and recurring litigation on issues ranging from squatters, dower rights, general hypothecs, mining rights, and succession. Typical was publisher John Neilson who testified in 1828 that in the Townships 'no one knows what law regulates them, no one understands the mode of conveyancing according to the law of England, except one or two.' Believing that French law prevailed on free and common soccage land, he had contracted with

persons upon the faith of their being possessors of land in [the Townships] under the laws of Canada; but it appears now, that according to the English law it was the eldest son that had it all, and they had nothing, being younger sons, and I have no security for my money.[28]

The Catholic Church was drawn into the debate by legal challenges to its right to tithe in free and common soccage lands that did not have canonical or civil status as a parish but were served by a priest as missions.[29] Resolution of these confusions by establishment of a universal system of law across Lower Canada would be a primary objective of law reform in the 1850s and an important backdrop to codification.

Given the bureaucratic, commercial, judicial, and imperial influence of the anglophone élite, its attitude to Civil law was crucial. We have already seen that, almost from their first days in the colony, merchants like James McGill took the initiative in demanding the legal rights of British subjects and chief justices William Osgoode and William Smith had insisted on the forced application of English Common law. These tensions increased in the 1790s. Anglophone leaders, fearful of fallout from revolutionary France, intensified demands for tighter alien laws, a school system based on an English model, English as the official language, an end to seigneuralism, and restrictions on the privileges accorded the Roman Catholic hierarchy under the Quebec Act. The implications for the Civil law of these increasingly abrasive attitudes were made clear by lawyer Ross Cuthbert, who attacked the Custom of Paris as 'outdated' and a product of 'the dark ages.'[30]

In the post-Napoleonic years, some anglophones shifted away from these blatant attempts at anglicization. In the complex social and legal conjuncture of the 1820s and 1830s, there was understanding, albeit often begrudging, of Burke's and Montesquieu's insistence that the only alternative to coercion of large populations was a legal system that reflected a people's past. In 1825 the English-language Quebec *Gazette* published an article favouring French laws of inheritance over English practice, and in 1831 Ebenezer Peck, an Eastern Townships' member of the House of Assembly, objected to his community's insistence on English law. J.C. Grant, a Presbyterian minister, told British authorities that it was not of French law that inhabitants of the Townships complained but 'more of the present system by which those laws are adminstered, the remoteness of their situation, and the great difficulty of access to the courts of justice ...'[31]

The colony's most important jurist in the first third of the century was Chief Justice Jonathan Sewell (1766–1839). His career demonstrates a growing appreciation of continental legal doctrine and of the scientific potential of French Civil law. His political, legal, and educational power, in conjunction with his judgments as chief justice, his compilation of the rules of practice for King's Bench and Appeal courts, and his pamphlet on French law (1824), made him the most powerful intellectual in the ordering of the Lower Canadian legal system before the rebellions.[32]

Son of a loyalist and former attorney general of Massachussetts, Sewell completed his clerkship in Saint John, New Brunswick. In 1789 he opened a law office in Quebec City and quickly mastered both the French language and Civil law. Through his law office, Sewell trained a generation of the colony's most important lawyers and judges: Edward Bowen,

Chief Justice Jonathan Sewell's evolving ideology makes him a central figure
in the history of Lower Canadian law. His promotion of the Civil law tradition
as conducive to social peace and harmonious capitalist relations was an
important factor in the changing position of the Château Clique and later
acceptance by anglophones of codification.

James Stuart, Jean-Thomas Taschereau, and Philippe-Joseph Aubert de Gaspé. This network, along with marriage to the daughter of Chief Justice William Smith, wealth from the richest practice in Quebec City, and a fine legal mind, assured his rapid ascent in the legal élite. He was appointed solicitor general and inspector of the king's domain (1793), attorney general and advocate general (1795), judge of the vice-admiralty court (1796), chief justice of Lower Canada (1808–38). At his death, Sewell left an estate of £39,209 and a library of 1120 legal volumes.[33]

Sewell opposed seigneurial tenure and Custom of Paris provisions for succession which he considered too egalitarian; 'inequality of property,' he noted, was 'the first cause and best support of an effective Aristocracy.'[34] He placed religion, language, and the law at the vortex of relations between the state and citizen:

The great links of a Government and its subjects are religions, laws and language and when conquerors profess the same religion and use the same laws and the same languages as the conquered the incorporation of both into one political body is easily effected. But when they are at variance in these points experience seems to have demonstrated in Canada that it cannot at all be effected while this variance subsists.[35]

In the revolutionary and Napoleonic years, Sewell was often shrill, baiting French Canadians for their ignorance, their religion, and their idleness. When in 1810 he announced the need to 'overwhelm and sink' them with English Protestants, the enraged assembly responded with impeachment proceedings.[36]

Because he was chief justice for three decades, his judgments dominate pre-rebellion case law. In 1809, for example, Sewell, in a nine-page judgment, ruled in *Pozer v. Meiklejohn* that suits between merchants such as George Pozer and artisans such as brewer Meiklejohn were subject to commercial rather than ordinary law, making English rather than French rules of evidence applicable.[37]

By the 1820s, Sewell's politics were moving away from anglicization and assimilation towards tolerance and co-existence with French Canadians. He read the *American Jurist* and *Comyn's Digest*, and he and James Stuart were the only lawyers in Quebec City to subscribe to the *Edinburgh Review* and *Westminster Review.*[38] Sewell's thinking had an increasingly strong Civil law bias, emphasizing the importance of Roman law, the law as science, and the need to reform legal education. Concerned with professionalization, he encouraged the first important publication of

Lower Canadian case reports by giving George Okill Stuart access to his judicial minutes.[39] He spoke in favour of the principles inherent in the Quebec Act, describing the union of French civil and English criminal law as 'the triumph of good sense over national prejudice.'[40] In 1824, Sewell gave the inaugural address to the Quebec Literary and Historical Society and his speech, 'Respecting the Early Civil and Ecclesiastical History of France,' was published as a twenty-two–page pamphlet. Noting the 'polished minds of [the] Romans' and the usefulness of written law as 'an effective remedy,' Sewell called for the establishment of a law school that would 'lay the foundation of their studies on a solid scientific method.' He concluded from Burke that the law was a science and 'the pride of the human intellect.'[41]

Some well-placed imperial authorities shared this view and supported a reform of Lower Canadian Civil law on a continental model. While nationalists were increasingly skeptical of Westminster's motives in measures such as the Union bill of 1822 and Canada Tenures Act of 1825, British authorities were not, as Phillip Buckner has reminded us, francophobes. In 1823, Robert Wilmot Horton, under-secretary at the Colonial Office, told Papineau that the Colonial Office had no intention of touching 'your laws, usages, institutions and religion.' Five years later, Horton was still emphasizing that British policy was to 'guarantee to the French population their laws and institutions in the seigneuries.'[42] Other officials went further, publicly expressing doubts about any sanction by Westminster of the Common law forms of conveyancing prevalent in the Townships. James Stephen, counsel to the Colonial Office, situated Lower Canada into a larger imperial context, favouring codification and 'the simple form of the Roman law' for land conveyancing:

Our English forms are peculiarly inappropriate to the circumstances of a colony, and most of all to those of a newly settled colony. Wherever English colonists have been fortunate enough to find any of the continental codes in force respecting the conveyance of land, they have clung to it with great eagerness, and have congratulated themselves in their deliverance from a heavy burthen. This is especially the case with the Dutch law in Demerara, the Spanish in Trinidad, and the French in St. Lucia.[43]

These attitudes of Sewell and certain imperial authorities were, however, part of a larger political framework that was characterized by deteriorating ethnic relations in the 1820s. Particularly threatening to Lower Canada's civil law system were the Union Act of 1822 and the Canada

Tenures Act of 1825. Louis-Joseph Papineau, easily the dominant nationalist of the period, had no doubts as to the motives behind the Union Act, predicting disastrous results for propertyholders if the legal systems of Upper and Lower Canada were united.

The wisest, the most unbiased, the most intelligent legislator would have difficulty amalgamating their respective codes without danger for property acquired under different legal systems. Every change in the ancient laws as well as each new law will necessarily have a relationship with those which are in force in one or the other colony and, according to how they will affect the one or the other code, will be viewed through jealous and prejudiced eyes.[44]

John Neilson, another important nationalist, also warned British authorities that the Canada Tenures Act had 'created alarm' among the peasantry who 'conceived [it] to be the commencement of a system to change the laws that regulate property, and which have regulated property since the establishment of the colony.'[45]

The Canada Tenures Act was greeted with particular satisfaction in the Eastern Townships where it was taken as confirmation of the validity of common law conveyancing practices. While French customary law was used in some contracts on freehold land in the Ottawa Valley, anglophones in the Eastern Townships had opted massively for American law, particularly New York forms of conveyancing.[46] The francophone legal élite, sensitive and increasingly disposed to viewing the law from a nationalist and scientific perspective, linked this expansion of Common law practices to heavy anglophone immigration into the Eastern Townships. In 1828 some 10,000 inhabitants from the townships of Stanbridge and Dunham heaped coals on these fears by petitioning for the 'enjoyment of the Law of England' over French law which they found 'disagreeable' and 'distasteful.'[47] Concerned particularly with property law, they called for registry offices, an improved mortgage system, a simple form of conveyancing, and the establishment of courts using English law to decide cases in the freehold areas. Several powerful anglophone jurists supported the petitioners. Samuel Gale noted that, although customary law was generally considered to apply to contracts and personal property in the Townships before the Canada Tenures Act, he had always considered it 'illegal'; as for real property he had always used the English form of 'lease and release.'[48]

Nor did settlers in the Eastern Townships restrict their use of American legal practices to land and succession law. John Samuel McCord was judge in Bedford, a district along the American border. Instead of using the French laws of obligations – in which he was in fact well versed – he referred, obviously in deference to the legal traditions of those appearing before him, to a Vermont treatise on contracts to determine where bills were payable and responsibility in contracts dealing with payments in 'kind' of cattle and grain.[49]

Pressures for a public registry system and reform of the French system of general, tacit, and secret hypothecs demonstrated another deepening division – between capitalists who saw land as a commodity and those who saw it as part of traditional social relationships. The former argued that hypothecs and dower as traditionally practised in Lower Canada 'operate against the freedom and safety of mutations,' 'destroy confidence in titles and securities,' and obstruct 'commerce and improvement.'[50] In 1821 Archibald Campbell testified that in his practice as a Quebec City notary he had seen many investors opt for 'English funds' because 'they are ignorant of the degree in which real property here may be charged with Mortgages.' Quebec City merchant Joseph Deblois was just as blunt noting that he feared lending because of his 'ignorance of the state of the Property of the Borrowers, and an apprehension that the money might be laid out on property already mortgaged beyond its value.' Thomas Lee, a notary himself, used the occasion to attack his colleagues, noting that registry would protect against the destruction by fire of notarial records and would force notaries to be 'attentive to business.'[51]

FRANCOPHONE ATTITUDES

In the 1820s and 1830s, defenders of French Civil law tried to deflect these complaints by pointing out that an English-style land-registry system would destabilize the peasantry and diminish the customary rights of minors and married women. In their view, registry and Common law conveyancing would replace the safeguards imposed universally by customary law with the individual interested acts of husbands. John Neilson, for example, spoke out against English Common law practices:

Wives would lose their privileges, children would lose their privileges; persons who have advanced money would lose their privileges … in reality, a great many of the poor people would be deprived of their only means of support, which is the land upon which they work.[52]

To social conservatives, the registration of land was part of a larger challenge to historical power relationships in the community, by expanding the knowledge of property transactions and family legal arrangements from the local community and its authorities to the state by means of the registry rolls. This conservatism was partly rooted in the mid-sixteenth–century ideology of the Catholic Counter Reformation. Besides its emphasis on marriage as a sacrament, the Council of Trent had emphasized publicity (the banns, the church celebration, the parish registry) which made marriage – and by implication its legal consequences – public knowledge in the community. Registers kept by the local notariat and clergy were, along with this public memory, the guarantors of the legitimacy of social relations. 'Marriage and guardianship constitute in our society a public estate,' Jacques Crémazie reported in 1846, echoing the Council of Trent. 'Notoriety attaches to their existence. Third parties are inexcusable for being ignorant of it.'[53]

To offset the danger to land security of secret hypothecs, conservatives in the assembly passed acts in 1824, 1825, and 1829 which streamlined the customary practice of voluntary sheriff sales. By this costly and time-consuming procedure, a proprietor could use the legal fiction of a seizure and hypothetical sale by the court to force holders of liens to declare their rights.[54] These acts did not alleviate pressures for a public land-registry system which would purge real property of secret encumbrances. After the failure in 1826 of a land-registry bill introduced by Joseph-Rémi Vallières de Saint-Réal, the assembly in 1830 granted five counties in the Eastern Townships the right to establish registry offices. This pluralistic solution led to further difficulties, with an 1836 Legislative Council committee pointing out that demands for a land-registry system would inevitably force its extension into seigneurial areas.[55]

These substantive differences were often aggravated by ethnic tensions – the francophobia of several Château Clique judges was particularly inflammatory. King's Bench judge James Kerr, for example, aroused sensibilities in 1831 with his assertion that Canadian law was 'unworthy of an English judge' and that in any case 'he did not know what the law of Lower Canada might be.'[56] Patriote Elzéar Bédard responded in kind, charging in the assembly that the

Judges were English, and did not understand our language, nor could not know our modes of proceeding – they therefore introduced a strange mixture of English and French practices, which has brought confusion and uncertainty into every Court.[57]

Language and procedural quarrels were daily fare across the period. Still a student in 1825, future codifier Augustin-Norbert Morin wrote a public

Denis-Benjamin Viger

Viger's landed wealth gave him the means to read and write broadly on
Lower Canadian Civil law. His determination to maintain the Custom of Paris
and the larger integrity of the Civil law apparently stopped him from opening
the law to codification.

letter to Justice Edward Bowen complaining of Bowen's refusal to honour writs written in French. Quebec City's most prominent francophone lawyer, Joseph-Rémi Vallières de Saint-Réal complained that, by law, summons were to be in the defendant's language

whence the Judges inferred, that Canadians born since the Conquest being English subjects, their Language was the English language, and that they could only be summoned in that Language, on pain of nullity.[58]

Across Europe, codification was linked to the nation state and the desire of legal élites for systematic and written bodies of national law. It is not surprising then that demands for codification originated in the 1820s among moderate nationalist elements. Those who saw the Civil law as an essential component of French Canadian culture were worried by a number of changes: ambivalent imperial policy; an aggressive Château Clique bureaucratic and commercial élite; expanding numbers of anglophones in the cities and Eastern Townships; frontal assaults on historical rights such as banal dues, *lods et ventes*, the system of hypothecs, and customary dower; and the growing legitimization of Common law practices on Lower Canadian soil.[59] Papineau, for example, insisted that seigneurial tenure and Civil law as national institutions were inextricably linked: 'feudal tenure and the laws regulating it,' he insisted, 'are only an infinitely small part of the civil laws which French Canadians want to conserve in their entirety.'[60] Papineau, despite his strong sympathy for the Napoleonic and Louisiana codes, did not support codification, preferring to maintain the seigneurial system and the Custom of Paris as they were.[61]

This link between social conservatism and a defence of Lower Canada's Civil law system is best seen in Denis-Benjamin Viger. Viger's roots were in the emerging francophone professional bourgeoisie. His father, master carpenter Denis Viger, sat in the assembly for the riding of Montreal-East; his mother, Charlotte-Perrine Cherrier, was the daughter of a prominent Saint-Denis notary. His cousins included Patriote leader Louis-Joseph Papineau, who clerked in his office, Jean-Jacques Lartigue, the first bishop of Montreal, and Louis-Michel Viger, president of the Banque du Peuple. Viger himself married Marie-Amable Foretier, the daughter of Pierre Foretier, Montreal's most important landowner. After classical studies at the Sulpician Collège de Montréal, Viger clerked with three prominent Montreal lawyers.[62] The second largest landowner in Montreal with property worth £1334 in 1825, Viger was able to live as a *rentier*, enjoying his

3000 volume library, and pursuing eclectic interests in politics, culture, and constitutional law.[63]

Particularly influenced by Montesquieu, Viger was a profound conservative and a lifelong defender of church, seigneurialism, and the Civil law.[64] Writing under the pseudonym 'le Canadien,' he published two pamphlets (1798 and 1812) attacking the French Revolution and emphasizing the loyalty of French Canadians since the conquest.[65] In his *Considérations* (1809), he examined the effects in Canada of the habitants' system of education, their morals, language, and law. Language, law, and property ownership were inextricably entwined and chaos would result if foreign jurisprudence was introduced.[66] Decades before codification became an issue, Viger announced plans (1812) to publish a two-volume dictionary of Lower Canadian civil jurisprudence, based on Ferrière's *Dictionnaire* with additional explanations of Civil law in Lower Canada.

In the 1820s he stepped up his campaign to protect the Civil law and he undoubtedly influenced young clerks like future codifier Augustin-Norbert Morin. Seventy-five years of British policy, and particularly the introduction of freehold tenure into the Townships, had resulted in a confused mixture of land law. Effectively combining natural law and nationalism in his testimony to a British parliamentary commission in 1828, Viger demanded extension of the Civil law across Lower Canada reminding colonial authorities that it was 'fluctuation' in British policy since the conquest

by which we have continually been threatened with seeing all our institutions which were dear to us destroyed ... [Britain] should have continued to let the French law prevail all over the country.[67]

Pride in the Civil law tradition, its rationalism, and its adaptability to Lower Canada's needs was clear in his testimony. Our law, he told the committee, is 'simple and well-defined.'

He emphasized that Civil law was synonymous with a unified legal system implemented by local, elected officials.[68] French Canadians, he argued, do not want

to keep themselves distinct from the people that surround them; they wish to live in peace and quietness with all who now are or who may hereafter become inhabitants of the province, and that no alterations should take place in the existing laws and institutions without the consent of representatives equally and freely chosen by the whole population. They think the province has already been too much divided into distinct parts.[69]

Unlike in France, in Lower Canada there was no link between proponents of codification and revolutionary demands for law reform. The Declaration of the Rights of Man and the demand for fundamental transformation of civil and family relations – for divorce for example – that marked French reform between 1789 and the establishment of the Napoleonic Commission, were absent in British North America. As the class and ethnic suspicions of the francophone leadership hardered, Civil law came increasingly to represent seigneurial tenure, Catholicism, the French language, and the patriarchal family. From the perspective of Joseph-François Perrault, for example, codes were a means of combatting the ignorance of peasants and immigrants and of instructing them in the values of seigneurialism and traditional rural life. Perrault remained a noted anglophile, was hostile to the Canadiens, and spent his professional life in the colonial judicial bureaucracy.

With his family's fur-trading business cut short by the conquest, Perrault worked as a merchant in Louisiana and then clerked as a law student in Quebec City. He was never admitted to the bar but in 1795 he was named protonotary, or chief clerk of the Court of King's Bench at Quebec City. Appointed by the influence of the English Party and opposed to the nationalism of the Canadiens, Perrault was committed to bringing together Lower Canadian French, English, Scots, and Irish.[70] Both a practising Catholic and founder of the Frères Canadiens masonic lodge in Quebec City (1816), Perrault was a leading proponent of educational reform. He sponsored free, secular, compulsory schools on the Lancaster model and in 1832 established a school of agriculture.

Like Viger, Perrault's interest in compiling, translating, and organizing Lower Canadian law stretched back to the French Revolution. In 1789 he translated into French those parts of Richard Burn's handbook, *The Justice of the Peace and Parish Officer*, that were relevant for Lower Canada. In 1806 he published a portable dictionary of the rules of the Lower Canadian legislature, in 1814 a students' manual in criminal law, and in the 1820s two pamphlets on education.

In 1832 Perrault published his *Rural Code*, a pamphlet striking in its reversal of the ideology of the French Revolution. While the French Rural Code of 1791 emphasized natural law and absolute property rights, Perrault's manual enumerated the seigneurial and religious duties of the peasantry; alongside firewood, tithing, jury, and market regulations were

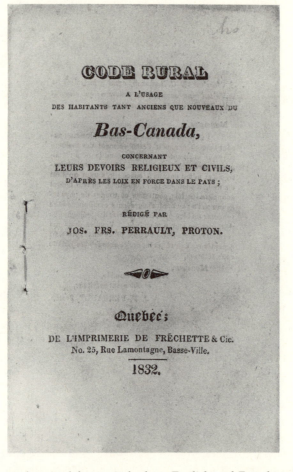

CODE RURAL

A L'USAGE
DES HABITANTS TANT ANCIENS QUE NOUVEAUX DU

Bas-Canada,

CONCERNANT
LEURS DEVOIRS RELIGIEUX ET CIVILS,
D'APRÈS LES LOIX EN FORCE DANS LE PAYS ;

RÉDIGÉ PAR
JOS. FRS. PERRAULT, PROTON.

Quebec:

DE L'IMPRIMERIE DE FRÉCHETTE & Cie.
No. 25, Rue Lamontagne, Basse-Ville.
1832.

Printed in pocket-sized format in both an English and French version, the thirty-four-page *Rural Code* was divided into three sections: religious duties, civic duties, the duties of public officers. Among the sixty-one subjects in the contents are hunting, firewood, the road *corvée*, banal obligations, galloping near churches, cemetery regulations, and behaviour in churches.

Joseph-François Perrault

day-labour rates and explanations of seigneurial dues. He outlined the religious, militia, and roadwork responsibilities of the seigneurial inhabitant as well as the obligations of male parishoners to serve as church-wardens.[71] Perrault also published an English version with a view to helping immigrants overcome their 'hostility to the feudal system' and their 'prejudices' against Lower Canada's laws and customs by coming to

know the laws, customs, and usages of the unknown country to which they have come to alleviate their suffering and to procure well-being and to free them from the prejudices that have perhaps been suggested to them.[72]

Most advocates of Civil law codification did not share Perrault's economic ideology. They were more often full participants in Lower Canada's capitalist economy sharing the liberal economic ideology of their landowning, professional, creditor, and entrepreneurial peers. Alongside deep concern for language, traditional social values, and historic institutions, they saw serious economic implications in the colony's Civil law confusion and polyjurality. Speaking from a broad sector of economic interests – trade, professions, industry, seigneurial and freehold landowners – some important francophone legal intellectuals advocated rationalization of the law and reform of hypothecary, dower, and contract law within a framework that respected customary privileges and pre-industrial seigneurial and ecclesiastical institutions.

From this perspective, the concerns of many moderate nationalists for the integrity of the Civil law were not simply defensive; proponents of codification came from diverse ethnic and social milieus with different elements perceiving varying national, professional, or capitalist advantages in codification. Some were legal professionals frustrated by the fact that crown patronage and lucrative commercial work was held by their Château Clique opponents. In Quebec City, for example, the number of lawyers increased from thirty in 1811 to eighty in 1831, but the legal work of British merchants remained in the hands of a few lawyers, particularly the partnership of Andrew Stuart and Henry Black.[73] Codification, a form of statutory law, was one way of increasing the power of the local legislature, where the professionals dominated, and of restricting judge-made law emanating from detested Château Clique judges. Patriote Amury Girod was typical in describing the outcome of court cases as a 'lucky-draw lottery.'[74]

Others approached codification from a perspective that reflected their interests as both nationalists and creditors. Debt recovery was the most important area of civil litigation in the first third of the nineteenth century. What Allan Greer calls the 'extreme ambiguity of ownership' led creditors to look favourably on registry laws and other means of enforcing proprietary and contract rights.[75] Denis-Benjamin Papineau, Toussaint Pothier, Elzéar Bédard, and John Neilson all promoted codification. Papineau's management of his brother's seigneury, Pothier's seigneurial and railway interests, Bédard's position as judge on the King's Bench, and Neilson's large publishing house gave clear class definition to their advocacy of codification. Their professional careers were on the line; their debtors had to be brought to bay, and their capital secured.

We have seen Neilson's defence of the Civil law in the registry debate. In 1828 he reported to British officials that a code would be educational: 'if there was a code drawn up, there would be no objection to the laws in Lower Canada, for the objections arise more from ignorance than anything else.'[76] Three years later, in a debate over revising and reprinting the provincial statutes in force, he reiterated Perrault's concern with immigration and the need for law which was simple and 'within the reach of all':

Ignorance of the laws was a great source of the abuses that prevailed in the Courts, and of the complaints that were made against the administration of law – it was that also that caused the multiplication of law-suits. Public opinion cannot be properly exercised, because the bulk of the people know not what the laws are; and on the other hand, being known only to a few, those few arrange amongst themselves, and do what they like with the others. In peculiar [sic] the English population have no knowledge of the laws that relate to property. The compilement of all laws that relate to property into one code would be particularly desirable.[77]

Calls for codification in the 1830s were increasingly linked to the moderate nationalist camp. Elzéar Bédard was typical in demanding a comprehensive codification of the Civil law in 1831. Participating in a rancorous assembly debate over the Canada Tenures Act and the prevailing system of land law in the Townships, he lashed out against judicial patronage and the inconsistencies of judge-made law. Codification, he argued,

ought to be set about immediately, for the longer we waited [sic] the more the evil was growing. The entangled state of the laws was now such that the whole may be said to depend solely and entirely on the will of the Judges.'[78]

Perrault's concern with educating the rural population about the rules of civic society was echoed by Louis-Joseph Papineau's younger brother, Denis-Benjamin (1789–1854). Justice of the peace and manager of his brother's seigneury at Petite Nation, Denis-Benjamin Papineau witnessed first-hand the difficulties caused in the Ottawa Valley by the confusion of the different legal traditions of French Canadian, British, and American settlers.[79] At Petite Nation, the Papineau books were laden with overdue seigneurial rents; in 1832 only ten of their censitaires did not owe them money.[80] As seigneurial agent, Papineau was in charge of forcing the payment of seigneurial dues to his brother, leasing sawmill sites and granting lumbering licences, stopping squatting and foraging on seigneurial lands, and competing for the censitaire's surplus with the other major creditor, an American merchant. In particular, the Papineaus, while inveterate defenders of seigneurial tenure, were concerned with the forms of land grant contracts, with effective debt collection, and with restrictions on their freedom in subdividing and selling their land.

Denis-Benjamin Papineau saw Lower Canada as in a 'state of transition' because of the immigration of peoples accustomed to 'different systems of legislation' and was frustrated by the legislature's inability 'to harmonize' society.[81] A social conservative, he was fearful of the effects of registration on dower rights, for example.[82] Identifying Civil law as the 'foundation of the whole social edifice' and using terms like 'solid,' 'homogeneous,' and 'well put together,' he proposed Civil law codification as a remedy for 'the abuse which may have crept in.'

If this foundation be solid, if the Legislative power be composed of materials homogeneous and well put together, the system of civil laws, that is to say the laws which regulate rights and duties, in a word the relation of individuals amongst themselves, although instrinsically imperfect, will always be sufficient to provide against actual wants; the Legislative power being always able to modify it according to the exigencies of the times ... But if the Legislative power has been constituted so as not to harmonize in all its parts, it follows that the wants of society are so much augmented from the absence of any remedy applied to the abuses which may have crept in, that a new codification becomes necessary. Codification will be the more necessary according to the different elements from which population will be composed, that is to say, of persons subject previous to their arrival to a new country to different systems of Legislation. When codification takes place then society is in a state of transition.[83]

Toussaint Pothier (1771–1845) was yet another who came to codification as a social conservative and capitalist. His father was one of the founders of the North West Company, and Pothier accumulated his capital in the fur trade.[84] One of the first petitioners for a Lower Canadian bank (1808), Pothier invested in the Lachine Canal, Montreal land, and in the Champlain and St Lawrence Railway.[85] He collaborated in projects with members of the entrepreneurial élite, such as John Richardson, William McGillivray, Peter McGill, and Josiah Bleakley, owned the seigneuries of Lanaudière and Carufel, and was an important land developer in the Montreal suburb of Saint-Laurent.[86] Well-known for his rigid social conservatism, his belief in a Canadian nobility, and his distrust of the popular classes, he became a legislative councillor in 1824 and accepted appointment to the Special Council in the post-rebellion years. Pothier was disdainful of both Papineau and Viger, but came to favour codification through his increasing hostility to British policy, which he saw as catering to the values of anglophone capitalists.[87] In 1836, the year that his railway opened, he petitioned the assembly for a comprehensive code 'that would incorporate and consolidate all the laws and existing provisions relative to civil matters' with a view to offsetting 'the delays, cost, and fluctuation of judgments – all due in great measure to the mixture of French and English law and practice.'[88]

Perrault, Bédard, Papineau, and Pothier personify both the diversity and the similarity of views among francophone supporters of codification. While some focused on its potential to block judge-made law, others emphasized its usefulness in facilitating capitalist activity by making law more efficient and by removing inconsistencies between French and English legal traditions. In the face of rural ignorance and heavy immigration, all were attracted to codification's educational potential. A code would be simple, universal, and French. And, sharing a profound social conservatism, they were aware of the ties binding codification to seigneurial tenure and rural and patriarchal values.

The Rebellions of 1837–8 abruptly stopped demands for a codification of Civil law that would in essence defend a status quo based on seigneury, social hierarchy, family, and rural life. As they became more radical, the rebellions unleased demands for reform that touched conservatives' raw nerves by putting in jeopardy fundamental institutions of French Canada: the landholding system, the Roman Catholic Church, marriage rights, and the Civil law. At a public meeting in Saint-François-du-Lac in 1837, there were attacks on customary dower and secret hypothecs. Seigneurial institutions were described as 'an immoral and unjust tax on industry' that depreciated landed property and 'discouraged capital and industry.'[89] The rebellions also led to renewed attacks on French Canadian institutions by anglophones. Facing flags marked 'Our two grand objects – Registry Offices and the Abolition of Feudal Tenures', James Holmes spoke to a 'loyalist' assembly on Montreal's Place d'Armes in October 1837:

There is not a man in the assemblage before me ... who was not interested in the subject matter of the resolution [in favour of registry], for, whether owner of real estate or not, the evil influence of the laws now in force in this province, affecting real estate, is of such a character to be felt by the labourer, the mechanic, the farmer, the merchant, by the entire mass of society: the merchant locks up his means immediately the instant he invests in landed property – whatever may be his necessities subsequently he cannot realize a shilling from that source simply because he cannot show that it is unencumbered.[90]

In the second, more radical phase of the rebellions in 1838, four clauses of the Proclamation of Independence (articles 5, 7, 9, 10) gave pause to authorities.[91] Its perfunctory demand for abolition of feudal tenure and seigneurialism 'as if they had never existed' raised not only the question of land tenure but the whole issue of vested property rights. The proclamation's attacks on customary dower and imprisonment for debt and its renewal of the call for a public land-registry system brought attention to the rights of married women, the nature and enforcement of debt contracts, and the implications of a registry system.

With the destruction of the Frères Chasseurs, the Proclamation of Independence – along with its radical property and nationalist expressions – was quickly relegated to the archives. Power was assumed by an appointed Special Council and experienced English liberals like Lords Durham and Sydenham. It was in this post-rebellion atmosphere of Union, of sharply trimmed nationalist sails, and of assertive clerical and capitalist authority that codification would resurface.

3

The Political Will to Codify, 1838–57

There are three prime principles of positive law; whose aim and interest is the profit and utility of man ... the maintenance, flourishing and peace of society, the security of property, and the freedom of commerce.

James, Viscount of Stair (1684)[1]

... feudal tenure is falling on all sides ...

Nicholas-Benjamin Doucet, *Fundamental Principles of the Laws of Canada* (1841)

But in a civil code, what old limbs can be trimmed off the ancient institutions! At first glance, feudalism ...

Revue de législation et de jurisprudence (1846)[2]

The crushing of the Patriotes facilitated severance of the historic link between the seigneurial system and the Civil law. While dismantling the former, reformers could impose coherence and ideological change on the latter. The collapse of the rebellions also allowed the ties between codification and nationalism to change. During the Union period, 1840–67, the meaning of codification changed. It became part of a political dynamic that included the initiatives of the authoritarian Special Council, the advent of bourgeois democracy in the 1840s, and expanding opinion in favour of a federal state in the 1850s. As one element in a move to general rationalization and institutionalization, codification promised a scientific legal basis and universality to Civil law. Ideologically, the Civil Code would emphasize the central position of the law of Obligations and define a new social contract in which the historical interests of region and certain customary privileges of married women, artisans, and seigneurs were subordinated to principles of equality before the law, individual freedom, freedom of contract, and the priority of exchange relations.

Of great importance in this process was the fact that codification and the law reforms surrounding it would be effected by a younger group of lawyers who, between the rebellions and Confederation, acceded to power in politics, on the bench, in the new university law faculties, and elsewhere in the colony. Pre-rebellion law reformers had emphasized the links between codification and politics. A code, they emphasized, would serve to block judge-made law emanating from arrogant anglophone judges, who were impervious to legislative control. Once they had power on the bench, in the party, and in cabinet, post-rebellion reformers worked to depoliticize the law, emphasizing rather what Gyula Eörsi calls a 'lawyer's spirit' – a rational, scientific, and ostensibly apolitical approach to legal reform and codification.[3] The marginalization of Patriote principles also broke the common front of law and language. Access to the subtleties of Civil law uniquely through the French language was abandoned, to the chagrin of nationalists, and passage of an English version of the code became an important benchmark in the institutionalization of civic bilingualism.[4]

Appointed by British authorities to act in place of the suspended Lower Canadian legislature, the Special Council responded with alacrity to class concerns. These included fear of popular resistance; the protection of capital, particularly that invested in immovables; and promotion of a bourgeois-dominated society based on equality and individual rights but one in which other élite elements – notably the episcopate – would have important privileges and responsibilities. As well, the council moved to establish a centralized, bureaucratic state that was equipped to educate, inspect, and discipline Lower Canada's increasingly disparate citizenry.[5]

The Special Council addressed fundamental issues of land and labour, the acquired rights of property, and the nature of sovereignty in Lower Canada. Its ordinances, 1840–1, intruded into family, marriage, and community relations – matters historically treated under the Custom of Paris. The council initiated broad schemes that were rational in origin and universal in scope. In his Common School Bill (1841), for example, solicitor general and future codifier Charles Dewey Day described his projected school network as part of a 'great general system of national education' which would embrace 'the whole population.'[6] The council introduced a universal land-registry system, set in motion the disassem-

Table 1
Motives for Codification

Agreed Principles, 1804–66

- acceptance of superiority of Civil law tradition over Common law
- codification to end polyjurality and confusion
- code to facilitate capitalist relations
- code to reinforce conservative social values towards family and marital authority
- importance of Napoleonic Code as model

Pre-Rebellion Principles	Post-Rebellion Principles
• predominance of seigneurial relations	• dominance of capitalist relations
• maximize integrity of customary law	• centrality given to law of Obligations
• defend privileges of seigneurs, married women, minors	• emphasize equality in contract
• insistence on relationship of Civil law to French language and nationalism	• emphasis on civic bilingualism and international qualities of a legal system with roots in Roman as well as customary law
• means of blocking judge-made law with legislative power	• process controlled by élite jurists and formally approved by legislature

bly of seigneurial tenure by establishing procedures for commutation on three seigneuries in the Montreal region, reinforced and extended central bureaucratic control into remote regions, and organized modern institutions, such as asylums, rural police, municipal governments, and schools for the popular classes.

The Registry Ordinance of 1841 epitomized the new political will to reform civil relations affecting the interests of manufactures, building societies, mortgage holders, and other holders of capital. Sylvio Normand and Alain Hudon describe registration as 'the first step towards the liberalization of real property.'[7] Drawn up by Chief Justice James Stuart, the ordinance secured titles by requiring registration of all conveyances, mortgages, and land transactions. As well as signalling the end of the secret hypothecary system, registration went against basic principles in the Custom of Paris by putting aside privileges of special-interest groups – seigneurs, women, minor children, heirs – in favour of simple priority by registration. The ordinance ended the priority given to customary dower rights: to be valid dower rights had to be registered by the husband. Even more important for the security of capital, it restricted the practice whereby every notarial deed constituting a debt bore a tacit general hypothec.

This legislation was not repudiated by the elected legislators who succeeded the Special Council later in the 1840s. On the contrary, the Reformers reinforced and legitimized the ideology of the council with a series of important acts: bankruptcy reform (1842, 1846),[8] reform of bills of exchange and promissory note legislation (1849),[9] the abolition of imprisonment for debt (1849),[10] amendment of the act regulating master-servant relations (1849),[11] the organization of the notariat and bar into corporate professions (1847, 1849),[12] municipal acts (1847, 1850),[13] the Seigneurial Act (1854),[14] the act settling the law governing lands held in freehold (1857),[15] and the judicial decentralization bill (1857).[16] School legislation in 1845 and 1846 strengthened the development of a universal elementary school system by linking it with expanding forms of municipal taxation. A variety of judicial acts, including the construction of regional courthouses and jails, and the insistence that judges reside in their judicial districts reduced regional particularism and brought uniformity to the administration of justice.

As for the registry system, deemed so essential to reassure capital invested in land in the form of mortgages, Louis-Hippolyte LaFontaine himself published a text of over two hundred pages attacking the Special Council's bill as a 'scissors and paste job,' a hopeless mixture of English and French legal traditions, written in language that was unintelligible to the masses. But he did not oppose registry reform and an end to secret mortgages; rather, he wanted an improved and more coherent law. In 1843 the assembly clarified and amended the registry act giving the population more time to conform and making it more universal in application.[17]

LAW AS SCIENCE

Sent to Canada in 1838, Lord Durham had revived familiar complaints about the Lower Canadian Civil law system describing it as

a mass of incoherent and conflicting laws, part French, part English, and with the line between each very confusedly drawn ... The French laws of evidence prevail in all civil matters, with a special exemption of 'commercial' cases in which it is provided that the English law is to be adopted; but no two lawyers agree in their definition of 'commercial.'[18]

This part of Durham's criticisms was echoed over the next years by important members of the bar and notarial élite. LaFontaine, Nicholas-

Benjamin Doucet, Charles Dewey Day, and Lewis Thomas Drummond called variously for institutionalized legal education and improved professional standards, for the rationalization of law through publication of law reports and digests and an end to Lower Canada's motley legal forms, and for translation into English of the Custom of Paris so all would understand it. In their demands for a scientific and market approach to the law, commercial lawyers like John A. Macdonald showed a familiarity with Jeremy Bentham, as well as American legal intellectuals.[19]

Lower Canada's most important professional body, the Montreal Bar Association, took the initiative in 1841. Its law reform resolution demonstrated that many of its members were beginning to favour a scientific approach to the law and, in the longer term, potentially codification.[20] The resolution was moved by LaFontaine, whose alliance with Upper Canadian Reformers like Robert Baldwin and Francis Hincks, represented the centrism of an increasingly important element in the francophone legal élite. Seconding the motion was John Samuel McCord, head of an influential anglophone family in Montreal and commander of the 1st Volunteer Brigade in the Rebellions. His doing so signified the shifting political interests of components in the anglophone community.

The resolutions criticized Lower Canada's judicial system, its 'obscure, vague and unconnected' laws of procedure, its confusion of lawyers' fees, its elderly and incompetent judges, and its inadequate court facilities. To offset the existing disorder, a reformed and unified Civil law system was needed:

the want of uniformity of judicial decisions is also much and widely felt ... [There are] a multitude of inferior local judges, adjudicating unconnectedly and necessarily creating as many distinct systems of jurisprudence as there are individuals.[21]

In 1841, the same year as the Montreal Bar Association's resolution, notary Nicolas-Benjamin Doucet's published his *Fundamental Principles of the Laws of Canada*. This bilingual edition of the Custom of Paris and parts of the Napoleonic Code was a further indication of the changing position of important constitutents in the francophone professional élite, as they left behind rural and seigneurial values in favour of urban and capitalist ambitions and accepted bilingualism in the law.

Of Acadian origin, Doucet (1781–1858) grew up and clerked as a notary in Trois-Rivières. The War of 1812 gave new dimensions to his career: he served as commissioner of oaths of allegiance, a captain in the Lower

Canadian militia, and a commander at the Battle of Châteauguay. By 1815 he had moved to Montreal where he strengthened his notarial practice among merchants like William McGillivray and Moses Hart with various government commissions as Indian agent, commissioner of seigneurial tenure, and justice of the peace.[22] A churchwarden of Notre-Dame Church, he used his office to display architectural plans for the Seminary of Montreal's new parish church; later, he served as president of the Montreal branch of the Quebec notarial association. With his strong links to the clerical, merchant, and professional élite, Doucet was one of Lower Canada's most successful commercial notaries, practising for fifty-one years and writing over 30,000 notarial acts.

Comparing the citizen to a blind man, Doucet was disturbed by the population's 'ignorance' of

the rules they are to follow in the application of the laws under which they live, and what they are to do in the intercourse they have with their debtors, their creditors, their neighbours, and how they ought to act when unjust demands, or insidious accusations are made against them.[23]

Doucet was particularly concerned by the notariat's lack of education and professionalism – critics referred to 'blundering' and 'ignorant' practitioners – and what he called the study of law from 'the wrong end.'[24] Writing for notarial clerks, Doucet mixed natural law and Civil law with loyalty to crown, constitution, and British liberty. He called for a broad education in the law:

If the student have enlarged his conceptions of nature and art, by a view of the several branches of genuine experimental philosophy; familiarized himself with historians and orators; if he have impressed on his mind the sound maxims of the law of nature, the best and most authentic foundation of human laws, reduced to a practical system in the laws of Imperial Rome; if to the qualities of the head he has added those of the heart, affectionate loyalty to the king; a great zeal for liberty and the constitution, and well-grounded principles of religion – the student, thus qualified, may enter upon the study of the law with advantage and reputation.[25]

The ideological separation between Doucet and pre-rebellion legal intellectuals, such as Joseph-François Perrault, is dramatically illustrated by the omission in the *Fundamental Principles of the Laws of Canada* of the title of fiefs. This division between seigneurialism and the Civil law was an

Table 2
Contents of Doucet's *Fundamental Principles of the Laws of Canada*, volume II (1841)

Introduction: Religious, Civil, Criminal, and Military Laws of the Natives, Still in Force in the Canadian Forests of the West
1 Of Persons
2 Of Things
3 Servitudes
4 Successions
5 Matrimonial Community
6 Dower
7 Lineal Redemption
8 Of Prescription
9 Donations, Inter Vivos
10 Wills and Testaments
11 Actions
12 Commercial Maritime Laws

Text of the Custom of Paris

essential precondition for the central place that capitalist principles would be given in codification.

Doucet's description of Canadian law, as illustrated by the contents of his two volumes (see table 2), took him across various legal traditions. Volume 1 was an ambitious survey of law and history treating the Origin of Things; Events of the Ages of the World; Laws and Customs of the Hebrews; the Legal History of Rome and Constantinople; the Laws of England; and Statute Laws. Volume 2 had an introduction to native legal traditions followed by the core titles of the civil and commercial code; his work finished with a bilingual presentation of sections of the Custom of Paris relevant to Lower Canada.

Given its importance to both Benthamites and American law reformers like David Dudley Field, it is not surprising that demands for an objective and scientifically based legal system were directed to revisions of statute law. In 1831, the assembly discussed the necessity of revising and reprinting provincial statutes in use. A decade later, a commission was established with a mandate to compile the some 1300 statutes and ordinances – often repetitive, overlapping, and technically unworkable – enacted in the period 1777–1841. The commission was to determine which were in effect in Lower Canada, and to present them in a corpus that would enable the legislature and public to ascertain 'in what its faults, deficiencies or uncertainty (if any) really consist.'[26]

Solicitor General Day and Attorney General Charles Richard Ogden named three anglophones, Alexander Buchanan, Gustavus William Wicksteed, and Hugues Heney, as commissioners, and one of Day's students, Francis Goschall Johnson, acted as commission secretary. After the death of Heney, the remaining commissioners, admitting that their understanding of the Custom of Paris was inadequate, dropped their compilation of those parts of the Custom applicable in Lower Canada. Their report simply reiterated the need for a reprint and official English version of it.

The commission's report was published in 1845 as *Tables Relative to the Acts and Ordinances of Lower Canada*. Since it did not abrogate previous law by being given the force of law, its legal significance was limited. In 1856, another commission was named to revise and consolidate the statutory law of Lower Canada and in 1861 the Consolidated Statutes of Lower Canada took effect.[27]

The 1845 report did indicate the confusion in statutory law. The commission had difficulty, for example, with overlapping laws between the Upper and Lower Canadian jurisdictions. In other instances, frustrated in ascertaining the status of certain laws, the commissioners were reduced to inserting question marks in their report. In the vital area of the regulation of markets and bread, the validity of eighteenth-century legislation could not be determined. A 1777 law on Forestalling, Regrating, and Markets (17 Geo. III, c. IV) had been superseded by an 1830 law; it in turn expired in May 1840 'so that the Ordinance [of 1777] seems to be again in force.' The status of another 1777 law, this one concerning Bread and Bakers (17 Geo. III, c. 10), prompted another of the commissioners' question marks. In addition to the issue of whether it was again in force once the law that had superseded it had expired, the commissioners could not determine whether powers over bakers had been transferred to municipalities.[28] With the growing importance of industrial production and of canal, steamboat, and railway enterprises, monopolies granted by the state over water-power and bridge sites became of great jurisprudential and economic significance. While in the United States a momentous body of jurisprudence on these matters was produced by the Marshall and Taney courts, the Lower Canadian commission was forced to report these issues as unresolved. Unresolved also was the status of the monopoly organized to construct the Montreal waterworks. Nor could the commission clarify the validity of deeds made in the absence of notaries in the Gaspé, of deeds related to the division of common lands in Varennes, and of old laws concerning customs at the port of Montreal. As for the

Special Council, which governed in the years after the rebellions, the commissioners concluded that many of its laws 'could scarcely be considered as more than experimental.'

In insisting on bilingualism in the law, the commissioners gave portent to what would become one of Cartier's major arguments for codification. They pointed out the imperative for a French translation of the criminal law and for an English version of the Custom: 'two systems of laws exist there, each of which, by reason of the language in which it is written is inaccessible to a large portion of the people whom it binds.'[29] This insular state of affairs was confirmed in 1849 when the Lower Canadian bar was officially established. Its act of incorporation did not insist on an understanding of French for bar admission; candidates were only required to be 'sufficiently acquainted with the English or French language and with the Latin language.'[30] Although in its early years the McGill law faculty emphasized a form of bilingualism, with professors who taught in French, there was ongoing resistance from within the anglophone – and presumably unilingual – professoriat to student demands for exams and lecture summaries in French. In the 1880s law courses in French died out at McGill.[31]

Of particular significance for codification was the structuring of the commission's *Tables* with four indexes organized by time, class, subject, and excluded materials. The first index located acts by date of passage; the second organized them into categories, such as constitution, education, penal, real property, and statistics. The third gave a general index of subjects – Abandon, Absentees, Absent debtors, and so on. The final index listed acts excluded from the report: acts that had expired, were private, or had not been passed in Lower Canada.

Another indication of the growing demand for scientific, written sources of law – what a McGill Faculty of Law announcement (1868) called 'coherency and certainty' – was the flurry of legal works published in the Union period.[32] New law journals were established: *La Revue de législation et de jurisprudence* (1846), *Lower Canada Reports* (1851), and *Lower Canada Jurist* (1857). The incorporation of the Lower Canadian bar (1849) and the establishment of law faculties in Montreal (1853) and Quebec (1854) created new markets for legal texts. Jacques Crémazie's *Manuel des notions utiles sur les droits politiques, le droit civil ...* (1852) and François-Maximilien Bibaud's *Commentaires sur les lois du Bas-Canada* (1859) were both published for law students. Using these treatises, law reports, and periodicals, Andrew Robertson produced a *Digest of All the Reports Published in Lower Canada to 1863* with the goal of contributing to 'a settled and uniform jurisprudence.' In 1865 the former secretary of the Codification Commission, T.K. Ramsay, published an index to reported cases.[33] Critics remained unimpressed:

Is there a country in the civilized world, wherein so few scientific books or pamphlets have appeared, as Lower Canada. Have we a solitary work on any branch of legal science written by a Lower Canadian, worthy of the name of a treatise on Law, and to which reference can be made in Court as of authority? ... With two different systems of law partially in force, no one has been found sufficiently patriotic or painstaking to write Commentaries on the Laws of Lower Canada worthy of a place on the shelves of a small library.[34]

Given the model of the Napoleonic Code and active codification movements in the German states and the United States, codification had obvious potential to provide a foundation for a scientific, written, and coherent Civil law system. The first known demand for codification in the Union period appeared in an anonymous article published in 1846 in the newly established *Revue de législation et de jurispurdence*. Whereas pre-rebellion intellectuals like Viger and Perrault had taken pride in the Civil law as 'simple and well-defined,' the author, writing in French, used the terms 'chaos,' 'disorder,' 'incertitude,' 'anachronisms' to characterize Lower Canadian law.

What old, anomalous and contradictory laws exist throughout our legislation! What disorder and uncertainty in the laws regulating persons, things, property, commerce, police! What anachronisms in the most important dispositions of our social structure! Who has a broad enough 'esprit' to embrace and understand the infinite variety of edicts, customs, brevets, ordinances, statutes, and jurisprudence of all sorts?[35]

Much more than a simple clarification of property and family law, the article argued, codification would be the means to resolve confusion over questions such as proof in commercial matters, the role of the jury, prerogative writs, contracts entered into in foreign jurisdictions, and the differing prescription jurisprudence of English and French law. Lower Canada had the worst of the old and the new: centuries-old French legislation, which was inadequate to regulate contemporary commercial matters, and a confused flow of recent laws concerning mortgages, bankruptcy, and municipal law.

The article wasted little time with seigneurialism or the Custom of Paris. Feudalism was a 'scab' but its eradication would have to include careful provision for the acquired rights of property. Married women's rights under the Custom of Paris were another impediment. In the process of codification, community of property, dower, substitution and *retrait lignager* (the right of an heir to take over an alienated property by paying the purchase price) would be subjected to imperatives of individualism and freedom of property. Codification would permit the harmonization of *ancien régime* French institutions with British public and constitutional law and institutions such as *habeas corpus*, mandamus, *quo warranto*, and *certiorari*. Organization of a code would also be the occasion to bring Lower Canadian commercial law into line with British, Upper Canadian, and American commercial practices. 'Cosmopolitan by nature,' the author contended, 'commerce must be regulated by systems uniform to participating nations.'[36]

Like seigneurialism, the French language was presented as another privileged *prima donna* that would be weakened by codification. It was a matter of 'simple justice,' the author concluded, that the code be 'rendered accessible to all' with an English version. How could immigrants, he asked, be expected to understand words such as *douaire, préciput, propre*, or *acquêt*?[37]

By the 1850s, confusion in the law was evident across the legal system. Justice Day, for example, tried to sort out whether perjury before a coroner's jury was to be decided by English criminal law or French Civil law:

the institution and duties arising out of it [the inquest] were derived from English law; how then could it be said, that a man obliged to discharge a duty under it should not be protected by the same authority? Could a man be compelled to do a thing under one law and made answerable for it under another? Two such opposite systems could not co-exist; either the law of inquest was the civil law of this country, or else the juryman acting under obligations imposed by English law must have the protection of the same system.[38]

The deepening penetration of capitalist relations into the countryside aggravated the situation. The controversy surrounding the bankrupt Montreal and Bytown Railway Company was typical: disposition of the company's assets in 1856 was blocked over the question of where the sale should be held. Part of the railway was on seigneurial lands and, by customary law, real estate *en roture* was to be sold at the church door of the parish. The railway, however, also ran on lands held in free and common socage, sales of which were normally held at the sheriff's office.[39]

DISMANTLING SEIGNEURIALISM

Seigneurialism and the laws encompassing it were not, as historians of nineteenth-century Quebec have reminded us, rigid structures that blocked industrial production or the accumulation of capital. R. Cole Harris, Jean-Claude Robert, Robert Sweeny, and Françoise Noël have shown the involvement of seigneurs like Louis-Joseph Papineau and Barthélemy Joliette in capitalist activities ranging from sawmills, to land speculation, railways, and industrial milling. Louise Dechêne has described seigneurial law as 'an ideal form' for urban landlords.[40]

At the same time, important elements of the seigneurial system blatantly contradicted the values of individualism and freedom of contract. *Banalités*, *lods et ventes*, and group rights to common lands implied monopoly and collective rights, which were anathema to capitalist relationships as perceived by the entrepreneurial and bar élites. Producers such as industrial millers demanded the right to buy wheat where they wanted and to use property in unrestricted fashion. Mutation levies on land improvements, seigneurial riparian rights over waterways and power sites, and a seigneurial domain blocking industrial expansion along the Lachine Canal, all served to encourage urban capitalists, rural land speculators, and industrial producers to subvert the intentions of customary law.

Nor were the concerns of capitalists limited to seigneurialism and other parts of the Custom of Paris. For years before the rebellions, legal professionals like Duncan Fisher and Bank of Montreal notary Henry Griffin privately advised clients how to avoid the full weight of French commercial usage and law by means of instruments such as limited liability clauses and penalty clauses in bills of lading. And as late as 1844 suits were before the highest courts contesting whether the maritime law of France or Britain applied in Lower Canada.[41]

For decades, direct challenges to the seigneurs had emanated from anglophone industrial entrepreneurs and urban land developers. William Fleming, Thomas McCord, and Thomas Porteous all disputed the seigneurial rights and even the property titles of the seigneur of the Island of Montreal, the Séminaire de Saint-Sulpice. In 1816 Scottish-born William

Fleming upgraded his windmill in Lachine, installing new vertical grindstones and winding gears that oriented the windmill's arms to catch the wind. When he began grinding the wheat of local farmers, which by seigneurial law should have been ground in its banal mill, the seminary sued. Unintimidated by the seminary or its appeal to seigneurial law, Fleming responded in court battles that lasted nine years. He contested the very property rights of the seminary, forcing it to consult Parisian lawyers and to produce letters patent from 1677.[42]

Born in Ulster, Thomas McCord, who had leased the Nazareth fief, was equally disdainful of the Custom and the traditions it enveloped. An entrepreneur for whom bankruptcy was a permanent shadow, McCord wished to convert his rural estate, with its manor, barn, stable, and flour mill into an industrial suburb along the proposed Lachine Canal. The religious communities whose estates surrounded his were offended by his aggressive individualism. In 1816 the seminary, whose domain at Saint-Gabriel was separated from its college by McCord's land, protested, urging him to respect the historic relations of 'neighbours.' In particular, they accused him of cutting hay along the road – a privilege traditionally reserved to the seminary – and of erecting fences that blocked access to the common.[43] Thomas Porteous was another who violated the niceties of seigneurial law by building a flour mill on land granted to him for the Montreal waterworks. Porteous planned to use his steam pump for milling as well as pumping water.

These entrepreneurs were able to hire the best legal advice. Commercial law firms like Torrance and Morris attacked customary law on a broad front, advising large land proprietors to stop paying seigneurial dues such as *lods et ventes*. Their firm regularly went to court to restrict seigneurial rights and, on the island of Montreal where commutation was possible after 1840, hurried their clients to commute their property into freehold.[44]

Seigneurialism in Lower Canada was partially extinguished in 1840 by an ordinance of the Special Council permitting *censitaires* in the Sulpician seigneuries of Montreal, Two Mountains, and Saint-Sulpice to commute their seigneurial dues of *cens et rentes* and *lods et ventes* into a fixed capital. Conversion into freehold enabled owners to avoid seigneurial dues on subsequent improvements to their properties, as well as facilitating its freer exchange and exploitation. Commutation in the 1840s was voluntary, was restricted to three seigneuries, and, by its very definition, limited to individuals with capital or the capacity to assume debt.[45]

The Seigneurial Commission of 1843 further exposed the weakened position of the seigneurial system. Whereas the 1836 Report of the Standing Committee on Lands and Seignioral Rights maintained the status quo, the 1843 commission addressed seigneurial tenure directly, determined to find an 'equitable means' of commutation.[46] The opinions of two of the commissioners on seigneurialism was well known. In his translation of the Custom of Paris published two years earlier, commissioner Nicolas-Benjamin Doucet had described feudal tenure as 'falling on all sides.'[47] Commissioner John Samuel McCord was the eldest son of Thomas McCord. In 1843, John Samuel and his brother had 247 property-holders (from whom they received rents) on their Nazareth fief and were working to develop their lands as an industrial suburb near the Lachine Canal.[48]

Tom Johnson has shown the commission's pivotal ideological role in eroding seigneurial property relations. Its report recognized the legality of seigneurial tenure under the Custom and the original attractiveness of a settlement system which placed 'within the reach of every man, the means of obtaining land, subject only to a small annual rent.' But seigneurialism, the commission found, was blocking 'progressive improvement' and had become a system in which only seigneurs could 'reap the advantage.' They concluded that the present position of the rural *censitaire* was particularly grim as he

toils through existence without the hope of relief, and transmits to his posterity a worthless inheritance. Under the operation of such a tenure, his right of property may become a mere delusion; as a moral being he is degraded, and his position is one of perpetual dependence.[49]

The solution – and central to what would become the ideology of the Civil Code – was the transformation of law into a neutral and scientific form, the apparent dispassionate servant of the entire citizenry regardless of status. While admitting the potential hostility on the part of *censitaires* who would be forced to compensate seigneurs for the loss of their seigneurial revenues, the commissioners reported acting 'calmly and dispassionately,' treating the issue as a 'purely legal question,' irrespective of 'individual hardships or what may be deemed vested rights founded on long and uninterrupted possession.'[50] Fairness and vested rights as determinants of legitimacy were giving way to principles based essentially on a person's voluntary entry into contract.[51]

These fundamental attacks on seigneurialism were echoed by the anglophone élite. A commissioner on the Seigneurial Court (1855) and later codification commissioner, Justice Charles Dewey Day described the 'feudal system' as decrepit and having 'outlived its age.'[52] W. Scott of Two Mountains focused on the 'evil effects' on manufactures caused by seigneurial water rights to the Saint-Charles River, privileges which had rendered 'useless' 'the finest water power in the world.' If seigneurial tenure was abolished, he maintained, 'Lower Canada would soon become as prosperous as any other country.'[53]

Of even greater political significance was LaFontaine's leadership in dismantling seigneurial tenure, a system he was on record as 'hating.'[54] Attorney general in 1842 and prime minister, 1848–51, he founded the Reform Party in Lower Canada; his tactics were based on the use of British constitutional practices and carefully constructed alliances with anglophone reformers, the Catholic hierarchy, and moderates in the francophone professional élite. When he was appointed chief justice of the Court of Queen's Bench in 1853, political leadership in Lower Canada passed to younger colleagues, first Augustin-Norbert Morin and then Cartier.

LaFontaine was instrumental to the francophone élite's abandonment of the rural idealism and strict nationalism of Papineau in favour of collaboration with anglophones and liberalized property and contract relations. Chairing the Seigneurial Court, Chief Justice LaFontaine borrowed directly from Montesquieu, describing seigneurialism as 'an exotic plant' which colonists had brought with them.[55] Imposing his views over the social conservatives led by Denis-Benjamin Viger, he deemed seigneurialism as incompatible with what he called a 'new form of government' and the 'habits of a people':

I am equally one of those who, forming a deliberate judgement of the changes which have since come into operation, in the condition, the wants and ideas of Canadian Society, are convinced that the laws which govern this tenure and the relations thereby established between seigneurs and censitaires (tenants) have ceased to be in harmony with the social usages of that same society. Now, laws which are not in unison with the habits of a people cannot long exist under our new form of government, above all when, however just and beneficial they may originally have been, they become, at a later day, although wrongly, to be regarded by the same people, not as creating a legitimate debt, but in the light of a tax to which, they easily convince themselves, they have yielded a free consent.[56]

Seigneurial Court (1856). Chaired by LaFontaine, this special tribunal of judges
was established in 1855 to rule on claims under the Seigneurial Act.
Justices Charles Dewey Day and R.E. Caron, soon to be named to
the Codification Commission, both sat on the court.

His argument was extended by P.-J.-O. Chauveau – later the first premier of Quebec – who told the assembly that seigneurialism was
'opposed to morality and the law of nature'; the right of property was
not 'sacred except in so far as it was useful – in so far it was sanctified
by labour.'[57]

LaFontaine also contributed to codification by insisting on the
separateness and indispensability of Lower Canada's Civil law system.
While jettisoning seigneurialism, he moved to protect Lower Canada's
institutional distinctiveness. Sensitive to suggestions that Lower Canadian private law might be assimilated by that of Upper Canada, he
reminded the assembly in 1847 of

the superiority of French civil law; it had existed and was found sufficient for all
the rights of the subject, for some five or six centuries, and he warned hon.
members from Upper Canada not to interfere with it.[58]

At the same time – and again opposed by Viger – he proposed that an official English version of the Custom of Paris be prepared and published alongside the French version.[59]

The centrality of the land question to Lower Canada's most fundamental values was not lost on defenders of seigneurialism. Viger praised its 'paternalism' and warned of the dangers of a system where any 'Tom, Dick, and Harry' or other 'roving proprietors' might establish mills with 'the most fatal consequences' for Lower Canada's water-power resources. He also anticipated that the dismantling of seigneurialism would serve as the inevitable prelude to a larger Civil law reform.[60] Lewis Drummond was another who was mindful of the ramifications of the end of seigneurialism. He too used the term 'paternal,' reminding the assembly that seigneurs were historically 'looked on by the law as trustees for the public.'[61]

It seems clear that the cathartic change from the values of feudalism to those of capitalism was played out on the land question – on the means of removing seigneurial dues, making commutation universal, and of indemnifying seigneurs. The Seigneurial Act of 1854 'for the abolition of feudal rights and duties,' fleshed out in subsequent acts, established *franc aleu roturier*, land tenure which was essentially the same as English free and common socage.[62]

The significance for the capitalist community of the institution of freehold property relations across Lower Canada has been rightly identified by historians like Blaine Baker, Fernand Ouellet, Jean-Pierre Wallot, and Jack Little. The Seigneurial Act did 'little to improve the financial situation of the habitants,' Little argues; they remained

in basically the same subservient position as before. The true beneficiaries were the commercial and industrial entrepreneurs of Canada East: as former seigneurs … their annual rents would not diminish and a government indemnity fund would compensate them …; as capitalists, it was now easier for them to speculate in land, to control timber reserves, and to build mills at water sites within the old seigneuries.[63]

Seigneurial law could now be excluded from the codifiers' mandate and, in 1857, the land law of *franc aleu roturier* was extended to the Eastern Townships.[64] With land law uniform and certain across Lower Canada, the codifiers could prioritize the values of growth, competition, individual rights, and freedom of contract, particularly in the importance they would give to the law of obligations. Commission secretary Thomas

McCord understood the larger significance of this transformation of property rights and its relationship to individualism:

The tendency of the age is make Things subservient to Persons, and to bring immoveables as well as all other things under complete subjection to the will of man.[65]

ATTORNEY GENERAL GEORGE-ÉTIENNE CARTIER

By the late 1840s there was growing support for codification as a method of law reform and a developing understanding among anglophone moderates of the political and cultural importance to Lower Canada of an autonomous and strengthened Civil law system. In 1850 William Badgley – no friend of Lower Canada's distinct Civil law – prompted an important codification debate with his introduction into the assembly of a new criminal code based on Edward Livingston's Louisiana criminal code of 1825.[66] And calls from merchants like George Moffatt for assimilation of Lower Canada's commercial law particularities under the Civil law into a uniform Canadian commercial law based on the Common law, could be balanced against those of Upper Canadian Solicitor General William Hume Blake:

If he [Mr. Blake] found any one endeavouring to do away with the English law under which he lived in Upper Canada, he should feel great jealousy; and as he should feel this himself, he would accord to others the same liberty ... Attempts to introduce laws applicable to both sections of the province could end in nothing but injury.[67]

Within Lower Canada, anglophones like John Sewell Sanborn of Sherbrooke spoke in defence of the Civil law over English Common law and the particular needs of 'new countries': 'we required laws suited to our circumstances, differing very materially from those of an old densely-populated country like England.'[68]

The Rouges included a plank in favour of Civil law codification in their platform of 1851 and, in the Legislative Assembly, members talked of its importance.[69] In 1855, Solicitor General Drummond introduced his municipal act in the form of what he called 'a sort of rural code,' emphasizing that it was written in 'language as simple, clear and intelligible as possible.'[70]

It was in this context that George-Étienne Cartier became attorney general of Canada East in 1856. Sensing a certain consensus among the legal élites, conscious of the capacity of careful law reform to encompass conservative social ideals alongside capitalist legal principles, and determined to entrench Lower Canada's distinct Civil law system, he brought a political will to codification.

Cartier's experience in the Rebellions in 1837–8, his role in the Saint-Jean-Baptiste Society and the Montreal City and District Savings Bank, and his marriage into a prominent Patriote family had all confirmed his credentials in French Canadian society. At the same time, the Cartiers – like many of their francophone peers – had a strong family history of loyalty to the British crown, an allegiance demonstrated in several wars and through their militia service. Cartier's anglophilism – evident in his collegiality with prominent anglophone jurists, in the increasing use of English in his own law records, and in his attractiveness to anglophone clients – surfaced in his strong support for bilingualism during the codification debate.

With its expanding commercial, service, and production activities, Montreal's economy was based on much more than international trade. The city's involvement in the countryside, in production for local markets, and in transportation to ports along the St Lawrence was reflected in Cartier's law business. Particularly before the mid-1840s, seigneurs, small merchants, forwarders, shippers, retailers, and early industrial producers appear among his clientele. With his surplus capital he became a *rentier*, investing in urban real estate – stores, a doctor's office, and apartments.

It was the conjuncture of political crisis and capital's changing approach to the state that provided Cartier with his professional niche. After the mid-1840s his general and local practice evolved into a 'Canadian' one in which he acted as broker between the interests of capital and the state, between francophone and anglophone interests, between pre-industrial and industrial institutions.

As attorney general for most of the ten-year period 1856–66, he was able to act directly on behalf of his most important corporate clients. These included the Seminary of Montreal – the city's wealthiest pre-industrial corporation and one whose wealth was based on land – and the Grand Trunk Railway, the very symbol of industrializing Montreal. In secret negotiations, he cajoled the former into accepting commutation terms for their seigneurial lands; he spoke for the latter in cabinet in the railway's recurrent appeals for legislation and railway subsidies. He helped usher out seigneurialism and was the most important Lower Canadian to promote a federal political structure. In cabinet, he played an important role in the municipal, educational, seigneurial, and judicial legislation that underlay the institutional state in Quebec. He was of particular importance to the anglophone community, reaassuring them, protecting their institutions, and reinforcing their rights within Quebec.

In 1837 Cartier and his Patriote peers acted on their beliefs. For any citizen – and particularly a lawyer – exile and a charge of treason against one is strong evidence of a fidelity to ideas. And although he mocked theoretical abstractions, there were fundamental political ideas behind his pragmatism and *bonne ententism*. Like most of his peers, Cartier was familiar with the literature of the *philosophes* and the revolutions. His library of 890 titles was rich in French, British, and American political economy, philosophy, and history; Voltaire, Rousseau, Montesquieu, Chateaubriand, Bagehot, Mill, Macaulay, Bancroft, Hamilton, and Marshall had prominent places on his bookshelves.[71] Although his law library was much smaller than that of Chief Justice Sewell and only one-third the size of that of LaFontaine, his 296 law titles show an easy ranging across language and legal traditions; three-quarters of his titles were in French.[72] He had Pothier in translation (as well as in French) and Blackstone in French translation. As well as English law classics like Chitty and Story, his library included Ferrière, Toullier, Troplong, Valin, Pardessus, Merlin, and Domat.

As he moved to centre stage of both bar and assembly, it was as a convinced conservative who supported the monarchy, who opposed a broadened suffrage, who insisted on the powers of an appointed Legislative Council, and who favoured moving the capital away from the urban turbulence of Montreal. This hostility to popular democracy was particularly strong on property issues. Property, he told an 1866 audience, is 'the element which must govern the world.'[73] His enemies perceived him in this ideological framework, and it was not by chance that he was nominated by a Molson in the elections of 1867 and his opponent was an advocate of a workers' international and of the socialist ideas of Proudhon.[74]

Like his mentor LaFontaine, Cartier was committed to the abolition of seigneurialism. Seigneurial tenure was 'absurd,' he told the assembly:

Fortunately, the question is not to be discussed by persons who are pennyless; but who are required by the constitution to possess a certain amount of property;

7956

George-Étienne Cartier

and he was happy to see it is not entertained by those who are ... actuated by the red republicanism and socialism of France.'[75]

Neither Tory nor ultramontane, Cartier's conservatism was rooted in the goals of his social class and profession. Using responsible government and the old boy network of family, school, bar, and Patriotes, Cartier and his peers were able to cut themselves in for an important share of power with Lower Canada's merchant, bureaucratic, and seigneurial élites. They built new alliances with industrial and moderate Catholic forces in the city, while in the countryside they were to win favour with the creditor community. In this process, Cartier walked an ethnic tightrope reminding francophone lawyers that his reforms allowed them 'to distinguish themselves' while presenting the process to anglophones as essentially one of efficiency.

Despite the political instability of the 1850s, the moment was opportune for fundamental law reform. Through the party system, the glues of patronage and moderate nationalism, and support from most Quebec bishops, Cartier was able to isolate both Tories and Rouges.[76] With increasing colonial control over administrative structures, the Cartier Conservatives extended power over both the seigneurial and freehold countryside with educational, municipal, colonization, tax, and transportation legislation.

Cartier was particularly attentive to the needs of his profession, clients, and social class. Long-awaited judicial reforms came in a rush while he was attorney general: the reduction of legal pluralism, the structuring of a legal bureaucracy, the revision of lawyers' fees, the increase in the number and salary of judges, and the reform of legal education. The formalization and expansion of the legal apparatus into rural regions was particularly important. Reform of the circuit court system and the confusion of local legal traditions through the introduction of district courthouses and jails and through a uniform, rationalized, and bilingual system of laws ensured expansion of the legal profession's power and prestige across Quebec. Codification was the final step in this process of modernization and uniformization.[77]

The perception of codification had changed fundamentally during the Union period. Its strongest pre-rebellion roots were among nationalists and supporters of *ancien régime* institutions, and it was closely associated with the defence of the French language, customary law, and seigneurialism. Under Union it became linked to the professionalization of the law with its emphasis on science, organization, and education, and to increasing pressure from capitalist interests. First with the Special Council, and then under responsible government with the leadership of francophone professionals like LaFontaine, the process of dismantling seigneurial tenure and separating it from Civil law was undertaken. This clearing away of seigneurialism, the subordination of nationalism to a bilingual vision of Lower Canadian legal culture, important measures to compile the law, and the formation of Lower Canada's first two law faculties, were the essential groundwork that permitted Cartier to initiate codification.

4

The Codifiers

we are in our hearts, by our laws, by our religion ...
monarchists and conservatives.

Augustin-Norbert Morin[1]

I have departed from our Law in this article ... The jurisprudence which had
grown up in France by which the courts constantly modified and disregarded
the clear stipulation of our contracts for the purpose of applying incertain
equity ... I have always felt to be an evil ... It is certain that the doctrine of
judicial interference with the plain meaning of contracts is regarded with
disfavour by modern jurists and it ought not to be continued in our law.

Charles Dewey Day[2]

In presenting cases, passing judgments, or writing a code, legal intellectuals use not just the strict tools of their trade but bring with them
instinctiveness derived from their own experience, training, social class,
and particular character. This blend in the codifiers of private and public,
of ambition and altruism, of the lofty and profane, of considerations of
family finances and sensitivity to the highest legal principles can be
discerned in the careers of the three codifiers.

Louis-Hippolyte LaFontaine – leader of the opposition (1843–7), prime
minister, and chief justice – was Lower Canada's most distinguished
politician and jurist and an obvious choice to chair the Codification
Commission. He had been Attorney General Cartier's mentor and, when

LaFontaine went into politics full-time, his junior partner, Joseph-Amable Berthelot, joined Cartier's law practice. Author of the important judiciary acts of 1843 and 1849 and of major appeal court judgments, LaFontaine had a passion for legal history, particularly feudal and Civil law, and published *Analyse ... sur les bureaux d'hypothèques*, a book-length critique of the Registry Ordinance of 1841. Pleading ill health because of his rheumatism, LaFontaine declined Cartier's request to preside over the Codification Commission in November 1857 and again a year later.[3] In 1859, Augustin-Norbert Morin, René-Édouard Caron, and Charles Dewey Day were named to the commission.

The three codifiers were born in the first twelve years of the nineteenth century.[4] All three trained as Civil law lawyers in Lower Canada, developing a strong sense of the Civil law's utility; this separated them from American proponents of codification, a group who remained Common law lawyers 'at heart.'[5] Unlike their elders, Denis-Benjamin Viger, Louis-Joseph Papineau, and Jonathan Sewell, their past did not include a memory of the French Revolution. But their world view was profoundly shaken by the Rebellions of 1837–8, a pivotal point in their social and ethnic perspectives.

The rebellions also brought sharp change to their careers. Day's prominence in prosecuting the Patriotes and as solicitor general earned him a judgeship in 1842. Caron and Morin established political and legal power bases on the givens of the LaFontaine compromise – collaboration in emerging parties with Upper Canadian reformers, the union of moderate French Canadian nationalism with the recognition of anglophone language and institutional rights in Lower Canada, the reform of Lower Canada's institutions, and full professional participation in the boardrooms and backrooms of the railways and other corporations wanting strong state support. They brokered, arbitrated, and conciliated the diverse interests that made up Lower Canada, serving clients, conciliating the increasingly heterogeneous population, wooing, disciplining, and educating the popular classes, and integrating regions like the Gaspé and the Eastern Townships into the emerging modern state.

Cartier knew Caron and Morin as friends and fellow travellers first in the boiler-rooms of nationalist politics in the 1830s and then in Liberal-Conservative administrations in the 1840s and 1850s. Their paths in government, commercial law, corporate directorships, and fraternal societies criss-crossed over the years. Morin and Cartier were particularly close since Morin's wife was a Cartier. Caron, Morin, and Cartier were among the moderates who distanced themselves from Papineau's politics of separation and defence of seigneurialism. They invested their careers – and here the contrast with men like François-Maximilien Bibaud is striking – in compromise between francophone and anglophone, in stabilizing class relations, and in meeting the political imperatives of an expanding capitalist economy. It followed that they agreed on the need to dismantle seigneurial tenure, to promote industrial development, and to collaborate with their Upper Canadian counterparts, such as Robert Baldwin, Francis Hincks, and John A. Macdonald. Their nationalist credentials were as moderates. Symbolically, Caron and Morin were pallbearers at the reburial in 1854 of the French *and* English soldiers who had died at the battle of Sainte-Foy in 1760.[6] While they insisted on the centrality of Roman Catholicism and the Civil law, they were willing to concede equality in Lower Canada to the language and institutions of the anglophone minority – principles entrenched in codification.

In terms of both status and pay, judgeships for a lawyer were the ultimate reward. Morin and Caron had both laboured for decades in the political trenches. Caron had been speaker of the Legislative Council for almost the entire period 1843–53; Morin had been co-premier, 1851–5. They had powerful roots in the provincial bar associations and were prominent in legal education, particularly in establishing Laval's law faculty. By the mid-1850s, both had acceded to the bench – Morin on the Superior Court for the District of Quebec and Caron on the Court of Queen's Bench.

AUGUSTIN-NORBERT MORIN

The roots of Augustin-Norbert Morin (1808–65) were seven generations deep in Canada and he was the fourth generation from Bellechasse county. His family farmed in Saint-Michel, thirty kilometres from Quebec City. Supported by his parish priest, Morin was able to leave Bellechasse for classical studies at the Séminaire de Québec.[7]

Nationalism was a strong force in his student experience in Quebec City and as a teenager he wrote for the newspaper *Le Canadien*. His writing attracted Denis-Benjamin Viger's attention and in 1825 he moved to Montreal to clerk in Viger's office. Even before his bar admission in 1828, Morin was close to the inner circle of Viger, Ludger Duvernay, and Papineau, and he acted as secretary at nationalist meetings. In 1825, signing himself 'a student in law,' he published a thirteen-page pamphlet attacking Justice Edward Bowen's refusal to accept writs in French:

our traditional legal system is absolutely clear that the language in which they are written is a legal language; these laws are in force in the colony for everyone and against everyone. The only exception to the Quebec Act of 1774 concerns lands held in freehold tenure.[8]

In 1826, Morin founded *La Minerve* although it was Ludger Duvernay who built it into a major nationalist newspaper. Morin remained editor until 1830 when, at age twenty-two, he was elected to the assembly in his home county of Bellechasse. He continued to write for the paper and in 1841–2 played a role in *La Minerve*'s revival.[9]

Through the 1830s, Morin was absorbed by the nationalist cause. He accompanied Viger to England; he edited the bills and manifestos – including the Ninety-Two Resolutions – of the Papineau group in the assembly; he was corresponding secretary of the Union patriotique. At the same time, he was well known as a nationalist poet, publishing 'La baie de Québec,' 'Dans ma douce patrie,' and 'Chanson patriotique.'[10] In 1836 he moved his law practice to Quebec. Here he led the minority Papineau forces against the moderate nationalists in trying unsuccessfully to establish a wing of the Fils de la Liberté. During the rebellions, Morin was imprisoned for three days but then released. Early in 1838, learning that a warrant for high treason had been issued against him, Morin fled Quebec City, hiding in a sugar shack in the parish of Saint-François. He was back in Quebec by the summer of 1838. He was never brought to trial although the warrant for his arrest remained in force; in October 1839, when the attorney general again threatened him with arrest if he did not leave the colony, Morin surrendered but after ten days was again freed.[11]

Morin was soon acting for LaFontaine in Quebec and was associated with LaFontaine's *rapprochement* with the Upper Canadian Reformers. Writing to Francis Hincks in May 1841, he put the Reform alliance into a context of compromise that characterized the rest of his career:

I am against the Union and its principal points as I believe every honest Lower Canadian must be. But I am not for violence or hate ... I want to convince the authorities of their error and give them the necessary time to repair it ... I am for peace, union, and harmony, if there is a possibility of achieving it.[12]

As the Reformers moved to power, Morin benefited from his status as LaFontaine's lieutenant. In 1841 he refused the solicitor generalship but was soon in the administration as commissioner of crown lands (1842–3) and speaker (1848–51). Morin was in the speaker's chair when the mob attacked and sacked Parliament in 1849. In 1851 he replaced LaFontaine, serving as co-premier in the Hincks-Morin and MacNab-Morin administrations until 1855 when he went to the bench. His administrations were characterized by deep divisions, particularly over seigneurialism and clergy reserves, and he is generally described as having failed to provide strong political leadership. François-Xavier Garneau, for example, thought Morin a poor choice as party leader: 'a man who was polite, studious and of simple tastes with the manners of an ecclesiastic rather than the passion of a conspirator.' An obituary described him 'as tender-hearted as a woman and as simple as a child. But for these – the infirmities only of noble minds – he might have been a great statesman.'[13]

Morin strongly defended the Catholic Church, the French language, and the colonization movement. Despite the hostile surroundings of Kingston, he made his first speech in the assembly in French and he worked to build the alliance between the Reformers and Catholic authorities. His correspondence for the period suggests a politician burned out in the mire of clergy reserves, separate schools, and ethnic politics. He found it difficult to break with Papineau over the question of seigneurialism; at the same time, younger nationalists like François-Maximilien Bibaud were disgusted by his alliance with the Tory Allan MacNab.[14]

In 1843, Morin married into a prominent Saint-Hyacinthe family. Albine-Adèle Raymond's mother was a Cartier, her father was a prominent merchant, one brother was superior of the Séminaire de Saint-Hyacinthe, and another represented Saint-Hyacinthe in the assembly. The Morins were childless and, with his health breaking down in the 1850s, he turned increasingly to his colonization project in the Laurentians. It was here in the village of Sainte-Adèle – named after his wife – that he died in 1865.

Throughout his long career, moderates in the Catholic episcopate perceived him as an ally – an important political asset during codification of the Civil law with regard to marriage and family. A strict Catholic, Morin was known as 'the Reverend' by his friends.[15] He sponsored colonization committees, drew up plans for an agricultural hospice where abandoned peasant children could learn farming, was president of the Saint-Jean-Baptiste Society (1847, 1851), and the Montreal City and District Savings Bank (1851). He drafted the School Act of 1845 which placed parish authorities, rather than lay municipality authorities, at the centre of the local school system. Morin always had a strong appreciation for the importance of libraries. His plan for a provincial library system included separate collections for francophone priests and Irish priests. He also envisaged separate libraries for Catholic girls with anglophone Catholics having their own facilities. He drew up lists for purchase by the Lawyers' Library, and promoted reconstruction of the Parliamentary Library which had been destroyed in the riots of 1849.[16]

Although increasingly enmeshed in the Union period's thicket of railway politics and changing corporate law, Morin carefully reaffirmed his belief in conservative social values: 'we are in our hearts, by our laws, by our religion ... monarchists and conservatives.'[17] His opposition to the abolition of usury conformed to historic Catholic principles and he was well known as a moderate on the land question. As attacks on seigneurialism multiplied in the 1830s, Morin stressed maintaining the status quo in the report of the assembly's Standing Committee on Lands and Seignioral Rights, of which he was sole author. Although the committee diligently solicited information on tenure, it avoided any advocacy of freehold tenure.[18] Two decades later, during the seigneurial debate, the Seminary of Montreal felt that Morin would be favourable to according them a generous settlement as recompense for the loss of its seigneurial privileges. Reviewing its work for widows and the Catholic poor, the seminary reminded Morin that he had always shown it 'good disposition.'[19] Even out of politics and on the bench, Morin continued to agonize over the separate school question, imploring John A. Macdonald to concede them as 'an act of justice.' During codification, he was the most sensitive commissioner to criticisms from ultramontanes.[20]

Morin's lifelong passion for the natural sciences and agriculture were reflected in his substantial library on agronomy and science. Morin was a member of the Institut Vattemare (1841), a philanthropic movement devoted to the establishment of libraries and natural history museums.[21] As early as 1840 he was accumulating property around the falls on the Rivière du Nord in the Township of Abercrombie. Located in a freehold area in the Laurentians to the north of the Montreal-area seigneuries, the region was a prime colonization zone with the first settlers arriving in 1840. Later in the 1840s, as minister of crown lands, Morin obtained some 3842 acres of freehold crown land in the area.[22] He built the area's first sawmill and carding mill, sponsored roads, and conducted agricultural experiments. The parish of Sainte-Adèle was established in 1852 and the municipality of Sainte-Adèle in 1854. He valued his Laurentian properties at £4000.[23]

As was typical of the leadership in the colonization movement, Morin linked colonization to industrial and railway development, tirelessly promoting mills, tanneries, bridges, roads, and railways in the Laurentians. Morin invested in colonization railways but apparently without much expectation of financial return. In 1857 he reported that he had lost track of £30 invested in the ill-fated Primeau wooden railway; of £62 promised to the Chemin de fer du Nord, he had paid up and apparently lost some £5. He still owed part of his £20 subsription for the Saguenay Railway while he described the £35 he had invested in the Rawdon Railway as 'probably lost.'[24]

As minister, Morin joined his colleagues in the various trunk railway projects that flourished in the 1840s. The key intermediary between the St Lawrence and Atlantic Railway and the state, Morin was the railway's vice-president (1846) and president (1848–50). He was also a director of the Colonial Life Insurance Company, the Montreal Mining Company, and was part of the Northern Pacific Railroad syndicate that planned an international line from Portland to Montreal, the Ottawa Valley, Sault Ste Marie and along the south shore of Lake Superior to the Missouri River.[25] These economic interests were reflected in his politics. He vigorously opposed annexation and American republicanism and was a strong advocate of free trade through Canadian ports, a policy that would channel products from the American Midwest along the St Lawrence route.[26]

As a capitalist Morin was no more successful in these larger railway enterprises than he had been in his Laurentian projects. Just months before joining the Codification Commission, in ill health and fearing that his wife would be left a pauper, he reported to her that he had lost £950 in the Montreal Mining Company, had sold what stock he had in the Grand Trunk (apparently for a loss or very little gain), and had paid back £200 which the St Lawrence and Atlantic had given him in stock. He did report annual dividends that the Colonial Life Insurance were paying him for £200 of stock which he had not paid up.[27]

Morin's personal papers make clear that he had never been financially successful as a commercial lawyer, land speculator, or investor. He remained in politics only with help from wealthy friends. In running for the assembly in 1841, he had met the land qualification by purchasing, but not paying for, land from the Boucherville family.[28] A decade later his finances – despite his judge's salary of £1000 a year – were still shaky and he undertook construction of his house on Rue d'Auteuil in Quebec City in 1857 by mortgaging his Laurentian property and by having his note endorsed by one of his Cartier relatives. George-Étienne Cartier's law partner, Joseph-Amable Berthelot, defended him in two important civil suits in Montreal where he was also in arrears for seigneurial dues.

Augustin-Norbert Morin
Clothed in his judge's robes, Morin holds the Ninety-Two Resolutions he
edited for Louis-Joseph Papineau. By Philippe Hébert, this statuette is in the
Séminaire de Saint-Hyacinthe, a fact that emphasizes Morin's strong link
through his wife to Saint-Hyacinthe's merchant and clerical elite.

In 1857 he offered to sell his cherished collection of agricultural books to the Parliamentary Library for £168. In the same year, he told his wife that his financial condition was so precarious that she might best renounce her right to his succession (and his debts), contenting herself with her dower right of £60 against his property.[29]

Morin's eclectic interests – journalism, politics, Catholic philanthropy, colonization, and agronomy – meant that the practice of law was rarely more than a part-time occupation. For a few months in 1842 he served as district judge of Kamouraska, Rimouski, and St Thomas, but he quickly resigned to re-enter politics. He did attract promising law students, including Hector Langevin, Joseph Doutre, and François-Magloire Derome, and he was involved in committee work for the bar: one formed to promote incorporation of the Quebec bar (1838), and another that established Bibaud's law school at the Collège Sainte-Marie. However, Morin was too active in politics to sustain a thriving commercial law practice and he never groomed a junior partner to act for him. In 1840 he and Cyrille Delagrave opened a law office in Morin's house, but the partnership apparently did not last. When Morin became speaker in 1848, his well-connected student, Hector Langevin, left to clerk with Cartier.[30] His important clients – ecclesiatical authorities in the Jesuit Estates question and the St Lawrence and Atlantic Railway – were apparently attracted to him for political rather than legal reasons.

In the 1830s, Morin was not an advocate of either radical law reform or codification; instead, his discourse echoed Viger's insistence on the dangers of Common law jurisprudence and on the inseparability of the Civil law and the seigneurial system. Lower Canada derived its 'particular' legal culture from this link, from its feudal form of land tenure, and from the complex and reciprocal family and social obligations inherent in customary law.

The inadequacy of English civil law for Canada was easily felt by all with an understanding of the colony. These laws – spread throughout the voluminous statute books of the imperial parliament or consisting of customs that varied from colony to colony around the Empire – were not of a nature to be ... easily applied in a country ... where land was held under another tenure; the reciprocal rights of seigneurs and censitaires having been conserved, it called for a particular jurisiprudence.[31]

Morin explained his legal ideology more fully in a lecture apparently prepared for Laval law students in the mid-1850s. Law, in a practical sense, he suggested, 'is the comparison of human acts and interest with the equity or the justice of the ruler which man in society has accepted … Law must flow from the conformity or differences of particular [human] acts with these natural virtues or recognized rules.' In his description of how judges needed sensitivity in adjusting laws that emanated from different sources to the complex reality of human behaviour, he appears to have been reiterating Savigny's sense of custom, history, and *Volksgeist*, or national spirit. Judges had to act not just by authoritative texts or precedent but by a careful balance of 'the art of reasoning' with a receptive state of mind – what Morin called a 'disposition' and 'volonté' to understand the deeper issues of the case.

To illustrate the complexity of exercising 'justice' in human society, he proposed a hypothetical inheritance case, the instance of a son who saw his inheritance from his father – land occupied by the family for generations – awarded to a stranger. Here he clearly juxtaposed custom to the formality of contract law.

If this son was a rustic closer to nature than educated in the order and functioning of society would he admit the two presumptions which formed the basis of his loss of possession – that the new proprietor had acted in good faith and could not be dispossessed without creating greater injustice, and secondly, that the natural heir had known the rule which would dispossess him after a certain delay and – not having acted – he had voluntarily renounced his rights.[32]

In 1854, Morin was appointed as the first dean of Université Laval's law faculty, as well as professor of natural law and the law of nations. With his appointment came an honorary doctorate of law from Laval. A year later, his nomination to the Superior Court brought complaints that he had not practised enough to be awarded a judgeship.[33] On the bench, his judgments received little attention in the *Lower Canada Reports / Décisions des Tribunaux du Bas-Canada* where the decisions of LaFontaine and Day dominated. Another complaint was that as co-premier and then judge, Morin was too busy to offer his courses regularly. 'Our judges are valuable for the honour they bring us,' the rector of Laval stated privately, 'but we need others for the work.'[34] To further complicate matters, Morin's always fragile health and financial situation both collapsed in the mid-1850s, and his correspondence shows increasing concern with death and bankruptcy.[35] His arthritis became worse, and in 1860, just three years after building a house on the prestigious Rue d'Auteuil in Quebec, Morin sold it, spending the rest of his life in a rented house on Rue Sainte-Ursule

Justice Morin's Library
Morin's 1800 volumes – donated to the Séminaire de Saint-Hyacinthe by his wife and still in the seminary's library – contained 227 titles in law, many of them multi-volume sets. His library demonstrates, however, that his real love was the rural economy, particularly husbandry. Among his 505 titles in agriculture were E.S. Delamer's *The Kitchen Garden* (n.d.), a *Mémoire sur les défrichements* (1741), and William Cobbett's *Cottage Economy* (1846).

in Quebec, in his wife's home town of Saint-Hyacinthe, or on his Sainte-Adèle estate.[36]

Aware that his reading in the law was inadequate for a judge and dean of law, Morin worked to educate himself. He travelled to Europe, researched in Rheinland law libraries, and drew up a 285-page bibliography, many of the titles being German works. He read Savigny and other works in German Civil and customary law and listed six German periodicals important for the study of Civil law.[37] His personal library presented another problem. Unlike his legal peers whose collections were concentrated in law and jurisprudence, Morin's passion was science and especially agronomy in which he had 505 titles.[38] In 1855, despite his financial difficulties, he spent some £350 buying law books from Jules-Isaïe Livernois's bookstore in Quebec City and the Bossange bookstore in Paris. From the latter he ordered Pothier's *Pandectae Justinianae* in Latin and two periodicals, *La Revue du droit français et étranger* and *La Revue étrangère de législation*. He also bought classics in English and American law – *Coke on Littleton*, Mathew Bacon's *New Abridgement of Law and Equity*, William Wetmore Story's *Conflict of Laws* (1834) and Stephen's *New Commentaries on the Law of England* (1841).[39]

When asked by Cartier in 1859 to serve on the Codification Commission, Morin replied that he would find it difficult to fill LaFontaine's shoes. He told Cartier that he was 'inapt' to assume responsibility for the Code of Procedure and that he would work 'only with hesitation' on the section dealing with English law; what was more, he did not want to be separated from his home and wife.[40] Nonetheless, he agreed to accept the appointment.

RENÉ-ÉDOUARD CARON

Codifier René-Édouard Caron (1800–76) was one of Quebec City's most prominent lawyers, specializing in large institutional clients. His parents, Augustin Caron and Élisabeth Lessard, were successful farmers, and his father represented Montmorency in the assembly. Born in Sainte-Anne-de-Beaupré near Quebec City, Caron was a contemporary of Morin at the Petit Séminaire of Quebec where teaching by the clerics was fuelled by vigorous rejection of the principles of the French Revolution. Caron clerked in the office of André-Rémi Hamel, was admitted to the bar in 1826, and then opened his law practice in Quebec City.[41]

By the 1830s Caron was active in politics, as mayor of Quebec City (1834–6) and as member of the assembly for the city's Upper Town (1834–6). Part of the group who revived the newspaper Le Canadien in 1831, Caron was strongly identified with the moderate 'Quebec party.' He resigned from the assembly in 1836 after disagreeing with the Patriotes and voting against Papineau; a year later he was named to the Legislative Council by Governor Lord Gosford. During the rebellions, he held a commission as captain in the Quebec artillery and later he became a justice of the peace (1846).[42] Although a leader of the opposition in Quebec City to the Union Act, Caron – like Morin and Cartier – adjusted to the reality of the Union and the politics of ethnic compromise, accepting nomination as mayor of Quebec City by the Special Council (1840). Caron was a strong supporter of the authority of both crown and church, organizing demonstrations of loyalty for several governors in the 1840s and signing the loyalty manifesto in 1849.[43] He served as speaker of the Legislative Council from 1843 to 1847 and 1848 to 1853.

His ties to the episcopate mixed spiritual, professional, and political interests. He and his wife were known for their piety: she hosted the Christmas party of the Sisters of Charity while he took pleasure in leading evening rosary. One of his major clients was the Séminaire de Québec.[44] With Morin, Cartier, and LaFontaine, Caron played a central role in cementing the alliance between the Liberal-Conservative Party and the Roman Catholic hierarchy. Caron was particularly close to Charles-Félix Cazeau, vicar general and the church's chief agent in negotiating delicate questions of education, Confederation, and minority rghts with the state.[45] Like Morin, Caron was active in education, serving on the board of the normal school in Quebec City (1836); and as a member of the Société des bons livres; as treasurer of the Quebec Bar Library; as vice-president of the Literary and Historical Society of Quebec (1844–5), the Union musicale (1834), and the Saint-Jean-Baptiste Society (1842–52); as president of the Library Association of Quebec (1845); and as honorary president of the Institut canadien (1848–52).[46]

With a successful commercial law practice and political career, Caron boosted his status with a good marriage. His wife, Marie-Vénérande-Josephine Deblois, was the daughter of Joseph-François Deblois, a well-known Gaspé entrepreneur, lawyer, member of the assembly, and later circuit judge.[47] One Caron son, Joseph-Philippe-René-Adolphe, sat in John A. Macdonald's cabinet and a grandson, Louis-Alexandre Taschereau, became premier of Quebec.

Caron had one of Quebec's most lucrative law practices and, according to Cartier, was involved in all of the important cases in Quebec City.[48] Caron was named queen's counsel in 1848; his clerks included François Évanturel, Télesphore Fournier, Cyrille Delagrave (Morin's partner in 1840 and secretary of the Seigneurial Commission, 1854), and Thomas McCord (secretary of the Codification Commission). Another student, Louis de Gonzague Baillargé, became his partner in 1844. Caron and Baillargé acted for the City of Quebec, the Séminaire de Québec, and other prominent Catholic institutions.[49] Caron was also a strong supporter of railways in the Quebec area, particularly the North Shore Railway and the Intercolonial Railway.[50] Caron's busy political and legal life left him little time for the intellectual side of the law although his library did include a copy of Montesquieu's *Spirit of the Laws*.[51] Caron was named to the Superior Court of Quebec in 1853, but his judgments – going by their inclusion in the *Lower Canada Reports* – were not particularly innovative. Promoted to the Appeal Court of the Queen's Bench in 1855, Caron was overshadowed by Chief Justice LaFontaine in his decisions in appeal cases.

Caron was a member of the Special Court established by the Seigneurial Act of 1854, and he contributed a sixty-four–page brief on fiefs and seigneuries, banal rights, and the ownership of waterways.[52] His memoir was important in the broad definition it gave to the property rights of seigneurs and, therefore, to their claims for indemnification. Reviewing the history of seigneurial tenure in Canada, he examined its governance by the Custom of Paris, the Edicts of Marly (1711), which obliged seigneurs to concede lands for dues (as opposed to selling concessions), and the Edict of 1732, which specifically prohibited seigneurs from selling

René-Édouard Caron

René-Édouard Caron's villa 'Clermont' (c. 1850)

This Joseph Légaré painting of Caron's estate in the Quebec suburb of Sillery gives a strong sense of the villa life enjoyed by the bar élite. Caron lived here as judge and codifier, selling it in 1873 when he moved into 'Spencer Wood,' the lieutenant governor's official residence. Day and Cartier had similar villas in Montreal while Morin built a townhouse on Rue d'Auteuil in Quebec's Upper Town. 'Clermont' was along the stately Chemin Saint-Louis and overlooked the St Lawrence River. Caron commissioned its design in 1848–9 by his law partner's brother, architect Charles Baillairgé. 'Clermont' was known for the beauty of the fruit and flower trees planted by Caron's wife, Marie-Vénérande-Joséphine Deblois, while Caron himself was a prominent member of the Quebec Horticultural Society and the Quebec Turf Club.

forest lands. In determining seigneurial indemnities, Caron argued that seigneurs had the right to compensation even for dues that were higher than permitted by law. He was equally liberal in his interpretation of the seigneur's right to what he called 'the lucrative privilege' of *banalité* and in describing non-navigable rivers as 'the property of seigneurs' and not of *censitaires* along their banks.[53]

With the completion of the Codification Commission's work, Caron resumed his seat on the Court of Queen's Bench. Hector Langevin wanted Caron named chief justice of the Superior Court in June 1866. Cartier, however, passed over him in favour of an anglophone, arguing that 'it would not be wise to excite the British element of Lower Canada' during the delicate Confederation negotiations.[54] Caron served as lieutenant governor of Quebec from 1873 until his death in 1876.

FRANÇOIS-MAXIMILIEN BIBAUD

The shared characteristics of the francophone codifiers – their generation and education, their involvement with railways and other entrepreneurial activities, their power in politics, at the bar, and on the bench, their willingness to compromise between customary law and capitalist principles of law, particularly freedom of contract, and their sensitivity to the demands of the anglophone minority – can be illustrated clearly by comparing them with their colleague, François-Maximilien Bibaud (1823–87). An outspoken critic of these compromises by the bar élite and defender of *ancien régime* legal and land institutions, particularly as they affected family and community, Bibaud was the most important legal thinker of the period and the founder of the law program at the Collège Sainte-Marie in Montreal.[55] By 1861 his program had conferred eighty-six bachelor of law degrees, and his graduates included Hector Fabre, Charles-Chamilly de Lorimier, and Louis-Amable Jetté. Bibaud wrote numerous works in law, history, and philosophy, including an abridged version of Blackstone, a translation of Justinian's *Institutes*, a treatise on contract, and *Essai de logique judiciaire* (1853). His biographers André Morel and Yvan Lamonde describe his *Commentaires sur les lois du Bas-Canada* as 'the only original, systematic exposition of the law in Canada East to be published before the codification of the civil law.'[56]

Son of Michel Bibaud, magistrate, historian, teacher, and founder of *La bibliothèque canadienne*, Bibaud received a classical education at the Collège de Montréal before clerking in the law office of Joseph Bourret and Toussaint Peltier. To counter McGill's expanding program – taught largely in English and emphasizing commercial law – Bibaud began teaching law at the Jesuit Collège Sainte-Marie in 1851, modelling his program on German faculties at Bonn and Leipzig.[57] Bibaud criticized his peers for having 'lost the secret of fundamental studies of jurisprudence' and of falling back on an easy reliance on the Napoleonic Code, and insisted on going back to the principles of Roman and natural law.[58] His teaching was based on the tutorial system and he tested his students with *Repetitoria* – oral exams in which students were interrogated by prominent jurists such as LaFontaine in Roman law and Cartier on contracts.

Cartier and Morin were important in founding Bibaud's program; they served on his organizational committee and lobbied the bishop of Montreal for a francophone school as a counterpart to McGill. In 1851, for example, *La Minerve*, Cartier's party organ, published Bibaud's lengthy attacks on William Badgley's project to codify the criminal law.[59] Badgley's proposed laws were, according to Bibaud, 'too specialized' and not based adequately on principles or a philosophy of law. England, Bibaud reminded his readers, was a country where cutting down a private tree was a capital crime so serious that not even the clergy could avoid trial in royal courts. Normally a strong supporter of property, Bibaud in this instance expressed concern for the dispossessed – the landless and native peoples – arguing that land 'belonged to no one' and noting that 'the state was more than the interest of proprietors.' He concluded by urging natural law, Roman law, and Catholic theology over the law of English Protestants; rather than Blackstone, Bibaud offered Grotius, Pufendorf, and Montesquieu as models for Lower Canadian law reform.[60]

Bibaud's strong defence of seigneurialism, seigneurial justice, and his inflexibility on the central importance of the Custom of Paris in Civil law inevitably distanced him from Chief Justice LaFontaine, Attorney General Cartier, and the codifiers. His essential ideological difference with the bar élite centred on his insistence on the importance to the French Canadian collectivity of the historic values inherent in feudalism and custom. In his *Commentaires sur les lois du Bas-Canada*, published in 1859 – the very year that the Codification Commmission began sitting – Bibaud warned that old law, particularly that dealing with family relationships, was being undermined by capitalist principles. The Registry Ordinance of 1841, for example, in allowing women to sign away dower rights, opened up 'sacred property' under the Custom of Paris to people's 'natural desire to contract.'[61] The abolition of *retrait lignager* in 1855 – a customary right that had permitted heirs and certain family members to retain alienated immovables by reimbursing the purchase price – also worried Bibaud

François-Maximilien Bibaud (1823–87)
This photo suggests Bibaud's strong personality and scholasticism. As well as
being noted for his legal writings and establishment of his short-lived
law school in Montreal, Bibaud was well known as a journalist, historian of
Canada, and polemicist.

who interpreted it as part of a larger deterioration of the rights of wives, children, and heirs.

Le retrait is completely contradictory to the genius of our Anglo-Saxon compatriotes who strive to distance themselves from any obstacle to the sure regulation of their business affairs and transactions; an Englishman who buys assumes that he becomes uncontested proprietor of his purchase.[62]

Bibaud's insistence on customary usages, his hostility to freedom of contract and other capitalist principles of English property law, and his contentious personality relegated him to the sidelines of legal power in Lower Canada. By the late 1850s, when the commission was named, Bibaud's role was limited to that of pamphleteer and teacher. In the institutionalization of the study of law, it was of great significance that Lower Canada's first – and most prestigious – law faculty was established at McGill where over one hundred bachelor of civil law degrees had been granted by 1866.[63] Because of the ultramontane versus gallican battle raging between Bishop Bourget of Montreal and episcopal authorities in Quebec City, Bibaud refused to consider any affiliation with Université Laval, and in 1867 his program closed.

CHARLES DEWEY DAY

The career of Charles Dewey Day (1806–84) emphasizes the political function of the law and the importance of profession, place, and status in a community beleaguered by immigration, urbanization, and class strife. His service on the commission alongside Morin and Caron brought ethnicity into line with class and guild as bearing walls of codification.

Day was the intellectual leader of the anglophone community as chancellor of McGill University, the most important judge after Chief Justice LaFontaine, and, it will be suggested below, the key member of the Codification Commission. Day was American-born, raised in a merchant's family, and shaped by the ideas of Lower Canada's pre-rebellion commercial and legal anglophone élite. His views on the European and American revolutions, seigneurial tenure, and registration of land were predictable. At the same time, he moved from prosecuting Patriotes in 1839 to being picked by ex-Patriote Cartier two decades later to be a codifier, a progression that illustrates the fundamental change in Lower Canadian class and ethnic relations in the post-rebellion period. His career served both his class and his ethnic community, strengthening the

Charles Dewey Day (1806–84)
The son of an American merchant, Day was Anglican and linked by marriage
to Bank of Montreal and Grand Trunk Railway interests. Solicitor general of
Canada East, named to the Queen's Bench in 1842 and to the Superior Court
in 1850, Judge Day was first chancellor of McGill University and one of the
founders of its law faculty before being named to the Codification Commission.

anglophone élite's separateness within a larger framework of compromise with fundamental French institutions, such as the Civil law. In 1865, as the Civil Code came to fruition, Day received academic laurels from his francophone peers – an honorary doctorate of law from Université Laval.[64]

Born in Bennington, Vermont, Day came to Montreal as a boy in 1812. His mother, Laura Dewey, was a member of Admiral George Dewey's family. His father, 'Captain' Ithmar Hubbell Day, operated a Montreal drug and commission business, Day, Gelston and Company, with two American partners. In Montreal the Days lived in a villa on the western slope of Mount Royal. By 1821 the family had moved to the Aylmer Road in Hull, where the elder Day was both an industrial producer and a merchant owning saw and fulling mills, as well as trading with Amerindians at the Deschênes Rapids portage.[65] Day was apprenticed by his father to a five-year law clerkship with another well-known American in Montreal, Samuel Gale. Vitriolic in his views of francophone society and Catholic institutions, a powerful landowner, and establishment lawyer for clients like Lord Selkirk, Gale was later named judge on the King's Bench.[66]

Admitted to the bar in 1827, Day practised in both Montreal and Hull, drawing clients from his father's circle of merchant and sawmilling friends. Day's political career was assisted by political contributions from timber baron Ruggles Wright in his successful election campaign for the Ottawa seat in the assembly (1841), and directorships such as that of the National Loan Fund Life Assurance Company in 1842 marked his advance.[67] After serving on the Codification Commission, Day left his judgeship in favour of several prestigious commissions and clients. He acted on the commission which determined the assumption of provincial debts by the newly established federal government, chaired the Royal Commission on the Pacific Railway scandal (1873), and acted for the Hudson's Bay Company in its claims against the United States.[68]

Marriage cemented his increasingly comfortable social position. With the death of his first wife Barbara Lyon, he married Maria Margaret Holmes, the daughter of Benjamin Holmes, general manager of the Bank of Montreal and vice-president of the Grand Trunk Railway. These family connections, his annual judge's salary of £1000, and his prestige as principal and then chancellor of McGill University placed him solidly in the anglophone establishment. The family lived in preferred anglophone neighbourhoods; from their Montreal residence on Victoria Street near Sainte-Catherine Street, the family moved in 1845 up Mount Royal to a home on Cote-des-Neiges. Summers were spent at Glenbrook, an estate on Lake Memphremagog.[69]

Like Sewell and Gale, Day attracted promising students who subsequently reinforced his legal network. Among his clerks were John Rose, who became Montreal's most important commercial lawyer and minister of finance; Andrew Robertson, treasurer and *bâtonnier* of the Quebec bar and editor of the *Lower Canada Reports*; and Lewis Thomas Drummond, who as attorney general was a crucial figure in the reform of Lower Canada's municipal and land law.

As a young lawyer, Day linked law and politics, combining Ottawa Valley and Montreal interests. A critic of Papineau's Ninety-Two Resolutions, Day was active in the Montreal Constitutional Association, seconding a resolution calling for strengthened British connections. He became more agitated as rebellion approached, describing the Patriotes as 'mad revolutionaries' and accepting a lieutenant's commission.[70] In 1838 Day was named a queen's counsel and he accepted appointment as deputy judge advocate for the Patriote courts martial. With *habeas corpus* suspended in Lower Canada, the treason trials – described by Murray Greenwood as 'one of the gravest abuses of due process in Canadian history' – began in November 1838. Day was highly visible, prosecuting Patriotes, such as Chevalier de Lorimier whom he described as a dangerous criminal deserving death on the gallows, and signing death warrants.[71]

With the trials completed and the legislature suspended, Day was named solicitor general in May 1840. He was a member of the Special Council that formulated ordinances concerning bankruptcy, the administration of justice, commutation of seigneurialism in the Montreal area, universal land registry, and the civil role of the Catholic Church in Lower Canada. With Attorney General Charles Richard Ogden, Day was instrumental in the establishment in 1841 of the Revision Commission to compile Lower Canadian statutes and ordinances – an important precursor to codification.

In 1841, Day presented a bill establishing common schools. These schools would form the foundation of a 'great general system of national education ... extending to the whole Province [i.e. Canada West as well as Canada East], and embracing the whole population.' The bill emphasized centralization, uniformity, appointed (as opposed to elected) school officials, and strict controls over texts, teachers, and curriculum. It was anathema to nationalists like Denis-Benjamin Viger, and it confirmed the Catholic episcopate's suspicions of Day's ethnic and religious motives.[72]

Hanging the Patriotes at the Montreal Jail in 1839 (Henri Julien)
In the fourteen trials in which 106 prisoners were tried for treason, 99 were
found guilty and, of these, 12 were hanged and 58 transported to New South
Wales. Day was paid £1170 for his professional services as deputy judge
advocate as well as £225 as an aid to publishing the state trials, and shared
£900 with three other deputy judge advocates for expenses in attending the
courts martial.

Day, who apparently spoke little French at this stage of his career, made
his feelings on language well known. In 1842 he shouted down LaFontaine for speaking French in the assembly. On the bench, Day was quickly
in an altercation with ethnic overtones over whether Justice Jean-Roch
Rolland's deafness affected his ability to discharge his duties.[73]
Like Perrault, Viger, Cartier, Morin, and others in the legal élite, Day
had a lifelong interest in education. He was a director of the Montreal
High School (1850), vice-president of the Montreal Horticultural Society
(1851) and the Anglican Church Society, and president of the Royal
Institution for the Advancement of Learning (1852–84); it was Day who
gave the address at the Provincial Industrial Exhibition in 1850.[74] The
fledgling McGill College became his particular mission; *pro tempore* principal, 1853–5, he was named McGill's first chancellor (1864) and held the
position until his death two decades later.

Before the bar was incorporated in 1849, the Advocates' Library of Montreal had an important professional role as well as educational and library functions. Day was admitted as a member in 1835, was vice-president in 1838 and 1841, and president in 1839, 1840, and 1845. When LaFontaine replaced him as president in 1846, it signalled a larger francophone presence in the Montreal bar élite.[75]

Although McGill had offered law courses since 1843, their influence had been uneven. The first instructor and later first dean of the law faculty, William Badgley, was one of Montreal's most important practitioners; he was attorney general, 1847–8, and *bâtonnier* of the Montreal bar, 1853–5.[76] As principal of McGill, Day was instrumental in the establishment of its Law Faculty in 1853. The links between the faculty and the merchant élite were direct: Badgley's father was a North West Company merchant; the family of Frederick Torrance, professor of international and Roman law, dominated the Montreal forwarding business; Day's father had been a merchant in Montreal and along the Ottawa Valley trade route.

While Badgley envisaged the disappearance of Lower Canadian Civil law into a pan–Canadian Common law system, Day strongly defended the Civil law. He also had a pluralistic vision of legal education in which students developed an understanding of what he called 'certain primary and fundamental principles.'

There are laws of God, of Nature and of common sense which must underlie and sustain all positive legislation. There are also general [maxims] and rules which have acquired a prescriptive authority and enter into the habits of thought and mode of reasoning of educated lawyers and constitute a kind of universal education.[77]

Under Day's pressuring, McGill's program became resolutely international; courses in 1856 included constitutional law, obligations, Civil law, Roman law, the origin of the laws of France, England, and Lower Canada, real estate and customary law, commercial contracts, legal bibliography, criminal law, and international law.

In 1842, Day left politics for the bench, first the Court of Queen's Bench for the District of Montreal and then the Montreal Superior Court after the judicial reorganization of 1850.[78] His accession to a judgeship was part of a political process that saw important elements in the older legal, merchant, and religious élite allied with the LaFontaine Reformers who moved to power in the 1840s. There is little evidence, however, that Day had significant social contact with francophone society and he apparently spoke little French when appointed to the bench.[79]

Earlier generations of anglophone jurists had emerged largely from Common law environments (Yale – Chief Justice William Smith, Lincoln's Inn – Chief Justice William Osgoode, Drogheda Academy, Ireland – Justice Edward Bowen, Oxford and New Brunswick – Chief Justice Jonathan Sewell), but Day clerked in Montreal. Like Cartier, Morin, and Caron, he was brought up in the Civil law tradition and his training, experience, and career had Lower Canadian horizons. Unlike several anglophone predecessors on the bench, he respected the indigenous law.

Although Day's papers have disappeared and the full contents of his library are unknown, it undoubtedly contained several thousand volumes. A few dozen of his most valuable books can be found in the McGill Law Library. [80] In French law, his library included Dumoulin on *Coutumes* (1615), Ricard's *Donations* (1713), Henriquez on the *Code des seigneurs* (1780), and the *Répertoire universel et raisonné de jurisprudence civile, criminelle, canonique et bénéficiale* (1784). He owned Azuni on the *Maritime Law of Europe* (1806), Lawes on *Pleading in Civil Actions* (1808), and Chitty on *Bills of Exchange* (1827). In addition to his own collection, we know that he borrowed books from the large library of the Torrance and Morris firm.[81]

During his seventeen years on the bench, Day heard hundreds of the most important cases in the Montreal District, ranging from the seigneurial obligations of industrial millers, to patent cases and the civil responsibility of the mayor of Montreal in the Gavazzi riots. His judgments – the most important of which were reported in the *Lower Canada Reports*, the *Lower Canada Jurist*, or in the 'Law Intelligence' columns of the Montreal *Gazette* and Montreal *Herald* – were clear expressions of legal formalism: strict interpretation of the law, primacy of written contract, equality in contract, suspicion of jury decisions and awards in civil trials, and protection for vested property, particularly the milling and riparian rights of seigneurs.[82]

The growing use of steam, machines, and large industrial shops and the growth of major industrial, transportation, and financial corporations brought new significance to warranty, injury, damage, employment contracts, and nuisance cases. The Grand Trunk, usually represented by Attorney General Cartier or his partner Joseph-Amable Berthelot, was a frequent litigant before Day. In the intimate world of bar and bench, Berthelot replaced Day on the bench when he was named to the Codification Commission. Day's decisions in several important railway cases involving industrial accidents and jury awards, hiring contracts, and negligence gave a narrow definition to the liability of industrial or transportation companies. Himself an insurance company director, Day took particular care in the instruction of juries in insurance cases, reminding them of the importance 'of the uniformity of principles.' Insurance companies 'run great risks for a small remuneration' and, if they were to remain in business, insurance contracts 'must be carried out by all concerned in them strictly according to their conditions and not on feelings of liberality or false sympathy for assumed hardship.'[83] In *Ravary v. the Grand Trunk Railway* (1857), he showed his suspicion of juries, denying their competence to assess compensation for workers killed on the job:

The idea that the Jury would be in a position to assess damages upon the basis of the mere fact of the death of a parent, he looked upon as perfectly untenable. The deceased parent might have been one [on] whom his family depended for support, but on the other hand, he might have been an aged man, or a man of vicious habits.[84]

A crucial part of Day's approach to contract was his insistence that it be applied equally, whatever the privileges of a particular group. In *Cuvillier v. Munro* (1848), for example, defendant Munro protested his arrest for debt on the grounds that as a legislator he should not be liable to arrest for civil process. After reviewing the laws of England, New York, Massachussets, Vermont, and Privy Council decisions of appeals from Jamaica and Newfoundland, Day categorically rejected the privilege of members of the assembly in terms that clearly established the rights of credit over the privileges of particular groups: 'the law which gives a universal right to a creditor is not to be defeated by a particular necessity.'[85]

Day's social conservatism and insistence on a literal interpretation of the law – what he called looking 'at the question as one of strict law' – was especially rigorous in matters affecting women or family. A fellow judge was particularly vexed with Day's strict interpretation in a paternity case, *Stewart v. McEdward* (1854). The plaintiff's sisters and brother-in-law were the only people in the house who could prove the material facts, but according to Day's reading of the French Ordinance of 1667, they – being members of the family – were only admissible as witnesses in cases of adultery or family violence (*sévices*). In dissenting, Justice George Vanfelson said that in an extreme case, such as the one being heard, the more flexible French civil procedure, which admitted family members as witnesses, should be used:

What, a man of depraved character, and of immoral habits, will be allowed to partake of the hospitality of a father, abuse his confidence and seduce his daughter in the dead of night, and will be allowed to go free, because no strangers can be found to convict him of the deed? I consider that to be neither law, justice nor reason.[86]

Leasing, construction, hiring, and sales contracts were also subject to Day's literal interpretation of the contract, constituting what he called 'binding law between the parties' and 'an inflexible rule.' In *Boulanget v. Doutre* (1854), for example, tenant Doutre abandoned his leased house, claiming that rain 'found its way through the roof onto the beds and clothes of the inmates … that after having so suffered all the winter and summer, he had … notified the defective state of the house to the plaintiff by a notarial protest.' In finding for the lessor, Day insisted upon the integrity of the lease and, citing Pothier's *Contrat de louage*, ruled that a tenant could only have his lease terminated by court order.[87] *Kennedy v. Smith* (1854) revolved around a construction contract, which stipulated that no charge for extra work would be made unless the order for such work was given in writing. At the trial, defendant Smith refused to answer whether he had given the plaintiff verbal orders to execute the extra work which constituted most of the claim. Day's judgment sustained his refusal to answer, noting that the contract had in fact removed the litigant's normal right to question his opponent:

The question was whether this stipulation in the contract was a binding law between the parties which excluded the plaintiff from the ordinary right of examining the defendant on interrogations to prove the extra work which had been done without any *written* order. The majority of the court held that it was. By this stipulation between the parties they had established an inflexible rule which excluded the admission of all kinds of evidence but written evidence.[88]

This emphasis on the 'written' was the central part of Day's decision in *Syme et al. v. Heward* (1856) in assessing whether merchant Heward could be committed to a sale of 1000 barrels of Upper Canadian flour by the act of his drunken broker, Robert Esdaile. To Day, the issue was not the degree of the broker's intoxication (an argument that Pothier insisted on), or the good faith shown by the plaintiff Symes, or the fact that Esdaile was known as the agent for Heward. Day's dismissal of the case was based on lack of written evidence that Esdaile 'was authorized to act as the agent of the Defendant' and the fact that the defendant had not agreed by 'any note or memorandum in writing of the sale of the flour.'[89]

This concern for the structure, integrity, and nature of consent in the contract was clear in *Bernier v. Beauchemin*. Before obtaining his patent for the manufacture of a 'new and improved double stove,' Bernier had sold some 200 stoves. Beauchemin had bought the stove and manufactured a copy. Day was categoric that patent could not be retroactive and could not usurp the absolute right of property inherent in the original sale contract:

If I buy a stove, and at the same time no prohibition to its manufacture and use exists by patent, my right of property enables me to use this stove, to pull it to pieces and find out how it is made, and manufacture a stove of the same kind and sell it. This right is based, independently of statute, on the broad rules of common sense, and cannot be taken away by any letter patent granted subsequently to my acquiring it.[90]

While Day's formalism was dominant in his contract law judgments, property law and particularly seigneurialism contained fundamental legal conundrums of balancing vested interests with capitalist definitions of property. And, Day made clear, once the land tenure question had been opened, radical property solutions were to be avoided. At the opposite end of the ideological spectrum from the rebels in 1838 who warned in their Proclamation of Independence that they would treat seigneurial tenure 'as if it had never existed,' Day insisted that seigneurialism be treated

in its legal aspect only; without regard to the interest it has excited abroad, to the unpopular and objectionable character of any rights, or of any class to which it relates or to any other extrinsic consideration whatever.[91]

At the same time, cautious reform of the Lower Canadian land tenure system was necessary and, as a member of the Seigneurial Commission of 1856, he gave a textbook definition of the transformation of land under bourgeois law. Describing the 'feudal system' as having 'outlived its age,' Day anticipated that it would cede to 'social progress,' to 'new ideas,' and to 'new men.' Critical in this transition from feudalism to free market were the 'private rights' inherent in seigneurialism; these had to be 'carefully ascertained and amply provided for.'

The state, as a matter of 'public virtue and national character,' would play a central role in compensating the rights of seigneurs:

But we are not to charge the sin or misfortune of its old age, upon the present generation of seigniorial proprietors. The public interests demand the abolition

of the tenure: but public virtue and national character demand, even more imper-
atively, that all private rights invaded by its abolition, should be carefully ascertained and amply provided for.[92]

Two premises dominate his judgments in seigneurial cases: his literal
interpretation of the law in seigneurial relations, and the integrity of
contract. In the challenge of a steam miller and distiller against the
seigneur of Blainville's right to assess the *banalité* (*Monk v. Morris*, 1852),
Day unequivocally upheld the seigneur's banal rights, noting that it was
'utterly untenable' for a steam miller to be exempted from *banalités*:

The principle of the right to prevent the building of other mills or to demolish
them when built, clearly is, that they infringe upon the Seignior's right, by
interfering with the banal mill. In connexion with the same point, is the pretension
that because the chief object and occupation of the mills in question are to grind
grain for manufacturing distilled spirits, and for commercial purposes, and not
to grind for the *censitaires* of the Plaintiff, they ought not to be considered to fall
within the prohibitions of the law. But the law makes no such distinction and the
Court can make none ...[93]

Justice Day's emphasis on what he called 'my grand rule' of maintaining the integrity of contracts was of particular significance in the countryside. Here the increased population density, changes in village
economies, labour mobility, new rural industry, and increasing integration in urban markets led *censitaires* to challenge seigneurs who increased
seigneurial dues or who sold rather than granting seigneurial lands as
provided for under the Edicts of Marly (1711).[94] In *Boston v. L'Eriger dit
Laplante* (1854), Day had to determine the legality of whether the seigneur,
Boston, could 'sell and concede land at the same time' on his seigneuries
of Thwaite and St James. Day found that, although it had never been the
intention that seigneurs sell concessions, it was not against the law to do
so. More important than seigneurial traditions of granting land was the
fact that peasants had entered 'voluntarily' into sale contracts with Boston. Refusing to force the seigneur to return the sale money, Day subordinated seigneurial law to capitalist property relations, particularly
freedom of contract:

The party who voluntarily contracts waives the right given by the *arrêt* (of Marly,
1711), and it is his affair. There might be several applicants for the same land and
one might pay more than another ... The error of law, its causing the nullity of

the contract, is where a party has performed something under the erroneous impression that he was compelled to do it, when in fact he was not. In the present case there was no compulsion, there was no obligation on the Defendant to buy the land, he did so voluntarily.[95]

Attorney General Cartier certainly knew Day personally in the small shop of Montreal lawyers and jurists where both were active in professional activities at the Advocates' Library and the newly established bar. He had also appeared regularly before Day on behalf of his Grand Trunk clients. Day's roots in the anglophone commercial bourgeoisie, his regional strength in Montreal and the Ottawa Valley, his power in the educational and bar élite, and his judgments consistently supporting property and freedom of contract, along with his conservative family values, gave him strong appeal to the attorney general as a codifier.

These biographies of Morin, Caron, and Day – and their contrast with that of François-Maximilien Bibaud – give a sense of the codifiers' milieu, ideology, and membership in an urban legal and political élite. Born in small communities in the early nineteenth century, each had moved permanently to Montreal or Quebec City by his teenage years. None was connected with the great landed families of the seigneurial or Château Clique élite: one was from a merchant family, two from farm families. Day's early education is unknown, but the two francophones shared a classical college education at the Petit Séminaire in Quebec.

Rebellion politics divided the three young lawyers in the 1830s. One was a prominent Patriote and was charged with high treason; two held military commissions during the rebellions. Day was prosecutor at the Patriotes' courts martial. All three sat in the assembly and each cut his administrative teeth in sensitive portfolios – solicitor general, co-premier, speaker – and moved to the bench with first-hand experience of Lower Canada's linguistic, class, religious, and ethnic realities. Day, renowned for his hostility to Patriote politics in the 1830s and to LaFontaine's promotion of French in the early 1840s, mellowed on the bench. Both francophones spoke English well. Caron was an anglophile with a deep respect for the crown and British institutions; the more nationalist Morin was also known for his tolerance and his sense of ethnic compromise.

Each had important family, professional, and political ties that allowed him to bridge ethnic, religious, and business communities. Day was the offspring of a timber merchant and director of an insurance company; the three had commercial practices that drew on seigneurial, merchant, and

Université Laval

Administered by the Séminaire de Québec, Laval established law as one of its first faculties along with theology, medecine, and arts. The law faculty opened in 1854 with Morin as its first dean; the only other law professor was Jacques Crémazie who taught civil law. Laval awarded each of the codifiers an honorary doctorate of law.

The law faculties at both Laval and McGill, where Charles Dewey Day was principal and later chancellor, expanded rapidly and by the late 1860s monopolized law school education in Lower Canada. Attendance at law school was not obligatory for admission to the bar, but the normal clerkship of five years was reduced to three years with completion of the course of study in a college or seminary and completion of a course of law in a college or seminary.

institutional clients. Their power and prestige lay less in land, international trade, or the Colonial Office than in emerging institutions of the mid-nineteenth century – political parties, business corporations, the universities, bar associations, and government departments, such as Crown Lands or Justice.

The marriages of the three added to their social bonding into important banking, merchant, clerical, and professional constituencies. Two were hired as lawyers by major church corporations: Caron acted for the Séminaire de Québec and Morin for the Jesuits. But their perspectives were not confined to pre-industrial religious institutions nor to the exchange and land sectors of the economy. Morin's substantial acreage originated in freehold crown land in the Laurentians; Caron was an urban landlord. Each participated personally in the colony's expanding capitalist activities – the railways, insurance or telegraph companies, and developing industries, such as mining. While the entrepreneurialism of Day, whose father-in-law was vice-president of the Grand Trunk Railway, was limited after 1842 by his judgeship, Morin acted as president of the St Lawrence and Atlantic Railway. Caron, particularly as mayor of Quebec, was known for his strong support of Quebec-area railways such as the Intercolonial and the North Shore Railway.

The three agreed on the need to dismantle seigneurial tenure but – sensitive to historic property rights – with full compensation for seigneurs. On the bench and in the Codification Commission, they accorded a central position to capitalist principales such as freedom of contract and security for mortgages, although Morin in particular worried about loss of the values, the reciprocal duties, and the centrality of land inherent in the Custom of Paris.

As well as their clustering of family, cabinet, and boardroom activities, they all had important professional networks through the bar associations, the law clerks they trained, and their roles in the founding of university law faculties at Laval and McGill. The organization of law programs, the hiring of faculty, and the crippling of Bidaud's law school were elements that gave legitimacy and institutional weight to the legal culture that would envelop codification.

Day had been on the bench for fifteen years; his fellow codifiers Morin and Caron were essentially career politicians who became jurists in the mid-1850s. Each represented a different constituency: Day, an anglophone, graduated from the rough school of Ottawa Valley politics to speak for Montreal capitalists. Caron's name was synonymous with the regional interests of Quebec City. Morin, successor to LaFontaine as co-premier, had a wide reputation for integrity and strong loyalty to the rural population, the church, and causes such as colonization. It was to their political maturity rather than judicial brilliance, to their solid social conservatism, and to their sensitivity to the subtleties of both customary and capitalist legal traditions that Attorney General Cartier was reaching out in naming them to the Codification Commission.

5

Politics of the Codification Commission, 1857–66

Although eighteen months have since elapsed [since publication of the
Codifier's *First Report*], no review or even notice ... has appeared in print
in the English language. This is doubtless to be accounted for by the fact
that copies have not been furnished to members of the profession generally;
otherwise surely the work would not have been received in silence by the
English-speaking members of the Bar.

Lawyer Thomas Ritchie (1863)[1]

This code can be considered a good code for a Catholic nation taking into
account the fact that it concerns a people of mixed religion.

Papal delegate (1870)[2]

The act establishing the Codification Commission was one of three law
reform bills enacted on 10 June 1857. With the 'Act for settling the Law
concerning lands held in Free and Common Socage' and the 'Judicature
Act,' codification would culminate a two-decade process in which Lower
Canada's legal culture was profoundly transformed. We have seen the
weight of this change: the collapse of seigneurial law; the realignment of
power among Lower Canada's social groups; institutionalization of the
education and corporate rights of legal professionals; measures concerning registry, bankruptcy, and statute consolidation; reinforcement of the
principle of equality in contract over the particular status of wives,
seigneurs, and others.

Despite these changes in the years between the rebellions and 1857, regional considerations remained of great political importance. As state formation, modernization, universal models, and fundamentality became central concerns of urban authorities in Montreal and Quebec, outlying regions, isolated and driven by particular ethnic and social dynamics, dug in their heels, insisting on the dignity of traditional ways, laws, and landholding. In the Eastern Townships, Nicolet, and the Gaspé, people resisted taxation, changes in land tenure, and the imposition of central-ized educational, municipal, and judicial institutions. Conscious in the post-rebellion years of potential defiance in the countryside, the Special Council had established rural police in the District of Montreal, a con-stabulary charged with reporting 'any intelligence, commotion, or impor-tant event':

Every member of the force will make himself acquainted with every road in and about his Section, and he will learn the name and residence, character, opinions and influence of every person of note therein.[3]

But as with the anti-rent farmers' rebellion in New York state, the extension of police, regional courts, and other forces of order did not settle rural unrest, particularly resistance to debt collection. Lawyer Peter Winter, noting his 'disgust and want of confidence' in the ability of a single judge – given the number of cases involving merchants and their debtors – to cover the entire Gaspé, reported to the government in 1842 that 'the judicature should be altogether withdrawn and abolished in the District.' In the period 1846–50, the peasantry aided by members of the landed élite rebelled against the emerging alliance of LaFontaine's Reform professionals with the local clergy. Laws imposing compulsory schooling and education taxes provoked widespread rioting and, despite the personal intervention of Bishop Bourget, barns and schools were burned, tax collectors and schoolmasters were subjected to charivaris, horses were maimed, and municipal tax records destroyed in rural areas around Trois-Rivières and Montreal.[4] In the Ottawa Valley, with its tradition of ethnic violence, Sheriff Louis-Maurice Coutlée of Aylmer noted with satisfaction: 'Received 25 soldiers equipment with rifles and ammunition to be used whenever required to enforce the execution of civil processes in this district.'[5]

Expansion and reorganization of the court system was intended to reduce these differences and to give regional judicial teeth to the central government. The Judicature Act of 1857 – known euphemistically as 'the decentralization bill' – divided Lower Canada into nineteen judicial districts. Up to £5000 was provided for construction of a jail and court-house in each new district; the central government designated the judicial seat in each district and imposed a common set of architectural plans and construction regulations. In judicial districts like Bedford, the courthouse and jail complex, completed in Sweetsburg in 1861, became the region's largest building, dwarfing churches, merchant estates, and manufactures. Along with this physical plant, the act grafted another powerful symbol of authority onto regional life – an element of what Robert Griswold calls 'moral theatre' – by obliging judges to live in their districts rather than in Montreal or Quebec.[6]

With a largely anglophone population in the areas first settled and a history of autonomy and political assertiveness, the Eastern Townships represented a particular political problem. Inhabitants of the Townships expressed their views on taxation, colonization, justice, and road policy through petitions, their political representatives, and participation in the rebellions. As late as 1849, important politicians, militia officers, and magistrates had expressed interest in annexation to the United States.[7] The historic separateness of the Townships in land tenure had been tacitly recognized in the Quebec Act, the Constitutional Act (1791), the Canada Tenures Act (1825), early legislation affecting registry offices (1831), and, as late as 1860, by its exemption from statute labour provisions of the Municipal and Road Act. The creation of a Legislative Council in Quebec was in recognition of anglophone fears of the majority in the assembly. The Townships' status was recognized in the British North America Act's provision giving protection for schools and by section 21 which, to protect the anglophone minority, designated Quebec senators to represent specific ridings.[8]

Confusion over whether English property law or French Civil law applied to lands held in free and common soccage led to important litigation on issues such as the validity of dower and general hypothecs that observed French forms – complicated issues still before the appeal courts in the 1850s in *Stuart v. Bowman* and *Wilcox v. Wilcox*.[9] Insisting on the principle that 'lands of every tenure should be as far as possible uniform,' the Act 'for settling the Law concerning lands held in Free and Common Soccage in Lower Canada' ended the pluralism of property law. Imposing, henceforth, French law on free and common soccage lands, the act specifically mentioned descent, inheritance, encumbrances, alienation, dower, and the rights of husbands and married women. In applying the same laws in all instances as those governed by the tenure of *franc aleu roturier*, it prepared the way for codification and its application across Lower Canada.[10]

The District of Bedford Courthouse
The Bedford courthouse in Sweetsburg illustrates the rationalization and
centralization inherent in the Judicature Act of 1857. It was built (1859–61)
according to a set of plans used in at least thirteen other courthouses across
Lower Canada including Saint-Jean, Rimouski, Huntington, Sorel, and
Arthabaska. A construction contract for the entire system of new courthouses
was given to contractors Sinclair and Skelsey.

ESTABLISHING THE COMMISSION

The third, and most important, act provided for the codification of laws
relative to civil matters and procedure. While the law of obligations with
its insistence on equality in contract relations would form the core of
codification, the act's preamble emphasized continuity, custom, and conservation, Civil laws being

mainly those which, at the time of the cession of the country to the British Crown,
were in force in that part of France then governed by the Custom of Paris,
modified by Provincial Statutes, or by the introduction of portions of the Law of
England in particular cases.[11]

Cartier used this sense of history and persistence to reassure nationalists about the strength of the Civil law:

Sweetsburg, 1864

Located in the Township of Dunham just over a kilometre east of Cowansville, Sweetsburg was named the district judicial seat in 1857. This 1864 map gives a sense of the scale of institutions in the village. The newly constructed Bedford courthouse and jail was by far the community's largest building complex dominating school, Anglican church, hotel, brick kiln, tannery, and artisanal shops.

It is French or Roman law that has the force to absorb and which itself will never be absorbed. It is the jurisprudence provided for in this law which prevails across almost all of Europe, which has been introduced into the United States, and there, as in England, has become the basis of law reform.[12]

He also presented codification as essentially housekeeping – a technical process to resolve discrepancies and to provide translations and authorities for existing law. Codification, he told the assembly, was not a cause for 'apprehension or uneasiness' since it involved 'less change in the law of the land than was sometimes affected by a single Act of Parliament.'[13] Morin used the same approach in reassuring ecclesiastics:

[Opponents] assume that the Code proceeds by means of repealing laws and that everything which is not found there is abolished, while this Code, to the contrary, proceeds by means of conservation and everything which is not expressly or implicitly abolished will remain law as before.[14]

But reassurance for social conservatives and Catholic authorities by emphasizing 'old laws' and the Custom of Paris represented only part of the act's preamble. By making explicit provision for a bilingual code, it recognized the political settlement of Lower Canada's collective identity. While codifiers in France and nationalists like Denis-Benjamin Viger emphasized the relationship between national culture and a monolingual legal system – Christian Atias, for example, describes the Napoleonic Code as 'a phenomenom of *savoir* and of *civilisation'* – the act used similar arguments of rationalism, simplicity, accuracy, and access in imposing official French and English versions of the codes.[15] Recapitulating arguments made early in the 1840s in Doucet's *Fundamental Principles of the Laws of Canada* and in the *Report* of the commission to compile statutes, the act noted that the great body of laws 'exist only in a language which is not the mother tongue of the inhabitants thereof of British origin': codes were to be 'framed and made in the French and English languages, and the two texts, when printed, shall stand side by side.'[16] The two commission secretaries were to be fluently bilingual barristers – one anglophone and one francophone.[17]

Again, Cartier, with his vision of nationality in Lower Canada, defended bilingualism and the language recognition granted to the anglophone minority. Describing the Civil Code as 'the most pregnant source of national greatness,' he insisted that codification must serve 'not only the interests of my people, but also those of the other inhabitants of Lower Canada, English, Scots and Irish.'[18] Cartier didn't hesitate to defend his anglophilism and what he saw as its political benefits:

M. [T.J.J.] Loranger has just stated that I want to anglicize my compatriotes ... Doesn't he know how much I have struggled against certain prejudices to obtain the Grand Trunk line on Lower-Canadian soil thus enriching my compatriotes ... Who regulated the difficulties with the Eastern Townships? Is it French or English laws which have been introduced there? Who had thought of the codification of our laws before me? The code will be written in both languages.[19]

Another factor of crucial importance was the act's mandate to the commissioners to codify all civil matters 'of a general and permanent character' with the exception of laws 'relating to the Seignorial or Feudal Tenure' – redundant in any case since the Seigneurial Act of 1854. As in several American jurisdictions, the codifiers might have been limited to commercial law or civil procedure. Their commission also contrasted sharply with German jurisdictions in the 1860s where regional diversity made it 'absolutely impossible' to codify land, family, or inheritance law.[20] In Massachusetts, a committee chaired by the influential Joseph Story admitted only the possibility of codifying criminal and procedural law and 'commercial contracts.'[21]

It was also of significance that the codifiers were to draft only *two* codes.[22] In the Code of Civil Procedure they were to reduce laws of a 'general and permanent character' pertaining to procedure in civil matters. The second code, the Civil Code of Lower Canada, was to incorporate laws relating to civil matters 'of a general and permanent character, whether they relate to Commercial Cases or to those of any other nature.'[23] This meant that, unlike France which had a separate commercial code, large portions of Lower Canada's commercial law were incorporated into the Civil Code.[24]

Legal historians have noted the importance of this unitary approach to organizing the Civil law. John Brierley describes Lower Canada's 'complete *mise en ordre* of the living elements of the private law' as the 'most fundamental feature of the operation.'[25] To Gyula Eörsi, separate codes of commerce such as that of France in 1673 – a form duplicated in the Napoleonic Commercial Code of 1807 – represented the coexistence of feudal and bourgeois economic power. The strengthening of what he calls the 'capitalist orbit' saw the collapsing of commercial law into Civil law, a critical benchmark in the decline of laws based on personal status (in this case, that of the merchant) before a law of obligations which formed the core of bourgeois codes:

A distinct commercial law, where it exists, is a passing episode in the history of civil law; when people become more and more versed in the know-how of modern life, and the up-to-date solutions created in commercial life are incorporated into the civil laws, it becomes extinct as soon as it is permitted by legal traditions and the considerable obstacles bourgeois codification is faced with.[26]

The act placed important restrictions on the commissioners. They were first to embody in the code only those provisions 'actually in force,' and secondly to cite specific authorities for these laws. Amendments, and the reasons for them, were to be presented separately. The form of the codes was to be based 'upon the same general plan' as the Napoleonic Civil, Commercial, and Procedural Codes. And the commissioners were to include, with 'as nearly as may be found convenient, the like amount of detail upon each subject' as the French codes.[27]

The act provided that commissioners and secretaries must be barristers of Lower Canada and strongly suggested that the commissioners should be judges. The government – as opposed to the assembly – was to name the commissioners and secretaries, who were to hold office 'during the pleasure' of the governor. Indeed, one commission secretary was apparently dismissed for political reasons. The codifiers were to make periodic reports to the governor and, in cases of dissent within the commission, a commissioner could submit a minority report. No time limit was placed on reporting: it was two years after the passing of the act that the commission held its first meeting, eight years before the Civil Code was presented to the legislature, and a decade before both codes were in effect.

REACTION TO THE CODIFICATION COMMISSION

Given its broad implications, it might be expected that codification would have been a matter of intense public and legislative debate. In Germany, the participation of parliamentarians and practising lawyers was actively solicited while professional groups such as the Congress of German Economists discussed the implications of legal unity. In 1860, German practitioners formed a lawyers' congress whose specific mandate was to examine the relationship between national unity and law reforms such as codification; for years it played an important role in German debates over nationalism and forms of law. When drafted (1888), the German code was the subject of an important public and ideological debate among a broad range of interest groups – artisans, the League for the Reform of Land Ownership, master builders, chambers of commerce, and the Farmers' League.[28]

In New York state, laymen as early as the 1820s were calling for law reform that would focus on codification; later the bar association appointed a special committee to defeat codification in the assembly. In Massachusetts, the bar represented the main opposition to codification, while in 1832 a local labour leader attacked the secrecy of the law, the fact that by professionalizing it was moving away from its roots in the trades, and the fact that for the popular classes the common law was confusing and incomprehensible. Many American reformers promoted codification as a liberal measure to accompany deprofessionalization and an elected judiciary. An anonymous correspondent to the Boston *Courier* (1832) described the common law as 'a great unexplored ark': 'Let the dark be made light, let the unclean be purified; and let the unknown be clearly revealed by a full and lucid written code.'[29]

Legislators in Germany and the United States echoed these popular concerns. In New York, the assembly closely followed a commission's revision of its statute law over a three-year period, adding and dropping clauses and on one occasion intervening to urge the commission to show greater boldness in its reforms. When a codification commission was established in the state in 1847, its report was rejected after an intense debate. In Massachusetts, the support for codification given by radical lawyers like Robert Rantoul made it the source of ongoing legislative storms during the 1830s and early 1840s.[30]

In Lower Canada, little provision was made for public discussion of codification. Never a democrat, Attorney General Cartier, in presenting the codification bill, emphasized the particular social conjuncture of the late 1850s, particularly the fact that seigneurialism had been resolved 'without having aroused, as in France, a bloody revolution.'[31] As with the Confederation proposals, he isolated codification from the assembly, special-interest groups, and professional bodies such as the bar or notariat.[32] There was apparently no question of following the practices of the seigneurial commissions of 1836 and 1843. In the first of these commissions, members of an assembly committee questioned individuals in reported hearings; in the second, questionnaires were sent to diverse social constituencies including the clergy, seigneurs, lawyers and notaries, physicians, merchants, and 'notables among the inhabitants.' In the case of both of these commissions, the interrogations as well as the reports were published.[33]

The legislature's only significant participation in codification was in 1857, when the commission was established, and in 1865 and 1866 at the end of the process, when it approved the codes. In 1857 opposition members took strong interest in the codification bill. Lewis Thomas Drummond interpreted it to mean that, as in France, codification would be entrusted to a council of the wisest jurists and he proposed that implementation of the act be supervised by an all-party committee of legal specialists. The Rouges attacked the undemocratic and élitist nature of the proposed commission. A.-A. Dorion argued that one of the three codifiers should be from the other legal profession, the notariat. He also wanted to put a time limit on the commission's mandate, pointing out that New York had drafted its code in less than eight months.[34] His brother, Jean-Baptiste-Éric Dorion, objected to the exclusion of elected officials from the codification process. His amendment, seconded by

Alexander Mackenzie, that codifiers be appointed by the assembly rather than the government was defeated fifty-nine to seven.[35]

Civil law reform had important pan-Canadian implications in that it emphasized Lower Canada's differences from the Common law practices of the rest of Canada. Establishment of the Codification Commission was of particular significance in the political conjuncture of 1857, a period when the Cartier-Macdonald government was considering Alexander Galt's federation proposals; a year later, Cartier himself accepted the principle of federation.

The coincidence of codification and federation was not lost on Upper Canadians. George Brown's Toronto *Globe* ran an editorial immediately after codification was announced in the speech from the throne, February 1857. Emphasizing codification's importance, the *Globe* railed against Upper Canadian lawyers who 'laugh at the announcement and declare it to be humbug.'[36] In the assembly, Brown commented that codification would 'separate the sections more than ever from each other': 'if they were to remain one people, it must be by the institutions of the two sections of the province being as much as possible harmonious.'[37] In his call 'to assimilate' the legal system of Upper and Lower Canada, Brown was supported by Grits like Malcolm Cameron who insisted on 'one system of laws for civil rights.'[38]

Brown's argument in favour of a general codification of Upper and Lower Canadian law in 'a system adapted to the whole Province' split his colleagues in the Lower Canadian opposition. Confident in what he saw as the evident superiority of Civil law over Common law practice, A.-A. Dorion supported Brown, noting that France had successfully codified its diverse customs into a single code. For his part, Lewis Thomas Drummond agreed with Dorion on the strength of the Civil law tradition noting that, with the dismantling of 'feudal tenure,' there was little difference between Civil law practices in the two Canadas. He was sceptical however, of opening Civil law to a larger Canadian reform process given the hostility of Upper Canadian lawyers to Lower Canadian institutions. Instead, Lower Canada should proceed with its own codification; once established, its code would be 'acceptable to the whole country.'[39]

Well aware of the political significance of Lower Canada entering Confederation with its Civil law reinforced, Macdonald and Cartier rejected demands for merging the legal systems of the two Canadas. They emphasized that legal diversity and political union were not incompatible. Noting the unity of England and Scotland despite their different legal systems, John A. Macdonald concluded that 'it was impossible to codify two systems entirely different.'[40]

Absence of significant participation in codification by the larger legal community reinforced the image of codification in Lower Canada as a closed bailiwick. The judiciary, for example, was an important and evident source of opinion on the commission's work. However, outside the commissioners who were themselves judges, the bench showed little enthusiasm for the codification process. Even before passage of the Codification Commission Act, Chief Justice LaFontaine tried to distance the bench from the process, petitioning the assembly that judges be excused from having to examine and comment upon commission reports.[41] As finally passed, the Codification Commission Act left the government the option of submitting codification reports to Queen's Bench and Superior Court justices 'if the Governor in Council shall think it advisable.'[42] Judicial opinion was particularly sought as to the correctness of the commissioners' interpretations of laws in force. Acceptance of 'Corrections' offered by judges was optional for the commissioners.

As the commission's eight *Reports* were produced, the provincial secretary's office circulated them in both languages to each of the judges and assistant judges of the Court of Queen's Bench and Superior Court. Judges had five months to submit commentaries. The response was minimal. Most, including prominent judges such as Chief Justice LaFontaine, William C. Meredith, Andrew Stuart, and John Samuel McCord, pleaded that their judicial workload prevented any in-depth study of the commission's *Reports*. My judicial duties, W. Meredith wrote in a typical reply, 'render it impossible for me.'[43]

Three judges, Dominique Mondelet of Trois-Rivières, D. Roy of Chicoutimi, and Peter Winter of New Carlisle, sent substantive suggestions, although the latter noted that his 'remote district' prevented him from enjoying 'the extensive public and private libraries' available to his urban 'brother judges.'[44] The most important commentary was Mondelet's eight-page report on Obligations and Book One. His comments centred on a perceived softening of family and patriarchal rights. He was particularly concerned about contracts made under threat of violence while in 'persons' he objected to any loosening of the obligation of children to fulfil contracts guaranteeing their alimentary pension to their parents, and secondly to any softening of Pothier's insistence on the power of the husband to control his wife's property.[45]

Prominent members of the bar, such as Denis-Benjamin Viger, had an interest in Civil law reform and legal education that dated from the previous century. Historically, many members of the bar had shown strong interest in Civil law reform. As early as 1830, the Advocates' Library in Montreal had established a committee to consider translation into English of 'some approved work on Civil Law,' and in 1833 Michael O'Sullivan, president of the Advocates' Library, offered to give a course on the Justinian Institutes. In 1841 the Montreal Bar Association had petitioned for reform of the Civil law system, and in 1857 it had responded quickly to the 'decentralization' bill forming a special committee: 'All are interested in it: the Public, the Judges, the Lawyers.'[46] In the early 1850s Cartier had been a member of the council of the Montreal bar. In 1857 his decentralization bill was strongly defended by Christopher Dunkin and Justice Charles Dewey Day. Soon to be named to the Codification Commission, Day warned the bar that 'it would never do to throw the bill in the teeth of the Attorney General in such strong terms.' Before the bar's petition reached him, Cartier had received three reports and a handwritten copy of the minutes.[47] Politicized over judicial decentralization and legal education, the Montreal Bar Association hardly mentioned the Civil Code in its minutes during the several years of codification. Although the association contained an increasing number of Cartier's political enemies, it was probably not without significance that Cartier's former law partner, J.-A. Berthelot, had been treasurer of the Montreal bar (1854), while his new partner in 1859, François Pominville, had been secretary and as late as 1864 was one of the eight members of the bar's governing council.[48]

Certainly, the government never encouraged any debate of codification by wide circulation of the eight volumes of codifiers' *Reports* among lawyers. Lawyer Thomas Ritchie, for example, noted that the commission's *First Report* had been 'received in silence' by anglophone lawyers; he attributed this to its limited distribution.[49] Frederick Torrance had the same complaint. With his office set of *Reports* in demand and circulating among several lawyers and important merchants like Hugh Fraser, Peter Redpath, and John Torrance, he wrote Commissioner Caron expressing his 'regret' that copies had 'not been sent to every member of the profession.'[50]

In 1864, having taken no public stand on Civil law codification, the Montreal bar finally established a committee to consider the impending Code of Procedure. Minutes of the bar do not make it clear that this committee ever met.[51] Two years later, frustrated with the bar's inactivity and with the proposed Code of Procedure already before the legislature, Thomas Ritchie declared that 'it was time, then or never.' His declaration prompted the Montreal bar to establish (June 1866) a new committee, which would hurriedly examine the draft code of procedure. It forwarded thirty-eight proposed amendments to a meeting of the Montreal bar on

19 July, 'but it being vacation, and the notice short' only ten members – far short of a quorum – attended.[52] Since the code received third reading on 27 July, their proposed amendments had no apparent effect.

Other interested legal constituencies remained silent. The Chamber of Notaries offered no public comment despite the obvious implications of the Civil law for their profession, including specific sections treating the notariat. Nor did criticism emanate from Lower Canada's two youthful law faculties – Laval and McGill – a fact probably attributable to the close relationship between the codifiers and law faculties.[53] At Laval, commissioner Morin was dean of the law faculty until 1866 and the professor of commercial law, Jean-Thomas Taschereau, was married to Caron's daughter, Marie-Josephine. Independent criticism was even less likely from McGill where codifier Day was chancellor, had been a principal founder of the law faculty, and was personally responsible for naming faculty members, like the commercial and criminal law professor, John Joseph Caldwell Abbott, and Frederick Torrance, professor of Roman law. One of Montreal's most important commercial lawyers, Torrance wrote a background paper for the commission on the law of married persons. With passage of the Civil Code, he wrote Cartier expressing his 'delight' and his willingness to write supportive editorials.[54]

Lower Canada's nascent legal journals did not play a significant critical role in codification; they too were dominated by élite networks. A Day clerk and later governor of McGill, Andrew Robertson, was member of the council, treasurer, and *bâtonnier* of the Montreal Bar Association during the codification period. As well, he published *A Digest of All the Reports Published in Lower Canada to 1863* and edited, with commission secretary Joseph-Ubalde Beaudry, the *Lower Canada Reports/Décisions des tribunaux du Bas-Canada*.[55] Secretary Ramsay was one of the founders of the short-lived *Law Reporter* and the *Lower Canada Jurist*. The latter was sponsored by the Montreal bar, was dependent on publishing subsidies from the attorney general's office, and had McGill professor Frederick Torrance as its managing editor.

This bonding in both the francophone and anglophone bar élites through marriage, militia, university, bar, neighbourhood, and church only partly explains the consensus in favour of codification. The bar élite's best clients came from the large institutions, railways, merchant houses, and industries – the core constituency in favour of the simplified, universal, and coherent Civil law system promised by codification. Nor, unlike many of their American peers, did members of the Lower Canadian bar apparently perceive codification's promise of simplicity and access to the law as a threat to their professional privileges. Indeed prominent lawyers such as Lewis Thomas Drummond insisted on the inherent superiority of the Civil law tradition, predicting export of the code as a model for Upper Canada.[56]

For other young lawyers in the 1860s – before the first Riel and New Brunswick schools crises – the code's emphasis on bilingualism corresponded to their vision of a larger Canada characterized by bicultural tolerance. Wilfrid Laurier, his bachelor of civil law degree in hand, expressed this feeling in his address to the McGill University convocation in 1864:

Two different legislations govern this country: French legislation and English legislation. Each of these legislations are not confined to the race to which they are intended but rather each rules simultaneously the two races, and, a fact worthy of note, this introduction in the same country of two systems of legislation entirely different has been done without violence or usurpation but simply by means of laws and justice.[57]

One major comment on the codifiers' first *Report* came in the form of a pamphlet, *Codification of the Laws of Lower Canada: Some Remarks on the Title 'Of Obligations,'* written by Thomas Ritchie in 1863. A well-connected lawyer who had defended the Grand Trunk's monopoly against the master carters of Montreal, Ritchie apparently wrote his pamphlet in the Torrance and Morris office. Highly laudatory of Day's work, Ritchie particularly approved the choice of the 'natural and philosophical' order of Pothier over 'the errors of arrangement' evident in the Napoleonic Code. Impressed by the title's search for 'pure, concise and unambiguous' language, he repeated Day's comments that definitions and axioms should be excluded from a code and restricted to scientific treatises.[58] Giving strong approval to the 275 articles in the Obligations title, Ritchie did offer fifteen pages of comments, most of them word changes, punctuation, and other clarifications.

The strongest critique of the code came from François-Maximilien Bibaud. In his *Corrigé du code civil*, he criticized its contradictions, its inconsistencies, and the unintelligibility of certain sections. In particular, he attacked Day for having picked articles 'with impunity' from Pothier's *Obligations*. He accused the codifiers of 'great temerity' in undertaking codification without a better understanding of Roman law: 'one can say without hesitation that the Commissioners do not seem to have even suspected its existence.'[59]

SANCTIONING THE CODE: LEGISLATURE AND CHURCH

From 1859 to 1864 the commission undertook the codification of Lower Canada's civil and procedural laws, a process treated in chapter six. In November 1864 the commission submitted its final report, and in January 1865 – in the very session highlighted by debate of the federation proposals, by the anglophone minority's pressing for increased language and school protection, and by Alexander Galt's resignation – Cartier introduced the Civil Code bill into the Legislative Assembly. Speaking for almost an entire day on 30 January and again on 25 August, on third reading, Cartier reviewed the history of the commission, its reports, and its amendments. In January Cartier spoke French; in August he addressed the assembly in English, reminding members that he had presented the bill in French. In any case, he told the assembly, most members understood English.[60]

Comparing the Civil Code to its Justinian and Napoleonic counterparts, Cartier emphasized the apparent consensus over codification. He recalled the general agreement with which the codification *Reports* had been received over the past four years and the fact that, despite criticism of details, the larger principles of the code had been accepted. Secondly, and an important factor given the Confederation debates, Cartier anchored the Civil Code as the centre-piece of Lower Canada's legal culture:

A code for us ... an indigenous code! Adopt this code which gives force to our nation and which will be of great utility in Confederation.

Finally, he presented the code as essentially 'only a repetition in a more methodical form of the law already existing in Lower Canada.'[61]

Since the Confederation and Civil Code debates occurred concurrently, Cartier and Solicitor General Langevin had to defend the autonomy of Quebec's Civil law system within the proposed federal structure. With the exception of municipally appointed magistrates, all judges were to be named and paid by the central government. And, although Quebec would have jurisdiction over its Civil law, Ottawa had the power to establish special courts, in particular a supreme court. Most difficult was the contradiction between the code's clear statement (article 185) on the indissolubility of marriage except 'by the natural death of one of the parties' and the granting under section 91 of the British North America Act of jurisdiction over marriage and divorce as a federal responsibility (provinces under section 92 did retain control over the solemnization of marriage).

The anxieties of social conservatives and nationalists coincided on the issue of divorce. An element in French codification, divorce came to strong public attention in the 1850s with the beginnings of British feminism, particularly the *cause célébre* of Caroline Sheridan Norton, and demands for reform of women's property and marriage rights. Ominously for those opposed to divorce under any circumstances, the Matrimonial Causes Act, an 1857 act permitting judicial separation and absolute divorce in England, was copied in several Canadian jurisdictions.[62] Within the Codification Commission itself, the issue had been carefully treated by codifier Caron who distinguished between the legislature's right, under British parliamentary tradition, to dissolve a specific marriage by a particular law and the Civil law. Since the latter took marriage to be 'indissoluble' except by death, it followed, Caron remarked, that divorce was 'foreign to our work.'[63]

Critics were not satisfied, and concern about the effect of the British North America Act on the values of the Civil Code came from several quarters. Sir Étienne-Paschal Taché reminded the public that divorce was 'antichristian and antinational'; writing later in *La Thémis*, lawyer B.-A. Testard de Montigny commented on the implications for women's sexuality if the institution of marriage collapsed:

On their side, women, seeing that they were not protected either by their virtue or by their affection, would abandon themselves without restraint to the most shocking behavior. And this is new proof of that truth, attested to by the experience of all ages: the excess of divorce leads the woman to adultery.[64]

In opposition, A.-A. Dorion warned of the implications of subjecting Catholic marriage to secular forces – mayors, the federal government, and the legislative will of a parliament – in which Protestants would form a majority:

What shall I say on the subject of marriage – the basis of all our institutions? Is it not dangerous to have it at the mercy of the Federal Government? ... before long, mayors will take the place of the *curés*, and will celebrate the marriage of their constituents. Our laws which regulate our marriages at present are very important to us, and are based on Roman law. These are the only laws suitable to Canadians, and the wise provisions characterizing them were the fruit of the experience of several ages. We should not incur the risk of any change in them by a legislature, the majority of whose members do not hold our opinions on this subject.[65]

Dorion voiced other concerns over the autonomy of Lower Canada's Civil law. Could the federal government, he asked, regulate mixed marriages, a matter before Quebec courts in *Connolly v. Woolrich* (1867) over the validity of a marriage *à la façon du pays* between a Cree and an Irish Catholic. Dorion also raised questions about the age limit of twenty-one (article 119) before which parental consent for marriage was required, an issue already before the courts in *Mignault v. Bonar* (1865).[66]

Other members questioned the language clauses of the British North America Act as they affected the court system and the appointment of judges by the federal government.[67] Cartier responded carefully, particularly to criticisms of section 101's provision for a federal appeal court. This central court, which would serve to coordinate jurisprudence, was necessary, he argued, to ensure 'a uniform and common' legal system concerning letters of exchange, customs, and promissory notes. As for the abilities of common law judges sitting on Civil law appeals from Lower Canada, he minimized the difficulties, noting that judges elsewhere in Canada were versed in equity law which had Roman roots similar to the Civil Code.[68]

The Civil Code bill was referred to a select committee chaired by the attorney general. Except for three notaries, committee members were lawyers.[69] Meeting in the Railway Room of the Legislative Assembly, the committee sat nineteen times in February and early March 1865.

The bill was divided into two, with proposed amendments separated from articles embodying laws in force. The committee concentrated entirely on the 217 amendments; eight of their nineteen meetings were spent on the first twenty-six amendments, all of which dealt with Obligations.[70] In committee, it was A.-A. Dorion who most actively challenged amendments. When he moved an important change to the amendment concerning delivery, debate was postponed. On resumption of committee hearings the following day, Commissioner Day – author of the section – was in attendance. Dorion's motion of opposition to the article was defeated eleven to seven. All three codifiers attended committee hearings for debate on their amendment concerning the witnessing and notarial authentification of acts. There was some debate over the fact that only males were permitted to witness notarial acts and over whether females should be permitted to witness a will.[71]

From April to July 1865 Cartier was absent in London and Paris, and in July codifier Morin died. Late in August the bill came back to the assembly for third reading; debate was restricted to 25 and 30 August.

A.-A. Dorion described codification as the most important bill since the Union Act. A journalist, observing that it was 'one of the most important questions ever treated by Parliament,' was surprised to find the public galleries almost deserted.[72] As in committee, there was no general debate but rather examination of particular amendments. Among the several amendments to which he protested, Dorion was particularly concerned by the 'ruinous' abandonment of old law concerning delivery in sales contracts. Here, he received support in the form of a petition from the Quebec City Board of Trade, virtually the only public protest against the code.[73]

Dorion also objected to the haste with which the committee had been obliged to examine the bill. Cartier responded that, although the committee had been restricted by the length of the session, it had had adequate time. He pointed out that the codifiers had proposed few amendments and that commission *Reports* had been published over four years. During this period, members like Dorion had not commented on the commission's work even though they had been part of the J. Sandfield Macdonald–Louis-Victor Sicotte government.[74]

On third reading, the Legislative Assembly made four changes (two proposed by Cartier) and, just before passage, Cartier moved three further amendments. The bill was passed by the assembly on 1 September and was approved without change by the Legislative Council a week later.[75] In the eleven months before the Civil Code of Lower Canada came into effect on 1 August 1866, the commission put the finishing touches to it, incorporating amendments made by the legislature and harmonizing these with other parts.

Codification of procedure had always been secondary to that of the Civil law, and in their initial meeting the codifiers apparently accepted Caron's suggestion to postpone procedure until their work on the Civil Code was well advanced.[76] In 1862, secretary Beaudry was assigned to draft the code of procedure and in May 1865, with the Civil Code before the assembly's committee, the commissioners examined his report. It received little amendment when presented to the legislature in June 1866 with the select committee on procedure meeting eleven times.[77] The bill received third reading in the assembly on 27 July and received first, second, and third readings in the Legislative Council between 30 July and 2 August; the Code of Procedure came into effect on 28 June 1867.[78]

The Code of Procedure's historian, Jean-Maurice Brisson, is critical of the commission's failure to use its power to propose amendments, describing the code as essentially a compilation of existing procedural practice. The ninety-five modifications which the commission did suggest were, he argues, largely 'questions of detail,' which left the code in Désiré

Girouard's terms as 'the product of an undigested mixture of French and English law.'[79]

Acquiescence by the Roman Catholic episcopate – or at least its non-ultramontane majority – was crucial to the political success of Civil law reform. Codification of civil status, marriage, and family matters were highly sensitive clerical matters touching nerves that stretched back to the Council of Trent. Aside from its potential infringement on canonical jurisdictions, codification challenged temporal and clerical authorities of different religious persuasions by forcing the harmonization of legal elements of Catholic and Protestant practices in areas such as marriage.

It is important to emphasize that it was the code's implications for family and marriage – and not its capitalist ideology – that concerned church officials. The participation and investment in banking, insurance, railway, and industrial projects by diverse constituencies in the church has been well documented. In Quebec City, the archbishop and Ursuline nuns bought shares in a local railway. For its part, the Seminary of Montreal, the city's most important landed institution, decided in 1841 that it should look to 'a public enterprise like the port, a canal, or a railway … as a less odious and more advantageous form of investment' than feudal forms of revenue, and throughout the period it participated actively in discussions with state officials over the terms of dismantling seigneurialism on its lands.[80] In the Union period, the seminary's feudal revenues were transformed into capitalist forms: urban rents, mortgages, bonds, and stocks. By the 1860s the church was increasingly dependent on capitalist revenues to finance its expanding parish and institutional responsibilities. Similar proclivities were evident among the ultramontanes, the strongest critics of codification. Ultramontane lawyer Joseph-Édouard Lefebvre de Bellefeuille, for example, was prominent in the Pacific Railway scheme of Hugh Allan.

The silence of moderates in the Catholic hierachy on codification was part of its larger compromise with the LaFontaine-Cartier reformers over issues such as responsible government, education, and seigneurialism. Catholic leadership had persistently supported established order with important interventions on the side of the state in the Rebellions of 1837–8, the Lachine Canal strikes of 1843, and rural unrest in the period 1846–50. The discreetness of most of the episcopate over the Confederation proposals and their pastoral letters in favour of authority after Confederation were further signals of the hierarchy's priorities. This loose ideological and political alliance of church and state was buttressed by private reassurances, appeals to moderate Catholicism, and personal, professional, and family networks. Attorney General Cartier, Solicitor General Hector Langevin, and codifier Morin all had direct family links to the Catholic hierarchy.[81] And they were employed professionally by the most important religious corporations: the Seminary of Montreal, the Séminaire de Québec, the Jesuits, Université Laval, and several of the women's orders. In reassuring Catholic authorities, the codifiers emphasized two elements: the code was untainted by revolution and, given Confederation and threats to Catholicism in Canada, it was a force for entrenching Catholic rights. In a widely circulated letter written to a Catholic official just days before the Civil Code was introduced in the assembly, Morin reiterated that the code was a 'means of conservation' and that contesting it would prove dangerous:

You will find no amendment [in the Civil Code] on matters which might affect religious matters ... If, however, one tried to go as far as [ultramontane critics wished] ... the experience would be, I would say, not only unfruitful but dangerous to the highest degree, especially in the contemporary situation, for the important interests which they pretend to safeguard.[82]

Lay authorities could also point to the protection of Catholic interests within the Codification Commission. One of the major differences between the two Catholic codifiers and their Protestant colleague occurred over whether civil death should be proffered on Catholics taking perpetual vows in religious communities. Day disliked the concept arguing that the 'ancient laws of France' concerning civil death for those in religious professions had ceased with the conquest. Caron and Morin strongly defended the Catholic position, overruling Day, and forcing him to submit a minority report.   In one of the commission's sharpest exchanges, they rejected Day's objections describing it as a conquest mentality that led to 'the opinion that the religious profession no longer exists legally in this province.'[83]

Even more crucial to Catholic authorities was the issue of marriage. All three commissioners rejected without difficulty the Napoleonic Code's treatment of marriage as a civil ceremony in favour of continuing to entrust the marriage ceremony to ministers of the various religious denominations. In affirming the Custom of Paris's treatment of marriage, the codifiers confirmed fundamental principles of the Council of Trent, leaving marriage as a sacrament for Roman Catholics and emphasizing that it was a public, religious event, publicized normally by bans, consented to by parents, and duly entered into parish records.

The codifiers did divide over the question of how to publicize the marriage act. The issue of clandestine marriages and of making marriage 'notorious' in the community had been an important concern of the Council of Trent.[84] As with civil death, the two Catholic commissioners again overruled Day. Publicizing marriage, Caron and Morin emphasized, was a means of 'hindering clandestine marriages which are, with reason, condemned by all systems of law.'[85] In addition to the importance of bans, they insisted that marriage should be celebrated *'publiquement,'* a term they translated as 'openly.' They thought that the word openly had a 'certain elasticity' that would discourage clandestine marriages while being 'suited to the various interpretations' that the different churches and religious congregations gave to it. Day however turned to authorities who interpreted *publiquement* more strictly to mean that the ceremony had to take place 'in church *en face de l'église,'* a practice he described as contrary to all of the Protestant denominations except the Church of England.[86]

The LaFontaine-Cartier alliance with the gallicans and the code's strong defence of Catholic principles was rewarded. When the *Second Report,* which included Persons, was published in May 1862, there was no official reaction from the church; two years later when criticisms did occur, they were restricted to ultramontanes. In 1864 ultramontane lawyer Joseph-Édouard Lefebvre de Bellefeuille published the first of three articles in *La Revue canadienne.*[87] Linking Napoleon to the French Revolution, atheism, and anarchy, he questioned the use of the French Civil Code as a model for the legal system of a Catholic population. During the assembly debate on the codification bill in 1865, these fears were echoed by three bishops, Joseph La Roque of Saint-Hyacinthe, Louis-François Laflèche of Trois-Rivières, and Ignace Bourget of Montreal.

The leading ultramontane, Bourget was already critical of the attorney general on issues ranging from the university question and division of the parish of Montreal to Cartier's private life. Seeing codification as the occasion to apply Catholic principles across the Civil law, Bourget denounced the code to papal authorities and proposed that articles affecting the church or religious life be submitted to the episcopacy for approval.[88]

Although this opposition was persistent, its political importance was minimized because of the historic tensions between the Rouges and ultramontanes. It was the gallicans who dominated the episcopate. Bishop Charles-François Baillargeon, president of the Provincial Council of Bishops, although uneasy with codification, told papal authorities that the Civil Code should be accepted as a reflection of 'the faith and piety' of the attorney general and his colleagues.[89] Also of importance in clerical acceptance of the code's position on church-state relations were the opinions of members of the bar élite like Justice Thomas-Jean-Jacques Loranger. In his *Commentaire sur le Code civil du Bas-Canada* (1873), he noted that marriage had been recognized as 'a religious and sacramental act and as a civil contract': 'the church alone has jurisdiction over the marriage tie and the impediments to its validity, and that the state alone has authority over its civil aspects.'[90]

Maintaining the upper hand, the gallicans published a treatise on parish law in the form of a code. Joseph-Ubalde Beaudry – a Cartier protégé, former francophone secretary of the Codification Commission, and principal author of the Code of Civil Procedure – had become lawyer for the Sulpician-dominated parish council of Notre-Dame. In 1870, he produced the *Code des curés, marguilliers et paroissiens accompagnés de notes historiques et critiques*, a work fiercely attacked by ultramontanes for its gallican perspective on church-state relations.[91]

Ultramontane criticisms of the code were expressed at the Provincial Council in 1868 but they did not carry the day. In any case, with the code already in effect, it was too late. In 1870 a papal delegate concluded that, given the fact that its jurisdiction included peoples of mixed religion, the Quebec Civil Code was 'a good code for a Catholic nation.'[92]

6

The Commission at Work

[My plan] is to put the civil laws in order, to distinguish the subjects of law
and to organize them according to their rank in the corpus of which
they are a natural part ...

Jean Domat (1689)[1]

The duty of the Commissioners is to prepare a series of articles, expressing
the practical rules by which civil rights are regulated and determined,
and not to theorize upon nice and unprofitable distinctions, however logical
they may seem to be.

Codification Commissioners' *First Report* (1861)[2]

This chapter examines the setting up of the commission, the dynamic
among the codifiers, and the process of codification. I leave article by
article examination of the code to labour, family, or commercial law
specialists, and emphasize instead the codifiers' delicate ideological task
of reinforcing traditional social relations through the bias of the family
while putting freedom of contract in a central place.[3] From this perspective, their work gives little sense of Lawrence Friedman's image of codification as a process of change, as 'a handy way to acquire new law, a
way of buying clothes off the rack, so to speak.'[4] Instead, we will see the
effects of the tight boundaries established by the Codification Act even
in amendments. The codifiers returned regularly to their mandate, noting
that they were charged, not to write new law, but to consolidate the old.

As Civil law jurists they sought to bring order to Lower Canada legal practice by turning to French or other authorities who in turn drew from Roman, customary, and natural law sources.

Central to this coherence with the past and with the larger hegemony of church and state was the codifiers' distancing of social relations – marriage and divorce are obvious examples – from revolutionary principles such as the Rights of Man, happiness of the individual, or equality among family members. Conservatives, they – and this certainly included the Protestant Day – were comfortable relying on Catholic legal intellectuals like Jean Domat and Robert-Joseph Pothier.

This reinforcement of central elements of pre-revolutionary Civil law was not at all incongruous with nineteenth-century concepts of freedom of contract. The codifiers, for example, did not hesitate in qualifiying the universality of certain principles. The careful definition of civil status – minors, women in marriage, civil death – permitted the exclusion of important categories of persons from equality before the law and, more importantly, freedom of contract. In titles such as Marriage, Separation of Bed and Board, and Paternal Authority, the code would emphasize pre-revolutionary marital and paternal rights. This was clearest in the rules governing marriage. With an expanding freedom of contract characterizing civil relations in general, matrimonial property regimes (and here there is a parallel with what Susan Staves found in England in the eighteenth and early nineteenth centuries) were separated from other forms of contract and made a distinct form of partnership subject to traditional patriarchal controls.[5]

But codification was not simply a renaissance of another historical time which, by ignoring nineteenth-century principles of persons, property, and work, would permit Quebec to languish as a reactionary, anti-capitalist backwater. The codifiers also had clear instructions to use the Napoleonic Code as a structural model and further to integrate commercial law into the body of the Civil Code. The French code's tripartite division (Persons, Property, Exercise of the Rights of Property), itself drawn from Justinian's Institutes, provided form for the Lower Canadian Civil Code. The codifiers would also imitate the French code by treating Obligations as their first order of business and by positioning it at the core of the code.

The Lower Canadian commissioners, it is worth reminding ourselves, were also to imitate the Napoleonic Code's rejection of feudalism, excluding from the Lower Canadian Code any 'Law relating to the Seignioral or Feudal Tenure.'[6] This, we have already seen, represented a fundamental shift towards property as a natural right, as *private*, as an *individual* right, and as a commodity that could be disposed of freely. Individuals, the codifiers reported, 'dispose as they please of the property belonging to them.'[7] Preliminary articles to the title 'Of Ownership,' reflecting both Pothier and the Napoleonic Code, gave powerful definition to these concepts of absolute property ownership:

Ownership is the right of enjoying and of disposing of things in the most absolute manner, provided that no use be made of them which is prohibited by law or by regulations.[8]

Two other articles (407, 408) emphasized that one could not be compelled to give up property except for public use and that ownership in a thing gives the right to all it produces.

This emphasis on persons over things was an essential part of freedom of contract; immovables, as commission secretary McCord put it, were brought 'under complete subjection to the will of man' while contracts – 'expressions of man's will' – were rendered 'definitive and reliable.'[9]

Charles Dewey Day, it will be argued, was the central codifier in this careful merging of absolute property rights with traditional family relations. He drafted Obligations – the code's pivotal title governing personal agreements – as well as almost all titles dealing with commercial undertakings. By writing the *First Report*, he obtained a head start in imposing his distrust of theory and definition across the code. His seniority and long experience on the bench, his strong personality and good health, his forceful writing, and his voice as spokesperson for the anglophone and commercial élite can be felt throughout the commission's work, even on titles written by his colleagues Caron and Morin. Nor should we underestimate the significance of Day's writing the central sections of the code in English. In the immediate discussions of his titles, he had the tactical advantage of working in his own language; he proceeded confidently, weighing translations carefully and working through the bias of words to protect the values of his particular constituency. At another level, he worked to break down the links between French law and French language ensuring the institutionalization of a compromise legal culture. At the political level, the voice and legitimacy he brought to the process was of great signficance given the influence of the anglophone minority and their insecurity in the federation and codification settlements of the mid-1860s.

FORMING THE COMMISSION

The months following passage of the Codification Act in June 1857 were characterized by intense political instability. When LaFontaine declined to chair the Codification Commission, Attorney General Cartier postponed naming it as the government struggled through its lack of majority in Upper Canada, its replacement by the short-lived Brown-Dorion administration of August 1858, and its 'double shuffle' manoeuvre on regaining office. Cartier's absence in England for several months in the fall further delayed the appointment of commissioners. Late in 1858 Cartier again asked LaFontaine to serve and, when he refused, asked René-Édouard Caron and LaFontaine's protégé, Augustin-Norbert Morin, to be on the commission. In a letter written from Toronto to 'mon cher juge,' Cartier asked Caron to serve. It is not clear when Day was asked, but in February 1859 the three commissioners were formally appointed by the governor general.[10] Two commission secretaries were appointed in the same month: Joseph-Ubalde Beaudry and Thomas Kennedy Ramsey.

French-language secretary Joseph-Ubalde Beaudry (1816–76) had clerked for Côme-Séraphin Cherrier and was admitted to the bar in 1838. One of the editors of the *Lower Canada Reports / Décisions des tribunaux du Bas-Canada*, he was described by Cartier as perhaps the best-versed lawyer in Lower Canadian jurisprudence.[11] Beaudry's career was as a legal administrator rather than practitioner: he was clerk of the Court of Requests in Saint-Hyacinthe, clerk of the Court of Appeal (1850), and clerk of the Seigneurial Court (1855). As Morin's health declined, Beaudry's responsibilities on the commission increased. He drafted the titles 'Of Privileges and Hypothecs' and 'Of Registration,' was one of the main authors of the Code of Procedure, and was named a commissioner when Morin died in the summer of 1865. A gallican, he later wrote the *Code des curés marguilliers et paroissiens* (1870) and finished his career as a judge of the Superior Court for the District of Montreal.[12] On becoming commissioner, he was replaced as secretary by Louis-Siméon Morin (1831–79), a well-known Conservative and, for a short period (1860), attorney general in a Macdonald-Cartier government.[13]

The first English-language secretary, Thomas Kennedy Ramsay (1826–86) was born into the Scottish landed gentry, received a classical education in St Andrews, lived in France for a few years, and emigrated to Lower Canada with his family in 1847. Ramsay clerked in the Montreal office of the well-known Conservative Christopher Dunkin and was

Codification Commission

With a backdrop of legal tomes and gothic pillars, the three commissioners are surrounded by their two male secretaries, quills in hand. René-Édouard Caron sits in the centre with Charles Dewey Day to his right and Augustin-Norbert Morin on his left. The francophone secretary, Joseph-Ubalde Beaudry is seated next to Day while Thomas McCord, the anglophone secretary, is next to Morin.

admitted to the bar in 1852. Bilingual, Ramsay later published in French, explaining that he wrote better in French than in English.[14] He established his reputation on the academic side of the law as a founder of the *Law Reporter* (1854) and the *Lower Canada Jurist* (1857), and after leaving the codification commission he published three legal studies.[15] The inventory of his library after his death confirms his strong interest in Roman law and pre-revolutionary French law.[16]

Despite his position on the Codification Commission, the always litigious Ramsay continued to be an outspoken Conservative and supporter of Cartier's politics. In 1862 this cost him his secretaryship when the new Liberal government of Sandfield Macdonald and Louis-Victor Sicotte dismissed him. Once the Conservatives were back in office, Ramsay's career revived. He served as crown attorney in Montreal, 1864–8, was appointed queen's counsel in 1867, and in 1870 was named to the bench, first the Superior Court and then the Queen's Bench where he remained until his death in 1886.[17] Thomas McCord (1828–86), scion of one of Lower Canada's most important landholding and legal families, replaced Ramsay as secretary. McCord's grandfather, Thomas McCord, was an important magistrate in Montreal, his uncle, John Samuel McCord, was Superior Court judge, and his father, William King McCord, was judge on the Court of Queen's Bench. Like Ramsay, Thomas McCord was groomed for an élite career in law. His family sent him to the Petit Séminaire of Quebec where he received a classical education, training in the French language, and an understanding of francophone and Catholic culture. His father apprenticed him to René-Édouard Caron; once named to the commission, Caron supported his former clerk's appointment as secretary. After the completion of the commission's work, McCord published the first commercial edition of the code, *The Civil Code of Lower Canada* (1867) and, like his fellow secretaries Ramsay and Beaudry, went to the bench, as judge for Bonaventure (1873), the Gaspé (1883), and as deputy judge of the vice-admiralty court (1884).[18]

Although the commission and its secretariat were in place early in 1859, it did not meet in formal session until October 1859, apparently because of Morin's ill health.[19] By then, however, much of the organization of material, the titles to be written by individual commissioners, the research duties of the two commission secretaries, and the commission's working policy on language had been decided.

Caron served as chair, organizing meetings, handling correspondance, and drawing up memoranda and agenda. Somewhat less esoterically, he rented and drew up the £170 annual lease for the commission's office space in Quebec – in a building he himself owned. The commission space consisted of individual offices for each codifier, a meeting room, secretaries' office and another for the clerks, waiting room, and an apartment for the resident caretaker and his family. A commission library was organized in the offices and Caron, former speaker of the Legislative Council, arranged to borrow books from the Parliamentary Library, a loan that included twenty-one cases of books on French law.[20] In Montreal, Day and both commission secretaries borrowed legal treatises, particularly American, from the library of the Torrance and Morris law firm.[21] Caron was also active on the issue of the commissioners' pay. By the terms of their appointment, the codifiers were to devote their full professional activity to codification, and Caron drew up a memorandum for inclusion in the minutes justifying their activity in the four months from their

The Commission's Offices
Located in Quebec's Upper Town along the main commercial street at
70 Rue Saint-Jean, the commission's offices were in a building owned and
renovated by Caron in 1851. The building's two lower floors were occupied
by Merrill's Dry Goods.

nomination in February 1859 to their first meeting in May. He also raised
the question of whether their £1250 annual salary entitled them to a daily
supplement of £4 for work on Sundays.[22]

THE COMMISSION AT WORK

Informal meetings of the commission were held on 27 May and 10 June
1859 with Day and Caron present. Secretary Ramsay was set to work
identifying customary and statute law no longer in force, and Beaudry
was assigned to analyse Lower Canadian jurisprudence through reported

decisions. By October 1859 Ramsay had completed his assignment and in 1863, after leaving the commission, he published his work as *Notes sur la coutume de Paris*.[23] The status of Beaudry's work is less clear since it apparently overlapped the work of a parliamentary commission which was published in 1864. Certainly by 1862 Beaudry had been assigned to drafting the Code of Civil Procedure.[24]

Two critical issues – the delegation of individual commissioners to draft particular sections, and the order of preparation of titles – may have been settled before the commission's first unofficial meetings. In his acceptance letter to Cartier, Morin had noted his lack of competence in commercial law and procedure, both strongly influenced by English law.[25] Morin was also handicapped by ill health and drafted only two titles (see table 3). 'Of Prescription' and 'Of Gifts inter vivos and by Will' were, however, among the most complex in the code, particularly in their integration of French and English law.

Day's correspondence with Cartier has not survived and one cannot be sure – given Day's roots in the anglophone élite and his strength on the bench in commercial cases – if it was understood by the attorney general that Day would write Obligations and many of the titles concerning commercial law. Given the sensitivities of nationalist and clerical politics, it seems unlikely that the anglophone commissioner would be assigned titles concerned primarily with marriage or succession. In the larger perspective of ethnic politics in Lower Canada, Day's duties can be interpreted as a legal equivalent to the tradition of according economic portfolios to anglophones. Strong supporting evidence that, from the first meetings of the commission, it was understood that Day would write Obligations is suggested by Caron's assignment to Day of all commercial authors to be consulted by the commission.[26]

In addition to drafting the crucial *First Report*, Day wrote almost all remaining commercial sections of the code. He wrote the entire *Fourth Report* (Sale, Exchange, Lease and Hire) and much of the *Sixth Report* (Mandate, Loan, Deposit, Partnership, Life-Rents, Transactions, Gaming Contracts and Bets, and Pledge). With the incorporation of commercial law into the Civil Code, it was Day who wrote the *Seventh Report* (Bills of Exchange, Merchant Shipping, Affreightment, Carriage of Passengers, Insurance, and Bottomry).

Besides chairing the commission, Caron assumed responsibility for drafting the Preliminary Title, one commercial title (Of Suretyship) and much of the code concerning immovables, persons, family law, and successions: First Book (Persons), Second Book (Property and Ownership), 'Of Successions,' and 'Of Marriage Covenants.'

Table 3
Commission Reports

Report	Date of Presentation	Subject	Author	Language
First	12 Oct 1861	Obligations	Day	English
Second	28 May 1862	Preliminary Title	Caron	French
		First Book (Persons)	Caron	French
Third	24 Dec 1862	2nd Book (Property & Ownership)	Caron	French
		Prescription	Morin	French
Fourth	25 Feb 1863	Of Sale	Day	English
		Of Exchange	Day	English
		Of Lease and Hire	Day	English
Fifth	19 Jan 1864	Of Successions	Caron	French
		Of Gifts inter vivos & by Will	Morin	French
		Of Marriage Covenants	Caron	French
Sixth	8 Jul 1864	Of Mandate	Day	English
		Of Loan	Day	English
		Of Deposit	Day	English
		Of Partnership	Day	English
		Of Life-Rents	Day	English
		Of Transaction	Day	English
		Of Gaming Contracts & Bets	Day	English
		Of Suretyship	Caron	French
		Of Pledge	Day	English
		Of Privileges and Hypothecs	Beaudry	French
		Of Registration	Beaudry	French
		Of Imprisonment in Civil Cases	Beaudry	French
Seventh	25 Nov 1864	Book Four (Commercial Law: Of Bills of Exchange Of Merchant Shipping Of Affreightment Of Carriage of Passengers Of Insurance Of Bottomry)	Day	English
Eighth	25 Nov 1864	Supplementary Report (corrections & changes)	all 3 codifiers	English & French?

Source: Based on McCord, *Civil Code of Lower Canada*, vi–viii, and Brierley, 'Quebec's Civil Law Codification,' 581–9; usually punctilious, McCord is circuitous in identifying which codifier drafted particular titles.

The Civil Code, it must be emphasized, was not prepared in the order it took in its published form. The codifiers drafted Obligations first; in the completed code, it appears as Title Three in Book Third. In publishing the code, secretary McCord concluded that Obligations was 'the basis of the greater portion of the whole Code.'[27] Obligations, the codifiers reported, 'comprehends the fundamental principles upon which a large proportion of civil rights and liabilities depends and furnishes rules of universal application in their adjustment.'[28]

The drafting of Obligations by Day and, once ratified by his fellow codifiers, its publication as the commission's *First Report* gave a central place in the code to contracts and to Day's interpretations and definitions. To a large degreee, his work co-opted ideology that might have formed much of Caron's Preliminary Title. As well, articles of 'Obligations' inevitably trespassed into titles drafted subsequently by other codifiers; the rules for actions in commercial matters, for example, were treated in Day's *First Report* and overlapped Morin's responsibility for Prescription.[29] And once accepted and published, 'Obligations,' in tandem with Day's strong personality, gave momentum and direction which other codifiers found difficult to contradict in subsequent parts of the code.[30]

Although commission reports, presentation of the code to the legislature, and physical evidence such as the photo of the commission suggest a team approach to codification, the essential work of drafting titles was accomplished by individual commissioners working with a secretary. In accepting nomination, Morin had made clear his reluctance to travel or to be separated from his family, asking that one of the commission secretaries be assigned to him. In 1860, he sold his house in Quebec City and moved to Saint-Hyacinthe where he presumably wrote his titles.[31]

For his part, Day apparently worked in Montreal where his family lived and where he had ongoing responsibilities as chancellor of McGill. We know for certain that Day returned to Montreal in early July 1859 with seventeen volumes borrowed from the commission library and, it was here, in the familiar milieu of commercial lawyers and McGill colleagues, and probably assisted by secretary Ramsay, that he drafted Obligations.[32] Later in the codification period he travelled to England.

While the individual codifiers worked on their sections, the commission met only sporadically in plenary session. Their first meeting was on 27 October 1859, and they then adjourned for four months, meeting on 21 February 1860 to discuss Day's draft of Obligations. After meeting regularly for two weeks they adjourned on 4 April coming together again

Legal Chambers

Drafting titles of the Civil Code was essentially a solitary task undertaken by a codifier, usually with the help of a commission secretary. The full commission met in its Quebec City offices, but the preparation of titles probably took place in legal chambers similar to those of Côme-Séraphin Cherrier.

on 12 December 1860. This pattern was typical of commission meetings throughout the codification period.[33]

DRAFTING TITLES

Following suggestions made by Caron in their spring meetings, Day prepared his draft of Obligations by dividing large sheets – one sheet per article – into four columns: 'Present Law'; 'Civil Code' (of France); 'Amendments'; 'Remarks.' In later drafts, commissioners moved to a simpler worksheet of only two columns, 'Existing Law' and 'Amendments and Remarks,' with the second column containing references to the Napoleonic Code.[34]

The first column, 'Present Law,' was, as we will see, of crucial importance: Brierley calls it the incorporation of 'the living law into a single
text.'[35] From the handwriting on the worksheets, it would appear that, in
some cases, the codifier himself wrote the 'Present Law' and its authorities; in other instances, commission secretaries apparently researched and
completed it for correction by the codifier in charge of the section.[36]

Serving as what Caron described as a 'canvas,' column two of the draft
for the *First Report* cited the relevant article of the Napoleonic Code.[37] The
French code gave not only form but allowed the codifiers to compare
'old' law to law post-dating the French Revolution. If the Napoleonic
article reflected Lower Canadian law it, along with supporting authorities, could be adopted with with what Day called 'mere changes of
expression and arrangement.' 'This article,' Caron wrote of domicile, 'is
comformable to the Roman law, and to the old French law as well as to
the Code Napoleon, from which this article is copied, saving the substitution of the word "person" for that of "Frenchman."'[38]

In other instances, the Napoleonic Code was useful in providing a
model for removing social distinctions under old law that contradicted
principles of freedom of contract. For example, old law as well as the
Louisiana Code gave particular status to servants. The commissioners
had several discussions over how to deal with various forms of employment. In Rome, 'painting was the object of lease and hire; Pothier holds
it to have been a liberal profession in France': 'the distinction between
the contracts,' the codifiers summarized 'when the service is to be paid
for, is so purely theoretical that for all practical purposes they may be
considered identical.' They concluded by following the Napoleonic Code
model of including employment under Lease and Hire.[39]

In columns three and four of the draft of the *First Report* and in column
two of subsequent reports, 'Amendments' were proposed, explained, and
given supporting authorities. Day for example, wrote:

I have stated in general terms the rule of our present law as given by Pothier and
have suggested as an amendment (art 45) the rule of the [Napoleonic] Civil Code
(art 1138) expressing it however more carefully as suggested by Toullier.'[40]

The Civil Code bill presented to the assembly in 1865 listed 217 amendments, and McCord, commenting on the code as finally passed, listed 201
articles containing new law. He divided these into six categories: free
disposal of property, wills, stability of rights, prescription, protection of
third parties, and improvements of the law.[41] The new laws were, in

secretary McCord's terms, 'not of a subversive character, or likely to disturb existing relations, or to clash with prevailing notions'; rather their aim was to 'harmonize with the ideas of the present day.'[42] Those in the most important category, according to McCord, were to 'facilitate the free exercise of man's domain over property' and to 'render contracts 'definitive and reliable.' Of less importance were new laws which protected the rights of third parties, while others remedied defects in existing laws.

Once the codifier had prepared a draft, clerks sent copies for individual examination by the other codifiers. The commission – the three commissioners and two secretaries – then met in formal session adopting, rejecting, or modifying each article.[43] Their decisions were recorded in two ways, formally in the minutes and informally in the notes each commissioner kept on his working copy.

Day was the only commissioner to submit a minority report. His 'statement of objections' to the *Second Report* took issue with five elements of the 'Persons' drafted by Caron and approved by Caron and Morin. Three of his objections centred on the capacity of Lower Canadian law – and hence of the commission – to determine who was a British subject. His other objections concerned the definition of civil death as it related to Catholic clergy, and the Civil Code's jurisdiction with respect to corporal penalties. Day was also persistent in defending the Protestant minority; on his worksheet of Caron's draft on the publication of marriage bans, for example, he wrote: 'Question: How do these bear upon marriage of Protestants?'[44]

Once approved, titles were translated by a secretary and returned for verification to the original codifier. In the final step, translations were read and approved before the commission. Translation was of paramount importance since English and French texts were to be equal in law. The commission itself operated in bilingual fashion, an issue which had first been raised in the taking of minutes. After considering several possibilities – keeping minutes entirely in English or in French, recording the language spoken, or translating them entirely into two versions – the last method was adopted with the minutes being kept in duplicate French and English versions and read and adopted in both languages.[45]

Day drafted his titles in English; the balance of the code was prepared in French (see table 4). There were special difficulties (what Caron called 'embarrassments') translating terms, particularly from French to English. In some instances, Scottish technical terms were used.[46] Day's notes show his wrestling with *dommages et intérêts*, which he finally translated 'by the word "damages" which I think fully renders the idea in English.'[47] We

Table 4

'Laws of the Country' as drawn up by Commissioner Caron[1]

1 The Custom of Paris, French laws in force and accompanying jurisprudence followed by the Parlement of Paris in 1663, date of the creation of the Conseil supérieur, which introduced or recognized the existance of these laws in Canada

2 Edicts and ordinances of the French crown promulgated for Canada, 1663–1759

3 Ordinances of the Conseil supérieur, 1663–1759

4 Laws, edicts, and ordinances promulgated by the French crown for France, which were registered in Canada by the Conseil supérieur

5 Statutes of the British Parliament passed since the conquest for Canada or which specifically named Canada

6 Laws promulgated by the military government, 1759–74[2]

7 Laws and ordinances passed by the Legislative Council from its creation in 1774 until its abrogation in 1791

8 Provincial Statutes of Lower Canada, 1791–1840

9 Ordinances of the Special Council, 1838–41

10 Acts applicable to Lower Canada passed by the legislature of the United Canadas since 1840

11 English criminal laws as they existed in 1774 and as revised by legislative acts

12 For matters not treated in the above categories, recourse was to be made to pre-revolution French jurisprudence such as Pothier; to Canadian authors such as Doucet, Crémazie, Lafontaine, and Bonner; to the jurisprudence of decisions from France and from Canadian reports such as Pyke's Reports, Stuart's Reports; Roman law adopted in France by Domat, Angers, etc.; finally to English public law applicable across the empire and affecting the rights of Lower Canadian inhabitants as British subjects. (abridged)[3]

1 *Notes générales*, 1–4 (trans.); see also Brierley's comments, 'Quebec's Civil Law Codification,' 547–52.

2 Caron does not think there were any such laws, an opinion confirmed by Brierley. *Notes générales*, 2; Brierley, 'Quebec's Civil Law Codification,' 549.

3 Caron notes that he included the public law clause as the result of a suggestion from Day.

have already noted that translation of the term *publiquement* in the title 'On Marriages' led Day to comment on the 'elasticity' suggested by the English translation 'openly' (article 156). Caron, in compiling 'Of the Distinction of Things,' was frustrated by the imprecision of the English term 'Things.'[48]

Day submitted his draft of Obligations in February 1861, and over the next year it was examined by the commission. With the *First Report* printed in both languages, submitted to the government, and circulated to all Queen's Bench and Superior Court judges in Lower Canada, the commission turned to Caron's draft of the Preliminary Title and Book First which was adopted in May 1862 and published as the *Second Report*. By the fall of 1862 the commission had approved 'Of Property' and 'Of Prescription,' which were published as the *Third Report*. In the winter of

1863, the commission worked on Day's titles on Sale, Lease, and Hire, which were submitted as the *Fourth Report*. The *Fifth Report*, devoted to Successions, Gifts, and Marriage Covenants, was approved in January 1864. The *Sixth Report*, to which Day, Caron, and secretary Beaudry contributed draft titles, was completed in July 1864. Other commercial law titles were drafted by Day and approved in November 1864 as the *Seventh Report*. In the same month, the *Supplementary Report* was published, and early in 1865 the Civil Code bill was introduced to the legislature.

AUTHORITIES AND IDEOLOGY

As part of his preparatory work, Caron drew up a memorandum listing twelve categories of laws in force in Lower Canada (table 4). Although the extensive research necessary to fill in each category was never undertaken, with the exception of the Custom of Paris, and was apparently made unnecessary by the drafting of specific sections of the code, Caron's memorandum emphasized the commission's intention to follow its mandate strictly, bringing coherence to existing law rather than using codification for legal innovation. The Codification Act, Caron wrote,

indicates the manifest intention of the Legislature to retain our ancient laws which are still in force, to innovate with caution and reserve, to distinguish the changes which one would like to make, and especially to carefully understand all laws which are still in effect.[49]

Caron saw the declaration of authorities as perhaps the codifiers' crucial task:

To know the laws of which the code must be composed, it was necessary to seek for them in the different sources whence they originate; sources so varied, and more numerous perhaps with us than in any other country.[50]

John Brierley has counted some 350 written sources in the seven published *Reports*.[51] Few of these are to Lower Canadian sources. In the crucial *First Report*, for example, only seven Lower Canadian sources were cited (six statutes and one reference to the *Lower Canada Reports*), and these dealt with relatively minor sections – testimony, oaths, and the authenticity of private writings.[52] In the *Sixth* and *Seventh Reports*, the codifiers relied on the Consolidated Statutes for authority on limited partnership and on Lower Canadian case law for rules concerning anonymous partnerships and fire insurance.[53] American sources were also important in commercial sections, particularly Story, *On Contracts* and *On Partnerships*; James Kent's *Commentaries*; Theodore Sedgewick, *Treatise on the Measure of Damages*; Simon Greenleaf, *On Evidence*; and the draft of New York's civil code.[54] Scottish sources, particularly Bell's *Commentaries on the Law of Scotland*, were utilized in several commercial sections. The authorities for insurance law were particularly diverse. In treating maritime insurance (articles 2492–567), which they drew largely from France's Marine Ordinance (1681), the codifiers spoke of 'uniform' and 'well settled,' 'fundamental rules' that existed internationally. Fire insurance was another subject in which 'principles are happily well settled' and, since English policy forms were used in Lower Canada, English law formed the basis of the seventeen articles. For life insurance, the codifiers turned to nine articles from the draft of the New York civil code.[55]

Despite this cosmopolitanism of commercial law sources, authorities in the Lower Canadian Civil Code were drawn overwhelmingly from pre-revolutionary French authorities among whom Charles Dumoulin (1500–66), Jean Domat (1625–96), and Robert-Joseph Pothier (1699–1772) dominated. Known as the prince of the French jurists, Dumoulin was important in unifying and systematizing customary law. Domat's *Civil Law in its Natural Order* was crucial in bringing Roman law with its emphasis on rationalism to the customary regions of the north, particularly Paris whose custom was applied in New France. Domat brought harmony between the Roman digests and codes and a natural order established by God.[56]

Pothier, professor of law at Orléans and often described as the father of the Napoleonic Code, combined what Jean Carbonnier calls the skills of the technician with those of the moralist.[57] Pothier's editor presented his treatise on the *Contract of Sale* as

not only a good book of law, but an excellent book of morals; a work of all countries and of all nations; a book, to which antiquity can present no rival but the Offices of Cicero, and which has no superior but the Gospel, and that because the Gospel is the very work of God.[58]

Paul Ourliac noted that Pothier was 'trained in Roman law but faithful to the moderate solutions of the common law of the custom.'[59] In the confusion of Lower Canadian politics and jurisprudence, Pothier's clarity, simplicity, and comprehensiveness were particularly attractive. Commission secretary Ramsay recalled the impact Pothier had on him as a young clerk in Montreal:

Anything we learned was picked up by the practice we saw in an office and the books we chanced to read. I was dismayed at the endless rows of dingy books, then rarely enlivened by the gay morocco bindings of the *nouveau droit* ... From the moment I opened [Pothier on Obligations], the dread of the dryness of law disappeared as by enchantment, and starting from one word there rolled forth a perfectly clear explanation of the whole of legal rights and liabilities.[60]

It is Pothier's *Mariage* and *Personnes* which led the list of authorities in the chapters on Marriage, Illegitimate Children, and Paternal Authority. Pothier, for example, was the code's first authority for its statement of marriage as indissoluble except by the natural death of one of the partners.[61] And once into his real strength of Obligations, Pothier was used by the codifiers to cut across the social landscape, defining the contractual rights of children, idiots, lunatics, and the inebriated. Married women can serve as our example:

For it is a consequence of marital power, that the wife be incapable of doing anything except it be dependently on the husband and by his authority. Hence it follows that, without his authority, she is incapable of making any agreement, and she can neither bind herself to others, nor bind others to her.[62]

The codifiers, particularly Day, were insistent in reasserting the virtually absolute legal incapacity of married women. Rejecting the Napoleonic Code's position that women were in an equivalent position to minors, Day restated Pothier's interpretation:

The rule is founded upon the doctrine of marital authority and should not be changed unless that branch of our law be essentially amended.[63]

The commissioners regularly alluded to Pothier's technical and organizational skills. In some cases, they used virtually the same language as the Napoleonic Code which in turn used the authority of Pothier. For example, domicile (one's permanent residence where civil rights are exercised) was a potentially confusing and yet fundamental legal question in a colonial society with diverse nationalities and an often mobile population. Where did youths have their legal residence in an apprenticeship, girls in domestic service, or wives who did not live in the same community as their husbands? Domicile could determine which courts a person could be summoned to, the place where a succession would be determined or a marriage celebrated. Here Caron, reporting that the provisions are 'simple and few,' relied essentially on the wording of the Napoleonic

Code and the authority of Pothier. Unemancipated minors had their domicile fixed with their parents; a married woman not separated as to bed and board could have no other domicile than that of her husband.[64]

The reliance on Pothier had an important influence on employment – a crucial subject given the changing relations of work in the transition to industrial capitalism. [65] The labour contract, the relationship of master-servant and employer-employee, negligence, the right to organize, and workmen's compensation, although subject to new conditions, were – barring statutory law – essentially subject to laws dating from the pre-industrial perod. In a pattern similar to that of the Napoleonic Code, the Civil Code largely ignored industrial work relations leaving these dis-putes to be settled largely on the basis of a strict interpretation of contract. And, although relationships in the workplace were assumed to take place in an environment of equal parties in contract, many employers had recourse to the criminal law to discipline servants and other employees.[66] Particular elements of labour law, such as the apprenticeship contract, were apparently left untouched, because in the jurisprudence of Pothier they were outside private law, falling under public law on guilds.[67]

Along with this strong reliance on pre-revolutionary authorities, the code was characterized by an absence of stated principles and definition. When the French codifiers began their task, they had to contend with the powerful ideological positions established by Jean-Jacques Cambacérès in his revolutionary drafts of the civil code and by Jean-Étienne-Marie Portalis in his *Discours*. In Lower Canada, Caron's 'Memorandum' served only as rough notes and, when the codification commission met in its first prolonged meetings, it was not over a theoretical statement but over Day's draft of Obligations.

In his draft, Day urged the codifiers to distance themselves from defi-nitions and principles. Since larger maxims, he insisted, could only be a 'directory' for judges, they were best excluded from the code and left 'where they now are in the great body of general principles and of right reasoning which surrounds and sustains all positive legislation.'[68] In seven articles that formed 'the preliminary dispositions' of the title of Obligations, the Napoleonic Code defined the meaning and types of contract. Day dropped this entire section, preferring Pothier's much sim-pler articles as the two general provisions of Obligations.[69] Day's approach was endorsed by all three commissioners:

The only definitions which should be adopted, are those which involve some rule of law, or are so inseparable from a particular rule, that by their omission it would become ineffectual or obscure.[70]

And in summarizing contract, the commissioners noted that they had 'avoided as subtle and useless, the questions so much discussed by civilians.' The duty of the commissioners, they reported, 'is to prepare a series of articles, expressing the practical rules by which civil rights are regulated and determined, and not to theorize upon nice and unprofitable distinctions, however logical they may seem to be.'[71] This approach served as a rehearsal for the rest of the code. Caron's preliminary title, for example, was extremely brief, explaining the code's promulgation, application, and defining a strict minimum of terms such as 'persons,' 'inhabitants,' and 'bankruptcy.'[72]

The exclusion of expressed principles did not mean, of course, that the codifiers ignored their work's ideological import. In their *Reports* and minutes, terms like 'evil' and 'revolting' betray the subjectivity of the codifiers. But, in general, issues such as sexuality – implicit in age of marriage, parental consent, illegitimacy, and separation from bed and board – were buried in the rhetoric of the patriarchal family as society's bedrock.

We shall see in chapter 8 that the rights of married women were determined with clarity. However, other contradictions between freedom of property and the sanctity of family relationships were less easily resolved. This was particularly so with gifts and wills. Testamentary freedom, permitted in 1774, had separated Lower Canada from the juris-prudence of both pre-revolutionary and Napoleonic France, the latter retaining (in both gifts and wills) 'the customary reservations in favor of the family relations which are inconsistent with the free disposal of property.'[73] The commissioners were not comfortable with Lower Can-ada's 'absolute freedom of disposing by will' which had led to 'gratuitous dispositions,' an apparent reference to the right to leave one's goods to a 'concubine' or to illegitimate children.[74] This posed a dilemma. Gifts *inter vivos* and wills formed part of the same body of the law of gifts and, in the interests of uniformity, should have been put together. The commis-sioners, however, despite 'their desire to keep within the path of the greatest freedom,' were reluctant to challenge the stability of the family by sanctioning gifts to concubines and illegitmate children, a posture which, as they put it, would have 'appeared immoral.'[75] As finally approved, the article was tortuous and detailed, emphasizing the sharp contradiction between freedom and morals. Gifts *inter vivos* to a concu-bine with whom the donor 'has lived' or to 'incestuous or adulterine children' were limited to maintenance; other illegitimate children were treated like other persons.[76]

To this point, the codifiers' work – despite important exceptions such as employment contracts – has been interpreted from the perspective of its essential faithfulness to a customary legal culture, old laws, and religious and patriarchal traditions. In these areas, Cartier could with justice present the code as simply 'a repetition' of law already in effect. The incapacity and dependence of married women, especially those in trade, provides a striking case study of the ideological and economic implications of this persistence of customary law.

7

The Persistence of Customary Law: Married Women as Traders

All persons are capable of contracting, except those whose incapacity is
expressly declared by law.

Article 985, Civil Code

Those legally incapable of contracting are:- ... Married women, except in cases
specified by law

Article 986[1]

I wish one of my girls was a son.

George-Étienne Cartier (1869)[2]

The news of my legacy reached me one night about the same time that the act
was passed that gave votes to women. A solicitor's letter fell into the post-
box and when I opened it I found that she had left me five hundred pounds
a year for ever. Of the two – the vote and the money – the money I own
seemed infinitely the more important. Before that I had made my living by
cadging odd jobs from newspapers, by reporting a donkey show here or a
wedding there ... [now] whenever I change a ten-shilling note a little of that
rust and corrosion is rubbed off; fear and bitterness go ... No one in the
world can take my five hundred pounds. Food, house, and clothing are
mine for ever.

Virginia Woolf (1928)[3]

Strongly influenced by Donald Creighton, much of Canadian legal and
business history is driven by the experience of the great merchants and

entrepreneurs. For example, in his provocative *Legacies of Fear: Law and Politics in Quebec in the Era of the French Revolution*, F. Murray Greenwood extols Creighton's 'magisterial' *Empire of the St. Lawrence*, expanding the Laurentian thesis to include the security issue as friction between merchants and the French Party led to development of a 'garrison mentality' among the English élite.[4] However, very different legal imperatives emerge if one puts international merchants and ethnicity to the side and focuses instead on wives in petty trade (traders, hawkers, tavernkeepers, shopkeepers), particularly their economic autonomy under the code – the 'money' factor as Virginia Woolf bluntly put it. Two perspectives provide the background to this case study of married women as traders: first, that of women under statute law, particularly their presence and responsibilities in public space and the treatment of married women under the Custom of Paris; and secondly, that of the codifiers in the context of Victorian gender relations. In addition, this particular period was marked by expanding industrial production, by new sexual divisions of labour, by the growing importance of capital and financial intermediaries, and by increasing state influence over the usual places of women's work such as the commons, the streets, the markets, the shops.[5]

WOMEN UNDER STATUTORY LAW AND
MARRIED WOMEN UNDER THE CUSTOM

One example sets the scene in a human scale. Widow Elizabeth Lyons had been one of the longest leaseholders of a bench in the new market of Montreal. From at least 1808 to 1814 she sold goods there and in 1819 she still appeared in a street directory as a dry-goods trader. In 1820, three years after the establishment of the Bank of Montreal, she ceded part of her business autonomy by granting a procuration to Benjamin Hall, noting that she had 'frequent dealings with the Banks at Montreal. That not being able to write or sign her name, her business and transactions suffer delays and other inconveniences.'[6]

To changing capitalist relations such as this and the importance of literacy for the autonomy of small traders must be added the role of the state. Hawking and peddling were traditional female trading activities increasingly subject to state regulatory power. In the terms of the Montreal Court of Special Sessions, that power aimed to assist 'the respectable class of traders who offer merchandise in their shops' considering the great number of Hawkers and Pedlars that are now in this city, some embarrassing the streets with their Tables and Hand Carts ... others going from house to house, withdrawing the domestics from the duties of their stations by tempting them to waste time and money.[7]

Increasing arrests of women for liquor or market violations were other indicators of tightening legal restrictions on their use of urban space. Elizabeth White, a stall-keeper at the Sainte-Anne market in Montreal was convicted of selling liquor without a licence while Marguerite Barsalow paid a £5 fine for buying and reselling two turkeys at the new market in contravention of market rules on regrating.[8] Reduction in the number of taverns in Montreal restricted another common female trading profession. Females represented 6.3 per cent of Montreal's 282 tavernkeepers in 1846.[9] Female prostitution was another economic activity subjected to increasing legislative control in the mid-nineteenth century. Although the Lower Canadian police act of 1839 had permitted police to apprehend suspected prostitutes, the Contagious Diseases Act (1864) went much further. Described by Constance Backhouse as 'a blatant form of sex discrimination,' it subjected women to medical inspection, forced treatment, and, if diseased, to compulsory hospitalization.[10]

The period following the American and French revolutions – with its emphasis on the Rights of Man and the responsibilities of citizenship – coincided with a time of narrowing civic duties for Lower Canadian women. Early in the nineteenth century, for example, women appeared on the Montreal assessment roles from which jury lists were drawn up but they did not appear on the jury lists themselves. This division between the universal responsibility for taxes and the gender-specific privilege of civic duty was confirmed in Montreal's act of incorporation (1831) which reserved the municipal vote to 'men' who fulfilled the age and property requirements. A provincial act of the same year excluded women from the civil and political rights accorded to male British subjects.[11]

The deteriorating franchise rights of Lower Canadian women in the 1830s and 1840s has been well documented by Nathalie Picard. Many propertied women, particularly widows, voted in provincial elections after 1792, and, in exceptional ridings such as Montreal West and Montreal East, female electors represented respectively 14.4 per cent and 9.5 per cent of the vote in 1832.[12] Although wives theoretically could not be enfranchised, confusion over the rights of married women with separation of property agreements left loopholes which some electoral officers interpreted as permitting married women to vote. An 1834 act disenfranchising women was abrogated in 1836, and it was only in 1849 that the legislature finally removed the vote from Lower Canadian women.[13]

Imprisonment for debt was another indicator of women's public capacities. Although at least six women had been imprisoned for debt in the period 1794–1828, changing debt laws in the 1840s reduced the contractual responsibilities of women.[14] After 1849, women (as well as men over seventy and the clergy) could not be imprisoned for 'reason of any debt or by reason of any civil action.'[15]

Philanthropic activities represented an important exception to the tightening of legal controls over female activity in public space. Historically, Roman Catholic female religious institutions had exercised considerable economic autonomy; by the 1840s, Protestant matrons were increasingly active in philanthropy, particularly in managing social institutions serving unwed mothers and orphans. To resolve the incompatibility of these responsibilities with their incapacity to act without their husband's authorization, married women in two Protestant institutions – the Montreal Lying-in Hospital (1843) and the Protestant Orphan Asylum (1848) – were permitted to act for these institutions without special authorization from their husbands 'any Law, usage or custom to the contrary notwithstanding.'[16]

Alcohol abuse was another area where the law provided for initiatives by wives. Along with employers, guardians, and other adult family members, a wife, under the Sale of Intoxicating Liquors Act of 1864, was permitted, by notifying sellers of liquor in writing, to have her husband banned from buying alcohol for one year. She was also able to bring actions in her own name against sellers of liquor who did not respect her notification and she could keep damages for her own separate use.[17]

The Custom of Paris, with its roots in feudalism and the Middle Ages, reflected a patriarchal view of marital, family, and community relations. This can be seen in provisions dealing with the husband as 'Seignior' with responsibility to administer family property, to choose the place where husband and wife would live, and to discipline children. Only in flagrant instances of physical abuse, economic neglect, or adultery in which the husband's concubine was kept in the home did old law provide for separation from bed and board.[18] In cases of a husband's squandering a wife's estate, the court could impose separation of property.

The husband's economic power is of particular interest to us. A married woman could not 'sell, alienate, nor mortgage her estates without the authority and express consent of the husband'; a contract made without the consent of the husband was null.[19] Although a woman could obtain extra protection through a prenuptial marriage contract itemizing her goods, which protected her from her husband's creditors and which provided for a dower, this practice – common among the Lower Canadian bourgeoisie – was increasingly unusual after the 1820s among couples from the popular classes.[20] Without a marriage contract, a wife's *propres*, property brought into the marriage or inherited, was automatically protected by the Custom; a husband administered his wife's property and benefited from its income but could not alienate it.[21] Studies treating domestic violence in Lower Canada, prostitution, the urban household economy, marriage ceremonies, and women in wage labour have amply demonstrated the larger implications of this female dependence.[22] The courts regularly reinforced this incapacity in money matters. Responding in 1862 to the codification reports, Dominique Mondelet of Trois-Rivières, reputed to be a progressive judge, summarized his understanding of marital authority: 'the wife even if separated as to property cannot enter into contract, even for the administration of her property, without being authorized by her husband or by the court.'[23]

This opinion, which does not appear to have been borne out by the Custom of Paris or eighteenth-century court documents, hints at the deepening patriarchy of judges. In any case, this incapacity would be confirmed in codification. In 1874, Justice Joseph-Amable Berthelot dismissed the suit of grocer Leduc who had sued his customer Doré to recover the cost of groceries extended to his wife. In his successful defence, Doré argued that his wife was 'not careful with expenses,' that he had asked the grocer not to extend her credit, and that he furnished her with adequate money for the upkeep of his family. If a wife was not satisfied with her husband's provisions, Judge Berthelot told the court, she had recourse to justice.[24]

Patriarchy was, however, only one of the anchors of legal ideology: the Civil Code, as we will see in chapter 8, was more than just a renewal of custom. It included a rational, impartial, and universal set of Civil law principles centred on the law of Obligations. This adaptation in the code to capitalist conditions would emphasize principles of freedom of contract, equality, and individual responsibility – what Jean Domat in 1689 summarized as 'wittingly and willingly.' This process of liberalization and universalization which included erosion of the historical privileges of seigneurs, minors, merchants, and artisans posed important legal conundrums concerning the rights of married women.

The expanding and increasingly important nineteenth-century business of life insurance provides a good example of the difficulties of balancing customary principles against those of contract. Article 282 of the Custom of Paris was specific in forbidding husbands and wives from benefiting each other 'in any way' except by mutual gift. Did this permit – the Life Association Company asked its lawyers in 1860, in a question that went to the very heart of the insurer's right to conduct business – a husband to make his wife a beneficiary of an insurance policy? Torrance and Morris responded that the company could essentially thwart the law since a policy was

manifestly an advantage granted by the husband to wife. But can anyone but the Company call it in question? Their contract was to pay to the wife and if they pay her is not the payment a good one discharging their obligation under the policy.[25]

In another instance, Torrance and Morris were asked if a widow in poverty had the right to surrender an insurance policy for a money consideration?[26]

The contradiction between customary principles of patriarchy and liberal values of equality was resolved by reinforcing the incapacity of married women as a *particular* exception to what P.S. Atiyah calls the *'generality* of contract law.'[27] Not unique to Lower Canada, this solution had parallels throughout western society. Although republican debates in the United States over egalitariansism and liberty prompted occasional attention to the issue of the women's franchise and married women's property rights and early American feminists like Elizabeth Cady Stanton saw the reform potential of codification, historians have convincingly demonstrated the persistence of patriarchal power.[28]

In France, Rousseau, Montesquieu, Voltaire, and others had challenged traditional views of marriage while, during the Revolution, Cambacérès' project for a civil code (1793) proposed marriage as an egalitarian and mutually acceptable contract that could be dissolved on the simple demand of the one of the partners. In family relations, the proposed code sharply diminished paternal power: relations between parents and their children (including adopted children) would be that of 'a small republic directed by a family council in an egalitarian spirit.' However, during the decade-long preparation of the Napoleonic Code, these revolutionary principles were subordinated to defence of property and an authoritarian and patriarchical vision of the family.[29]

Nor did the emphasis of John Locke and other liberals on individuals as free and equal alter historic principles of coverture in English law. Blackstone's *Commentaries on the Laws of England* confirmed that family relations under the Common law lay, as Mary Lyndon Shanley put it, 'outside the general principle that all legitimate authority must be based on consent': married women could not sue, sign contracts, nor make wills without their husband's permission. The latter also had privileges in child custody, in the right to his wife's body, and in double standards in matters such as adultery.[30] Nor, according to Susan Staves, did changes in English married women's property law bring fundamental change in this reality: 'they [judges] were comparatively free to reimpose patriarchal structures after those structures had been challenged by contract, and reimpose them they did.'[31]

Lawmakers in Lower Canada shared these attitudes to the dependence of married women, their need for protection, their aptitude for domestic activities, and their inaptness for civic responsibilities. Issues such as the ability of married women to work as autonomous traders and the ability of a husband to grant his wife some fiscal autonomy through a procuration were only particular and limited exceptions to this sharply gendered world-view. While legal provisions for the incapacity of married women originated largely in the Custom of Paris, new registry and bankruptcy laws affected married women's rights. One effect of the Registry Ordinance of 1841, for example, was to end the priority of customary dower rights, making them dependent upon registration by the husband.[32] Husbands who did not register outstanding claims were subject to charges of fraud and imprisonment until damages were paid. Reflecting back on the ordinance, Justice W.C. Meredith concluded that it had been for the 'public good' that married women and their children had been deprived 'of certain rights which tended to obstruct the alienation of real estate.'[33] Other contempories were less sanguine. One critic, John Bonner, described its 'harshness towards married women, minors, and privileged creditors':

Though its prime object was merely to establish Registry Offices, it sweeps, in fact, over the whole field of the Law of Real Property ... To the Lawyer, to the Notary, to the Merchant, to the Landholder, to the Capitalist, to every one who may be placed in the position of borrower or lender ... a thorough knowledge of its provisions would seem indispensable ... On the rules it establishes depends the scanty pittance of the widow: the ignorance of a single clause or paragraph may snatch from the orphan the means which parental foresight and affection had laid up for his maintenance ... In whatever sphere of life we are placed – by whatever social ties we are bound – whatever responsibilities we have accepted – and whatever domestic authority we exercise – it is our bounden duty ... to acquire a personal knowledge of a Law on which so much of our happiness and their welfare depends.[34]

The ordinance, by increasing security for property loans, facilitated the growth of mortgage companies like the Montreal Building Society (1845) and the Montreal Permanent Building Society (1858). However, like much of the Special Council's work, registry law was regularly ignored because of the costs involved, the distance to registry offices, and cadastral difficulties.[35] This led to recurring complaints from lenders who saw mortgaged property still vulnerable to claims of customary dower. This problem was taken up by the codifiers and, in a new law (article 2116), the Civil Code reinforced registry so that customary dower could only be preserved by registration of the marriage contract with a full description of immovables subject to dower.

Changing bankruptcy law demonstrated the same tendencies. By an 1843 statute all traders had to register their contracts of marriage at the district registry office; new marriage contracts had to be registered within thirty days.[36]

This combination of customary and statutory law led to the perception among lawyers that Lower Canada was more restrictive of married women than American jurisdictions. Reporting in 1859 to a Vermont client seeking information about power of attorney regulations, the Montreal law firm, Torrance and Morris, pointed out the particular dependence of wives in Lower Canada:

under our law the husband must be party to the power [of attorney] (tho it be given to himself) in order to authorize his wife. Every deed executed by a wife must be authorized by her husband not merely by his presence and being a party to the instrument but also by the instrument having the sacramental words 'A B wife of C D by her said husband duly and specially authorized as testifed by his signature hereto.'[37]

THE CODIFIERS AND GENDER

The codifiers had a strongly gendered sense of the relations between men and women. The female virtues were obedience and domesticity; the natural male roles were to provide leadership and order in the family. These views would be reflected in the codifiers' definition of the person, of rights to contract, and in their pronouncements on marriage and divorce. Untouched by feminist influence – not a significant force in Quebec before the 1880s – they reflected values shaped within all-male parameters of university, bar, and courts.[38]

In a society in which 84.8 per cent of the population was Roman Catholic, values of the Catholic élite were fundamental to this perspective.[39] Cartier, Morin, and Caron all had close ties to the hierarchy. Morin, whose vision of female education included libraries for Catholic girls segregated from those of boys or Protestant girls, was the first dean of the law school at Université Laval; the establishment of Laval was described by Philippe Sylvain and Nive Voisine as 'the crowning of the clergy's hold on the intellectual evolution of Quebec.'[40] Adding to this perception of law and society in the 1860s was the expanding political influence of ultramontanism with its insistence on conservative social values and subordination of the secular to the religious.

The effect of this environment on gender and family relations, on female sexuality, on the social role of women, and on the isolation of women from an increasingly rational and scientific world was made more compelling by acceptance in 1854 of new dogma surrounding Immaculate Conception and by the expanding cult of the Blessed Virgin. Mary's suffering, innocence, and obedience was presented as a female model in this sermon handwritten by a Montreal priest in 1871:

Mothers, why not imitate the Blessed Virgin? ... You sweep the floor, you cook the dinner, you mend your children's clothes, you keep things in good order in the house. Why not do all this in a spirit of love of God. All those actions the Blessed Virgin performed. They were very ordinary actions but they were sanctified by the spirit of love and charity which animated the Blessed Virgin.[41]

Sanctity of the marriage sacrament and male authority within the family were central elements in this ethic. The father was 'king of the family' and, as the ultramontane Le Nouveau Monde reminded its readers in 1869, foremost among his rights was the 'natural' and 'inviolable' right to 'control the education of his children, to shape their morality and their hearts, to mould them to his own image.' The influential bishop of Montreal, Ignace Bourget, buttressed this image of the father as 'the only sovereign of the child' and as the 'supreme arbiter.' Fathers initiated children to the 'hard facts of life'; mothers were responsible for the transmission of religious values. Édouard-Charles Fabre, Bourget's successor and Attorney General Cartier's brother-in-law, was also troubled by the dangers of extramarital sexuality in urban society and by the expanding female presence in public space.[42]

These gender attitudes were not, however, the prerogative of one particular religious group; the social conservatism of the two Catholic codifiers was strongly echoed by their Protestant colleague. Charles Dewey Day had a particular fixation with marital authority and, on several occasions, differed with his fellow judges over the priority he accorded it over laws of domicile or moral views concerning wife-beating. In December 1837, Marie-Clothilde Pinsonnault, while in exile with her husband in Albany, sold some of her own property (*propres*) in Huntington County. Following New York law, she contracted the sale without her husband's authorization. When the validity of the sale was disputed in November 1856, judges of the Montreal Superior Court divided. In dissenting, Justice Dominique Mondelet accepted that the deed should be judged by the real estate law of New York.

Interpreting the issue in opposite fashion, Justice Day gave priority to what he called the 'essential' and 'universal' character of marital authority:

the chief object of that law [Custom of Paris provisions asserting marital authority in contracts by the wife] was to regulate the status of husband and wife, and the protection of the property of families; the mere fact, that questions concerning real estate were sometimes involved, did not of itself determine the nature of the law ... The capacity of [a] wife involving the necessity of marital authority was a personal statute; and, being such, must be measured, not by its consequences, but by its essential character, which was universal, running into territories where other laws prevailed, and governing the alienation of real property within such territory.[43]

Nor, Day argued in another case, was the primacy given under the Custom to marital authority alleviated by flagrant wife-beating. When a man named Caissé assaulted his wife, 'struck her with his fist, and threatened to beat her and take her life,' Emerance Hervieux complained to a magistrate and a true bill was found against her husband. Her error in law, however, was to seek refuge at her brother's house; in a subsequent civil suit, the grieved husband successfully sued for damages resulting from the concealment of his wife. Finding in the husband's favour, Day noted that, 'however strong may be the moral reasons,' the brother could not cite 'bad treatment' as a 'legal defence.'[44]

Day was also adamant on the rights of fathers in cases of separation from bed and board. While granting the action of a woman named

Guernon demanding separation from her husband for ill-treatment, Day refused her child custody noting that 'it is against all principle to deprive the husband of the children where no cause is given.'[45]

Day carried these opinions forward to the Codification Commission where he vigorously defended marital power. His favourite authority was Pothier:

For it is a consequence of maritial power, that the wife be incapable of doing anything except it be dependently on the husband and by his authority. Hence it follows that, without his authority, she is incapable of making any agreement, and she can neither bind herself to others, nor bind others to her.[46]

Rejecting the Napoleonic Code's position that women were in an equivalent position to minors, Day reasserted Pothier's interpretation: 'The rule is founded upon the doctrine of marital authority and should not be changed unless that branch of our law be essentially amended.'[47]

Day's attitudes largely merged with the conservatism of his fellow Catholic codifiers giving consensus on the biological determinism of gender, the centrality of the patriarchal family, and the nature of motherhood, marriage, and domesticity. While some democratization of domestic relations characterized certain American jurisdictions in the post-revolutionary period, the Lower Canadian commissioners emphasized that male authority was both economic – the codifiers described it as 'the exorbitant power of the husband over the property of the community' – and physical.[48] The latter, with its ring of feudal dependence was expressed succinctly in article 174: 'A husband owes protection to his wife; a wife obedience to her husband.'

Throughout the code – registry, customary dower, succession, marriage, and separation from bed and board – patriarchy and marital autority were regularly confirmed. Writing the section on domicile, Caron reiterated the emphasis on Pothier by insisting that a wife, unless separated by the courts from bed and board, could have no other legal domicile than that of her husband. Divorce, we have already noted, was 'foreign' to Lower Canada and was not recognized in the Civil Code.[49]

Noting that the conjugal community was 'so essentially different from every other partnership,' the codifiers rejected articles of the Napoleonic Code that restricted the husband's right to dispose of property of the marriage community by gifts *inter vivos*.[50] Day lobbied hard in these discussions concerning the rights of married women. In the case of a separation from bed and board, for example, he objected to a wife's right as a defendant to any claim of *saisie-gagerie* upon the movable effects of the community.

These powers often blatantly contradicted economic and human realities. Were there extenuating circumstances that obviated a wife's exclusion from contracting? Should she be able to contract if her husband was absent, if he was jailed, or if alone she found it necessary to 'establish' a minor by signing an apprenticeship contract? In all of these instances, the codifiers opted for the strictest interpretation of patriarchy in which only judges could replace the power of the male head of household. If the husband's authorization was not available, 'that of a judge can always be obtained, and there seems to be no reason why the wife should be exempted from seeking the one when she cannot procure the other.'[51]

Separation from bed and board – possible under old law – was continued with only minor change. Wives (or husbands) could initiate actions. In instances of 'outrage, ill-usage or grievous insult' by either spouse, of a wife's adultery or a husband keeping his concubine in their dwelling, or of a husband's 'refusal to receive his wife and to furnish her with the ncessaries of life, according to his rank,' the court could award permission for the couple to live apart. Although marriage was indissoluble while both partners lived, separation from bed and board carried with it separation of property and gave the wife the right to choose a domicile other than that of her husband. In determining custody, the codifiers followed the Napoleonic Code: while the case was pending, children remained provisionally with the father unless the judge ordered otherwise. Final custody was normally entrusted to the party obtaining the separation although the court could award children to the other party or to a third person.[52]

The code said little about the civic or public responsibilities of women. Two of the three commissioners did feel that, in order to conform to the practice followed in notarized wills, women should not be able to witness a will using the English form. As enacted, the code confirmed that women were not permitted as witnesses of notarized wills but that they could witness written wills made according to English form.[53]

MARRIED WOMEN IN TRADE

Wives had always assisted their husbands in the boutique, market stall, or artisanal shop, but large numbers of women also operated businesses on their own. European estimates of the percentage of grocery shops operated by a woman alone range from one-third to one-half.[54] Spinsters and widows with capital, businesses, *rentier* property, or seigneuries were, along with female religious communities, visible and important economic forces in nineteenth-century Quebec. For their part, married women in the bourgeoisie who benefited from prenuptial marriage contracts had the legal means to maintain their property and to ensure their old age. And, under the community of property regime, a woman married without a marriage contract was assured, on the death of her spouse, half the property of their community – an important consideration if the husband had accumulated property.[55]

Less visible but perhaps more important in terms of their numbers and social significance were spinsters, wives, or widows active in small businesses involving foodstuffs, alcohol, lodging, or clothing. Petty commerce had an historic attraction for women, and customary law enabled married women to operate therein with legal and economic autonomy.

In medieval France and England, married women could trade independently of their husbands and married women operated autonomously as pawnbrokers, booksellers, and army provisioners.[56] Many of the autonomous females in petty commerce in Lower Canada were operating as the real heads of their households. Aside from the well-documented phenomena of spinsterhood and widowhood, it is clear that separation, desertion, or the bankruptcy of husbands left many women supporting large families.[57] Lower Canadian court records show significant numbers of women suing for separation both for reasons of physical abuse and the bankruptcy of their husbands. Of seventeen cases in which females were plaintiffs before the Queen's Bench of the District of Montreal in February and April 1843, three were cases of separation.[58] Census records also indicate that adult males were regularly missing from the households of many female traders. For example, peddler Eleo Phagan of the Sainte-Anne suburb in 1831 headed a household of two, both of whom had emigrated to Canada within the past six years. Phagan declared herself an unmarried women of less than forty-five years; her household included a female under fourteen.[59] At the other end of Montreal in the Quebec suburb, grocer Lise Martin headed a household of six in which there were no adult males. Again, the census taker reported no married individuals in the household but one unmarried female over forty-five, and two unmarried females between fourteen and forty-five. The household included two girls and a boy under fourteen. Grocer Adèle Létourneau's household had almost the same profile (six people of whom three were unmarried adult females and three were children under fourteen). A. Charbonneau also operated a grocery and alcohol outlet in the Quebec suburb. She declared herself to be married and head of a six-person household, five of whom were under age fourteen.[60] The census of 1842 gives similar examples of female grocers, tavernkeepers, and other traders heading large households.[61]

To understand the legal and business position of married women in trade, we must differentiate between two distinct legal categories – the female trader and the feme sole trader (in French, the *marchande publique*).[62] The former was recognized under the law as a 'trader'; she might be single, a widow, a wife separated in property from her husband, or a wife operating a trade with her husband's permission.

Included in this larger category of female trader was the feme sole trader, a married woman who had permission of her husband – 'authorization express or implied' according to article 199 of the Civil Code – to operate a trade with legal and economic autonomy. The ability to enter into certain contracts was perhaps the most obvious sign of this status. In both London and parts of France, local custom (confirmed in the custom of London, English common law and the Custom of Paris) recognized and protected the married woman who operated as a feme sole trader. The status was also recognized in several of the Thirteen Colonies.[63] Under the Custom of Paris, the feme sole trader was a married women (under either community or separation of property) who conducted a trade independent of her husband. Under the French Code of Commerce a woman could only be recognized as a feme sole trader with the tacit consent of her husband.

In Lower Canada, article 179 of the Civil Code left ambiguous the situation concerning the nature of consent. Authorities agreed that a woman married under the community of property needed her husband's approval but F. Langelier suggested that a separation of property regime allowed the wife to operate as a feme sole trader as part of her right to administer her own property.[64] Once recognized as a trader in the community, the female trader could, without the authorization of her husband, make contracts *concerning her trade* including purchase and sale of merchandise, the hiring of employees, and the making of promissory notes. (Although the French Code of Commerce permitted a feme sole trader to mortgage her real property as part of her trade, Lower Canadian authorities do not seem to mention it.) These rights were limited, however, and under the Lower Canadian Civil Code the feme sole trader could not appear in court without authorization of her husband:

176. A wife cannot appear in judicial proceedings, without her husband or his authorization, even if she be a public trader or not common as to property; nor

can she, when separate as to property, except in matters of simple administration.[65]

Both French and Lower Canadian authorities agreed that the feme sole trader must act in business independent of her husband. (Under both Common and Civil law, a wife could act as agent for her husband without the status of feme sole trader). Pothier was particularly insistent on the independence of the wife's business.[66]

These conditions emphasize that the rights of the feme sole trader were determined in large part by her marriage regime. If married under the community of property, her husband was responsible for contracts made by his wife; if married under the separation of property, the husband was not normally responsible for his wife's legal commitments as a feme sole trader.[67]

While most feme sole traders had limited capital and were from the popular classes, there are important examples of prominent entrepreneurs apparently establishing their wife's status as feme sole trader to protect their own businesses. The family of Augustin Cuvillier – important auctioneers and commission agents – used that device over two generations. In October 1811, Marie-Claire Perrault, a mother of seven, announced that she had formed a commercial establishment, Mary C. Cuvillier and Company, and intended 'on her own responsibility, to carry on the different brandes [sic] of Auctioneering, Brokerage and Agency.' Her entry into business in May 1811 coincided with severe problems in her husband's affairs and, according to Cuvillier's biographers, she was 'a front for Cuvillier's own business.'[68] Her storage, auctioneering, and commission business was apparently successful with advertisements for fireproof storage for flour, pork, or other valuables and auctions of dry goods. She continued as a major auctioneer and commission merchant into the 1820s.[69]

Forty years later, her daughter-in-law, Marie V.L. Duchesnay, apparently filled the same role for another generation of Cuvilliers:

wife of Maurice Cuvillier of Montreal in the District of Montreal esquire, separated from him as to property by marriage contract and trading at Montreal aforesaid under the name or form of Cuvillier and Co. the said Maurice Cuvillier for the purpose of authorizing his said wife.[70]

Again, although not permitted by law, Duchesnay seemed to be acting for her husband; in an 1862 shipment of 1700 boxes of tobacco to Liverpool, she endorsed the bill of exchange with her husband acting as her attorney.

Three important phenomena come together in the period of the Civil Code: the power of women in commercial and political public space is diminished, contract as an essential accessory to economic power is increasingly significant, and the Custom's emphasis on the legal impotence of married women is reiterated in the Civil Code. A broad series of articles of the code concerning the definition of persons and of marriage regimes separate married women from the universality implied in the general emphasis on freedom of contract. Our example of married women as traders demonstrates that a wife's autonomy in trade depended in large measure on permission granted by the husband. This coexistence of patriarchy and liberalism within the code mirrored the period's social conservatism and helps explain the subordination of married women over the following century in a society undergoing rapid capitalist development.

8

'Wittingly and Willingly': The Law of Obligations

Covenants ought to be made wittingly and willingly.

Jean Domat (1689)[1]

Every conflict between systems of jurisprudence, between economic régimes, between ideologies, finds it most vigorous expression in the issue of contract.

Mostapha Mohamad El-Gammal (1967)[2]

... the title *Of Obligations*, which because of its importance, as being the basis of the greater portion of the whole Code, it had been decided to commence with. For the same reason, this title was, even more than any of the others, the subject of long and careful examination and discussion.

Thomas McCord, commission secretary (1867)[3]

Technically oriented legal historians generally emphasize that the aim of a compilation of law such as a code is essentially reform directed to improving the organization and accessibility of the law. In these interpretations, doctrinal and conflictual elements are subordinated to the techniques of coordinating a corpus of private law in an essentially consensual environment.[4] From a political perspective, in which Law reflects a particular social conjuncture, however, the Civil Code resulted from a specific historical moment that included the implementation of bourgeois democracy, a fundamental redefinition of property rights through the dismantling of seigneurialism, and Confederation.

As the treatment of female public traders made clear, the major ideological compromise in the code was between a customary legal culture
and a rational, universal Civil law system with its roots in Roman law.
While the former corresponded to community perceptions of authority
in basic social institutions like marriage and the family, the latter facilitated expanding capitalist relations, particularly as they pertained to
contract and the law's perceived impartiality and universality.[5]

The consolidation of the traditional social framework of civil society,
particularly in 'Persons,' the first book of the Civil Code, was accompanied by a second agenda – the placement of the law of Obligations at the
core of the code. This formed part of a larger nineteenth-century reform
of Civil law across much of the west in which growing emphasis was
given to the free market and the treatment of labour and property as
commodities. Exchange relationships were increasingly expressed in written instruments and enforced by the apparatus of the liberal state.[6]

The Lower Canadian codifiers were unabashed in the importance they
gave to the law of Obligations, describing it as 'the fundamental principles upon which a large proportion of civil rights and liabilities depends,
and [which] furnishes rules of universal application.'[7] Commission Secretary McCord went further in integrating the law of Obligations into the
mid-nineteenth–century emphasis on individualism and the increasing
liquidity of immovables. He saw contracts replacing immovable property
as the major source of social stability:

It is one of the characteristics of the olden legislation that it appears to have had
in view Things before Persons. The conservative spirit of the law seems to have
clung to immoveables as the safest basis of social stability, and its policy tended
to restrict rather than to encourage the conveyance of real estate … In modern
society, the frequency and multiplicity of transactions have become so great that
real property now changes hands as rapidly as moveables did formerly. Agreements and promises are practically dealt with as representing the objects to which
they relate. The tendency of the age is to make Things subservient to Persons,
and to bring immoveables as well as all other things under complete subjection
to the will of man … Some of these provisions [of the Code] are intended to
facilitate the free exercise of man's dominion over property. Some by rendering
contracts and other expressions of man's will definitive and reliable, are calcu-
lated to furnish elements of stability …[8]

The law of Obligations had its roots in Roman law's great emphasis on
the sanctity of property rights and on the protection of those rights as the

primary function of the state.[9] Although it largely disappeared from Gaul with the barbarian invasions, the decline of commerce and credit transactions, and expansion into the Frankish kingdoms of feudal, canon, and German customary law, Roman law revived at the end of the eleventh century with the recovery of Justinian's *Corpus Iuris Civilis*. Concurrently with formalization of France's various customs in the thirteenth century, legal intellectuals began studying Roman texts in universities in Bologna, Montpellier, Orléans, and Toulouse. As written law expanded across the south of France, Roman law was incorporated as part of this region's customary law.[10]

Its penetration into the north (*les pays coutumiers*) was slower, but even here its usefulness in counterbalancing custom, family, and feudalism was demonstrated. By the fourteenth century, notaries in the north were employing Roman law to reduce the importance of seigneurial investiture; in the Île de France, Roman authority was used to facilitate exchange by permitting inheritances to be freely sold.[11] As French royal authority expanded in the fifteenth century, the influence of Roman law accelerated with courts across the *pays coutumiers* recognizing the superiority of the law of Obligations in commercial matters.

By the sixteenth century, when customary law was given written form and royal authority, Roman law, particularly the law of Obligations, was firmly ensconced. While the Custom of Paris dealt with land, succession, and family law, civilian law in the Prévôté de Paris governed many other aspects of contract. French law became more complex with the expansion of royal authority into areas untouched by custom especially the important ordinances of Louis XIV and Louis XV: civil procedure (1667), the criminal ordinance of 1670, the Merchant Code (1673), the Marine Ordinance (1681), the Slave Code (1685), and Henri-François Daguesseau's ordinances on *donations* (1731) and wills (1735).[12]

The importance to the Lower Canadian codifiers of Jean Domat and Robert-Joseph Pothier has already been noted. Trained by the Jesuits and then in Roman law, Domat in his *Civil Law in its Natural Order* successfully synthesized Christianity and rationalism using Roman law as his model for reason. While Domat endorsed freedom of contract, he qualified this endorsement by emphasizing Christian qualities of love and charity.[13] A half century later, Christian elements of contract were subordinated in favour of natural law, first by Chancellor Henri-François Daguesseau (1668–1751) and then by Pothier. Daguesseau defined the threefold natural duties of man as being to God, himself, and his fellow man.' Obligations grew out of the latter.

Justice holds Rome's Justinian Institutes in one hand and, in the other, the
Napoleonic Code with its inscription 'equal justice intelligible for all.' The
code, the citizenry is reminded, 'by its simplicity brought more good to France
than the mass of all the laws that preceded it.'

The whole rests on legal volumes among which Pothier's *Traité des Obligations*,
Domat's *Traité des lois civiles*, and the *Coutume de Paris* figure prominently.

Pothier's early work, *Commentaire de la Coutume d'Orléanais* (1740), and his Roman study, *Pandectae Justinianae in novum ordinem digestae* (1748), were followed in the 1760s by a series of specific treatises: obligations, sale, hiring, partnership, loan, deposit, mandate, pledge, insurance, gaming contracts, marriage, community of property, dower, property and possession. Pothier's analysis, organization, and clarity made him the dominant authority both in France and Lower Canada and, with the translation into English of Obligations in 1802, his work rapidly became important in both Britain and the United States.[14]

Emphasizing rationalism, individualism, and freedom of contract, Pothier provided a clear, and essentially secular frame for Lower Canadian contract law:

Contracts produce obligations ... We shall take notice now of a principle which is peculiar to the effect of contracts and of all agreements. This principle is, that an agreement has no effect but with regard to things that are the object of the agreement, and only between the parties. The reason of the first part of this principle is obvious. The agreement being formed by the will of the parties, it can only have effect on what the contracting parties intended and had in view. The second part of the principle is not so obvious. The obligations, which arise from agreements and the rights that result from them, being formed by the assent and concurrence of the will of the parties, it cannot bind a third person, nor give a right to a third person whose will has not concurred in forming the agreement.[15]

Pothier based Obligations on canonical and humanist sources and especially on natural law, which obliged man to fulfil his promises: 'natural law requires that each should perform what he promised, and repair the injury which he occasioned by his tort.'[16] He differentiated between two kinds of obligation: 'imperfect' or moral obligations were those 'accountable to God alone' and included charity and gratitude. Excluding these from his treatise, Pothier concentrated on what he called 'perfect' or legal obligations – '*personal engagements*, giving to him, with whom they are contracted, the right of requiring the performance of them'; these were obligations enforceable by legal process and sanctions of the state.[17]

In giving centrality to Obligations in the Lower Canadian Civil Code, the codifiers were only following the pattern of the Napoleonic Code; similarly, in Germany, states such as Dresden set up commissions to draft their law of Obligations.[18] In Lower Canada itself – despite our historiography's emphasis on the Custom of Paris as authority – jurisprudence, treatises, law libraries, and the content of law courses show diverse influences alongside the Custom of Paris, including Domat, Pothier, the law of Obligations, and merchant law.[19]

OBLIGATIONS IN LOWER CANADA

Historians such as John Dickinson have shown the importance in both rural and urban New France of cases involving debt, sales disputes, labour agreements, as well as seigneurial, family, and property cases. In Notre-Dame-des-Anges for example, those disputes represented 67 per cent of the total cases heard in the seigneurial court in the seventeenth century and 28 per cent in the eighteenth century. Throughout the New France period, debt provided the largest number of cases before the Prévôté de Québec.[20] Most of these cases were between urban merchants and artisans with peasants and seigneurs representing a much smaller percentage of cases. In the period 1785–9, seigneurial debt represented 6.9 per cent of peasant debt in inventories after death as compared with 34.2 per cent merchant endebtment.[21] These debts usually represented transactions between familiar parties; for example, F.-A. Bailly, an important merchant and creditor in Varennes, 'lent to people whom he knew well and who for the most part, lived within a short distance of his house at Cap Saint-Michel.'[22]

Until the late eighteenth century, written instruments were more common in urban or international commercial activities than in exchange and debt relationships in the countryside where contracts were most frequent in the fur trade. While written instruments were common in marriage and land-concession contracts, credit relationships between merchant, seigneur, and peasant were usually noted in the form of book debt, which was interest free; in disputes that went to court, statements under oath were given precedence over a merchant's ledger. Although seigneurs might prefer to be paid in cash, many debts were paid in kind or in services.[23] Allan Greer has drawn attention to the imbroglios concerning work contracted informally in the peasant society of the Lower Richelieu, citing, for example, a lawsuit between a boarder and his lodger over the amount of work expected in return for room and board.[24]

These social and credit relationships were strongly influenced by a hierarchy of privilege that included seigneurs, builders, wives, and others. The significance of this credit is evident from the elaborate system of marks that large creditors used in their books to indicate the reliability or solvency of individual debtors.[25] Louise Dechêne has interpreted seig-neurial relationships as vigorous, rigid, and exploitive; Louis Michel inserts these credit relations into a gentler mid-eighteenth–century per-spective in which the relationship between rural merchant and creditor represented

a variety of capitalism which was only slightly parasitical. Far from being founded on upheaval, it prospered in the existing agrarian structures profiting from the possibilities offered by the colonial situation.[26]

A complete analysis of the impact of debt relations in New France awaits its historian, but it would appear that contract law was still diffuse and permeated by the family, community, and Christian considerations that were central to the Custom of Paris. The creditor's security, for example, remained qualified by customary privileges, particularly those of the debtor's wife and minor children. Although the Ordinance of 1667 gave priority to written instruments as proof and the Merchant Code of 1673 set out regulations for commercial relations, the practice of oral agreements and practical, local arrangements remained strong.[27]

Several studies of the period from the conquest to the Rebellions of 1837–8 have emphasized the increasing penetration of formal contract into credit relations. In the post-conquest decades oral promises and book accounts were often replaced by written instruments drawn up by a notary, which imposed fixed time and payment conditions. These con-tracts brought the law of Obligations into full play between creditor and debtor. Debt-recognition contracts were assignable, were increasingly guaranteed by specific hypothecs, and bore legal interest.[28] Robert Sweeny has described the increasing use of notarized contracts in the post-Napoleonic period as part of a larger process of 'alienation' in which the legal professional, his clientele of urban merchants, and his ideology of contract and credit relations penetrated into the firewood-producing areas around Montreal, its peasant network, and its family strategies. Seigneurs were another powerful group of creditors who turned to notar-ial contracts to enforce payment of debt. When seigneur Napier Christie Burton died in 1835, his estate manager used the occasion to pressure endebted *censitaires* to sign debt-recognition contracts bearing 6 per cent interest. Françoise Noël links resistance to these measures to growing support for the Patriotes in the Upper Richelieu Valley. While he was in exile after the rebellions, seigneur Louis-Joseph Papineau increasingly turned to obligations and court judgments to force payment of seigneurial arrears. And by 1841, the Seminary of Montreal – the most important seigneur in the Montral region – employed a full-time notary who travelled around the seminary's three seigneuries writing and enforcing debt-recognition contracts.[29]

This treatment of seigneurial land increasingly as a commodity in the early nineteenth century took other forms, which further permitted the expansion of the ideology of contract into relations historically governed by custom and old French law. With population pressure and the growing value of domain lands (held, for example, as pine forests), the practice of certain seigneurs of keeping land off the market for speculative reasons or of adding conditions to land concessions was increasingly contentious. Although edicts of 1711 (Marly) and 1732 apparently denied the sale of unconceded seigneurial land while obliging the seigneur to make grants, seigneurs such as Napier Christie Burton, as land became scarce and more valuable, coupled sales contracts or other financial considerations to concessions.[30] Although *censitaires* reacted angrily to what they perceived as an abuse of long-understood principles governing seigneurial relations, lawsuits showed the weight accorded by the courts to freedom of contract.

In 1845, for example, L'Ériger dit Laplante entered into a mixed sale and concession contract for land on the seigneury of Thwaite and Saint-James. In addition to the sale price, he was to pay seigneurial dues including the *cens et rentes* and an annual corvée of a day's work or its equivalent in cash. Several years later and still owing over £88 of his purchase price, L'Ériger dit Laplante stopped paying, arguing that a sales contract was incompatible with seigneurial law. In settling the suit in seigneur John Boston's favour, Justice Day gave a strict and literal interpretation of the Edicts of Marly, noting that the seigneur was forbidden to sell only in the edicts' preamble and not in the body of the text. Day went on to give priority to contract. L'Ériger dit Laplante was under

no compulsion, there was no obligation on the Defendant to buy the land, he did so voluntarily. He had two modes of getting it; one pointed out by the law, the other by voluntary contract, and he cannot now urge that he did not know there was another course open to him.[31]

Lesion – loss or injury sustained by a minor – was another area where Lower Canadian lawyers used Roman law as authorities: 'It isn't necessary,' Elzéar Bédard argued in appellate court:

to report ... on the excellence of Roman law, the source of our law. The analogy which exists between the formalities required by our law for the alienation of the property of minors and that required by Roman law is too striking to pass unperceived.[32]

Contract was also given superiority over traditional procedural rights such as the right to interrogate the opposing party in a civil suit. In their building contract for a house, Kennedy and Smith agreed that all alterations or additions to the contract would be made in writing. When the builder sued for costs of £316 incurred for extra work assigned orally by the owner, the defendant refused to answer interrogatories, arguing that the contract was a 'binding law between the parties' which excluded the ordinary right of examination to prove that the extra work had been assigned orally. In his judgment, Justice Day ruled that their contract had established 'an inflexible rule' which justified the refusal to answer interrogatories.[33]

Commercial and maritime law present other examples of the diversity of Lower Canadian authorities and the presence of Roman law. We have seen that pre-capitalist societies were characterized by pluralistic legal systems in which merchant law (bills of exchange, bills of loading) was normally a separate body of law reserved for those with the particular status of merchant. France's Merchant Code (1673) was applied to New France but, after the conquest and particularly after the Quebec Act of 1774, its validity was the subject of recurring litigation.[34]

Further evidence of the importance of non-customary law is provided by the book orders of practitioners. Arthur Davidson, a young Scot admitted to the Lower Canadian bar in 1771, rose rapidly through the bar élite until he was appointed to the bench in 1800. A strong advocate for the anglophone merchant community, his library orders for 1780 show important purchases in Roman and natural law: Justinian's Institutes, Claude de Ferrière's *Les institutes de l'Empereur Justinien*, Domat's *Civil Law in Its Natural Order*, Samuel Pufendorf's work on the law of nature, Hugo Grotius's *Le droit de la guerre et de la paix*, and seven volumes of Montesquieu's works.[35] He was particularly concerned, he wrote to his London bookdealer, to have the latest editions of Pothier and particularly, as a practising lawyer, his indexes.

The price of Pothier's works compared to what I have understood to be the price of them in France in former times is certainly very high; but I am very glad and much obliged to you to have them, tho not the last and best edition, which I am informed has a *general* index, a matter of the greatest advantage to a lawyer, to say nothing of the almost endless *errata* my edition has. For which reasons I wish exceedingly to have the last and best edition, with a General Index in the same form. The one I have I can readily dispose of; and so I could of others, if I had them.[36]

The importance of the ideology of contract can also be traced through law treatises. In the eighteenth century – as epitomized by Blackstone – the law of real property dominated. Although he treated contract briefly, property represented one of the four volumes in *Commentaries* leading to Pollock and Maitland's succinct summary that contract 'appears as a mere supplement to the law of property.'[37] The same weighting is evident in the Custom of Paris which treated contract in a variety of sections without hinting at the ideological importance of the law of Obligations.

The customs contain almost no dispositions on contract ... One cannot find – even in embryonic form – a general theory of Obligations; contracts are simply based on practice ... Our old Law of Contracts consisted of measures disparate in form and spirit.[38]

Indeed, with its secret transfers and sales, its system of general and occult hypothecs, its emphasis on family and other privileged creditors, and its dependence on the property relations of feudalism, the Custom of Paris underscored principles antithetical to individualism and freedom of contract. This subordination of contract to social class and feudalism is also clear from pre-rebellion treatises such as Henry Des Rivières Beaubien's *Traité sur les lois civiles du Bas-Canada* (1832). Although following the same framework as the Napoleonic Code, he included a title on fiefs and his book on persons described ecclesiastics as 'a distinct class' who had special rights against their creditors. Instead of treating contract in a separate title, Beaubien spread it throughout his treatise.[39]

Contract came into its own in Lower Canadian legal treatises written in the Union period – two decades characterized by the decline of nationalism, by the collapse of the ideology of feudalism, and by rapidly evolving economic and social relations involving canals, railway shops, strikes, and big capital. Written for notarial students, Nicolas-Benjamin Doucet's *Fundamental Principles of the Laws of Canada* (1841) included an English translation of the Custom of Paris and, with its undigested mix of Huron, Hebraic, Confucian, canon, customary, Roman, and maritime authorities, served as a half-way house. His treatise dropped feudalism but did not treat Obligations systematically. His short statement on 'Obligations and Actions' was drawn from articles 89, 94, and 95 of the Custom of Paris.

This ambiguity soon disappeared as contract law steadily gained momentum while seigneurialism vanished from both treatises and law curricula. Commissioner of Catholic schools in Quebec City, Jacques Crémazie's manual (1852) emphasized natural law, laws 'God has established between men.' Contract had a central place with a chapter entitled 'Contrats ou Conventions, et des Obligations qui en résultent.'[40]

François-Maximilien Bibaud went further, offering a specific course in his law school on Obligations and drawing a dramatic scenario: Roman law was 'the veritable masterpiece of the human spirit' while the Custom of Paris and statutory law – devoid of principles – were simply 'bizarre' and 'barbaric' collections of 'discordant' facts.[41] Bibaud's 1859 textbook devoted a full title of sixty-three pages to Obligations, as well as describing particular contracts such as sale, exchange, lease, mandate, deposit, and partnership.

The Faculty of Law at McGill College – ambitious to be seen as Lower Canada's dominant law school and well aware of the academic needs of its constituency – had offered a course on commercial contracts in the 1840s. In 1853, the same year that the law faculty was formed, Frederick William Torrance was named professor of Roman law. Scion of a leading merchant family and trained in Edinburgh, Torrance was partner in a leading commercial firm. This linking of classical studies and university to commercial law and merchant capital was part of the mid-century realignment of power. In his introductory lecture on the legal system of Rome, Torrance described Roman law as one of the 'more complete and self-connected systems' of jurisprudence and underlined its 'vital importance' to the Lower Canadian lawyer. Civil law, he noted, showed 'proofs of the highest cultivation and refinement' and he went on to laud civil law intellectuals especially Domat and Pothier, 'immeasurably the superior of Blackstone.'[42]

Back in his law office, Torrance and his partner Alexander Morris helped clients minimize the effects of secret hypothecs. Like Day, they pushed contract into areas traditionally covered by conventions in the Custom of Paris. They chipped away at banal rights, helping clients transform fixed and traditional milling relationships into limited and specific contractual arrangements. This had the effect of permitting contracts between individuals to override customary practices. They also went to court defending a contractual mode for voluntary seigneurial commutations. Torrance forwarded a copy of his firm's precedents on contracts to the Codification Commmission and, when the draft of Obligations and other codifiers' reports were published in the early 1860s, Torrance and Morris began using them as authorities – years before their enactment – thus providing evidence for the attorney general's later statment that the code 'has been used and applied as fast as it came out of the hands of the codifiers.'[43]

OBLIGATIONS IN THE CIVIL CODE

Obligations are not a distinct book in the Civil Code but form a title of 274 articles within Book Third, 'Of the Acquisition and Exercise of Rights of Property.' As originally proposed by the commissioners, 'Of Obligations' contained 275 articles, 21 of which contained amendments to existing law and five of which consisted of new law.[44] To establish a valid contract the parties had to be legally capable of contracting, they had to give their consent legally, there had to be something forming the object of the contract, and there had to be a lawful cause or consideration.[45]

To Day, principles of natural law were implicit in his writing of Obligations. He argued, for example, that the code should not contain a statement declaring that contracts had the effect of law upon the parties; instead, 'there is in the law a higher and more compulsive contract than in the contract which only subsists by the law.'[46] Day's dislike of expressed principles, and his reliance on natural law, became more pronounced as he advanced further into his draft of Obligations. Theory and definitions were 'useless declarations' that should be 'purged' permitting perception of 'the common sense effect of the contract':

The attempt to provide rules ... for directing ... the mind of the judge in his search after the true meaning of a contract through its obscure and doubtful expression is obviously unwise and hazardous. There is a moral impossibility of providing any series of such rules at once so prescient and comprehensive as to be applicable without exception and so varied and numerous to meet all possible combination of difficulties.[47]

This reliance on self-evident principles hid fundamental relations of power. From the outset, Day emphasized the integrity of contract and insisted on a strict application of the will of the contracting parties. Contract was to dominate over considerations of property or the particular status of the merchant, artisan, or seigneur.[48] The key to this relationship was the freedom of the individual to enter the contract and significant parts of the title were devoted to defining consent, nullity, and lesion in contractual situations. For example, fear of injury suffered by a contracting party was a cause of nullity; but 'mere reverential fear of a father or mother, or other ascendant, without any violence having been exercised or threats made' did not invalidate a contract.[49]

The codifiers' concern with the universality of civil law had important repercussions on the structure of commercial law. We have already noted that it was a separate branch of jurisprudence in France and Lower Canada, a tradition confirmed in the Napoleonic codification by the enactment of a separate Commercial Code. In England, however, by the time of Lord Mansfield's death in 1793, much of the merchant law had been absorbed into the mainstream of common law.[50] In Lower Canada, the codifiers' mandate charged them to include commercial law in the Civil Code, a fact that would give further centrality to the ideology of Obligations. Day in particular saw no reason for merchants to continue having a special status. Examining laws of evidence, Day's *First Report* called for 'uniform rules which apply in all cases':

Nothing tends more to perplex and retard the administration of justice than the existence of conflicting rules for different classes of person or things ... There seems really to be no sound reason why the sale by a merchant of his goods to any amount may be proved verbally, while a sale by a farmer of his goods of the value of twenty-six dollars must be proved in writing.[51]

As the author of both Obligations and the entire book on commercial law, Day worked to integrate the two, subordinating, wherever possible, commercial law to Obligations. Rules of proof, for example, had been defined by statutory law and were outlined in 'Of Obligations'; unless expressly limited, they were to apply in commercial matters. Only in instances where the code did not make provision for the proof of facts concerning commercial matters was recourse to be made to the laws of England.[52] Day was also responsible for the preliminary disposition of the book of commercial law, stating that 'the principal rules applicable in commercial cases' which were not contained in the book of commercial law were to be found in 'Of Obligations,' 'Of Sale,' and other parts of the Third Book.[53]

In his organization, his avoidance of definition, and his emphasis on natural law, Day relied heavily on Pothier noting that deviation from Pothier in the Napoleonic Code 'has in every instance been for the worse.

I have therefore returned to his order.'[54] Using Pothier's framework, Day wove contract into a position of priority over customary laws which were, as we have seen, more regulatory, more hierarchical, and more attuned to community ethics.

We have noted that, on the judicial bench, Day was well known for the priority and rigour with which he interpreted the letter of contract. That strictness was transmitted to his draft on Obligations with its emphasis on limiting actions. Day was particularly concerned by judge-made law that might interfere with the integrity of a contract and the intention of the framing parties. The terms of contracts, the *First Report* stated, were to be enforced in full: 'the doctrine of judicial interference with the plain meaning of contracts is regarded with disfavor by modern jurists.'[55] Day was particularly bothered by the permission granted to judges by authorities such as Dumoulin and Pothier to diminish the damages specified in contracts. To offset what he called an 'evil,' Day – supported by Caron – in 'Damages resulting from the inexecution of obligations,' argued for the use of the Napoleonic Code which removed this discretionary power from judges. Morin, who preferred the old rule as 'safer and more equitable,' was overruled by Day and Caron.[56]

DELIVERY

Insertion in the code of new law based on the principle that consent and not delivery was sufficient to convey ownership was crucial in the expansion of capitalist relations permitting full play to individual will and future market conditions:

A contract for the alienation of a thing certain and determinate makes the purchaser owner of the thing by the consent alone of the parties, although no delivery be made.[57]

This principle applied to sales as well as gifts *inter vivos* and exchange.[58]

By the Roman principle of *traditio*, the transfer of ownership was a two-part process that involved the transfer of title (by sale, gift, or exchange) and delivery of the thing. Delivery could take several forms. By *traditio longa manu*, the transferor placed the thing in the hands of the transferee; *traditio clavium* was a symbolic delivery in which keys were handed over. Since delivery was one of the necessary elements of a sale, there was also the practice of the *quasi traditio*, or implied delivery, if the purchaser was already in possession of the thing.[59]

The relationship of delivery and ownership had been a frequent matter of dispute in Lower Canada. Disputes, such as *Bonacina v. Seed* centred on third-party rights.[60] On 15 January 1850 in a notarized sale, Bonacina bought furniture from Bowie for £228; delivery was symbolic in the marking of a chair and table. Bonacina then leased the furniture to Bowie. The furniture was subsequently seized as part of Bowie's chattels by Seed, one of his creditors. On appeal Justice Smith, relying on the Custom of Paris, found for Bonacina. Justice Day was much stricter in his interpretation, reviewing the Roman law of tradition using Pothier's *Sale* to show that marking the chair and table did not constitute delivery in Lower Canada.

Given the capital involved in advances and the seasonal nature and dangers of the trade, timber figured prominently in delivery cases.[61] When timber rafts broke up, burned, or were seized by third parties, the issue of what constituted a delivery at law became significant. In 1844, for example, Levey paid defendant Lowndes £488 for 14,000 feet of birch timber, which Lowndes was to collect north of Quebec City and pile on his wharves for delivery to Levey during the navigation season. Levey paid Lowndes in December 1844, and five months later the timber was destroyed in a fire on Lowndes's wharf.[62] Defendant Lowndes argued that Levey was at risk for the timber which had been piled separately for Levey on the wharf. The court found that delivery had not occurred since it had not been measured and verified by Levey.

The new law on delivery was an ideological beacon, emphasizing the importance of human will and commodity exchange. It facilitated the alienation of movables and capitalist speculation on future markets by dispensing with actual delivery in favour of promise. The sale of immovables presented similar dilemmas since there was uncertainty as to whether the Roman law of '*quoties*,' that is, the actual possession of landed property, applied under the Custom of Paris. Although Domat suggested that Roman tradition was part of the jurisprudence of France, natural law jurists such as Grotius and Pufendorf argued that the consent of the parties completed the sale without delivery; in 1726 the Parlement of Paris ruled that the law 'Quoties' was not applicable in the Vicomté de Paris.[63] Alan Stewart has demonstrated the great difference between title and actual possession of land in the Montreal suburb of Saint-Laurent. For over 50 per cent of sales during the period 1786–1810, possession and title did not coincide, delivery being delayed for months and even years in many cases.[64] Further complicating the situation in Lower Canada was the question of whether French or English conveyancing law was applicable in areas of free and common socage.

This issue of *tradition* of immovables struck at the very heart of property conflict between large land proprietors and squatters. For members of the Château Clique and other large proprietors, land sales and transfers formed part of their larger speculative activities and accumulation of family wealth. Real property was a commodity and delivery was an obvious impediment to the mobility of land.

In 1838, in *Bowen v. Ayer*, the Lower Canadian Appeal Court found that, following the practice in customary parts of France, it was not necessary to take actual possession of the property to ensure ownership.[65] Thirteen years later the issue again came to appeal in *Stuart and Ives* when lower courts in the Saint-Francis District apparently overturned *Bowen v. Ayer* by requiring delivery. In 1835, James Stuart purchased some 9000 acres of 'wilderness' land from his wife. In Stuart's absence, parts of this purchase were settled and cleared. One 200-acre farm was eventually sold for fifty dollars in an unnotarized conveyance to Eli Ives. For twelve years, Ives occupied and improved the land before being sued by Stuart – chief justice, baronet, and author of the colony's land-registry law – who claimed the land and £92 in compensation for Ives' 'wrongful' possession. The appeal court, after reviewing Roman law, English and French conveyancing practices, and *Bowen v. Ayer*, concluded in Stuart's favour. 'The mere naked possession' by squatters was 'inconsistent with the first principles on which the right of property rests' while the delivery of wild lands was 'impracticable and wholly useless.' *Tradition* in remote lands could be achieved by a symbolic delivery. 'Could it be imagined,' the court concluded,

that for the valid conveyance of these lands, it was necessary that the vendors and vendee, in person, or by duly constituted agents, should have gone into the forest, on each of these lots, and have given and received livery of seizin?[66]

The code's establishment of contracts without delivery cleared this confusion and, like the dismantling of seigneuralism, emphasized the treatment of land as a commodity and the dominance of the individual. Across the gamut of civil relations affected by the code, individual rights as expressed through the free will inherent in every valid contract were given precedence over the old law with its sense of balance and over the traditional authority of the state, community, and family.

9

Conclusion

Neither the codifiers nor himself desired to disturb the past. They only sought
   to legislate for the future.
                         Attorney General George-Étienne Cartier (1865)[1]

Everything is either the Immaculate Conception or workers' lunches
                                            Gustave Flaubert[2]

Canadian historiography often serves to level our past with French Canadians frozen in a reactionary time warp. Important anglophone intellectuals repeatedly depict Quebec culture as peopled with 'aristocrats' and
'sows.'[3] Among these recurrent images, Civil law has its place as an
illiberal, un–North American form of jurisprudence that has blocked
creation of a homogeneous Canadian society in which all citizens would
'abide by the same laws.'[4]
   Among other distortions, this depiction serves to deny the historicity
of codification, which emerged from a complex dynamic of changing
property, social, and political relations in the first half of the nineteenth
century. Codification can only be understood as operating in tandem with
the decline of seigneurialism and the accompanying breakdown of feudal
relations, the treatment of both labour and immmovables as commodities,
and the preparation in law of a changing capitalist environment dominated by what Willard Hurst called 'property in motion.'[5] The legal
process of codification was also an intimate part of a particular political

history that included the Rebellions of 1837–8 and the crippling of the Lower Canadian nationalist movement, the suspension of parliamentary institutions for several years and rule by an authoritarian Special Council, and, ultimately, the successful implementation of responsible government and the movement to a federal structure. The essential political significance of the Lower Canadian Civil Code was its protection of property interests, particularly through the contract, along with a system of customary law that reinforced traditonal family relations. This was accomplished within an emerging Canadian federal state that refused to be monolithic in its private law. From this perspective, the Lower Canadian Civil law system was not foreign, feudal, or static but an inherent, integral, and original element of Canadian federalism. This is particularly relevant given the Civil Code of Quebec that came into effect in 1994.

Part of the institutionalization process of the 1840s and 1850s, codification was perceived by members of the Lower Canadian bar elite, both anglophone and francophone, as an effective vehicle for reinforcing their vision of property rights, individual liberty, and family relations. In this interpretation, the fundamental changes in legal authority and structure that we witnessed in the decades before Confederation were integral to the implementation of what European historians comfortably call 'bourgeois law.'[6] Along with the codification of Civil law, this process included the dismantling of seigneurial tenure, the implementation of a centralized judicial apparatus in all regions, the establishment of a state-run land registry system, and the codification of judicial procedure. Codification helped give scientific legitimacy to the legal profession. With implementation of the codes of Civil law and civil procedure in the immediate pre-Confederation period, incorporation of the bar, and the decentralization of judicial institutions, lawyers became increasingly conspicuous in regional élites across Quebec.

Ideologically, bourgeois law implied universality and formal equality before the law, freedom of individuals to contract their labour and property, protection of capital through increased publicity for contracts, particularly those concerning immovables, and a broader use of written instruments. Nor was this *embourgeoisement* of the law simply an affair of the market-place. The entrenchment of patriarchy, which was part of the process, was accompanied, as we have seen, by a slippage in the public presence of women in Quebec, and a reinforcement in law of their functions within domestic, family, and philanthropic parameters. Married women were particularly vulnerable in this process, which saw a reassertion of marital authority. Excluded from important female professions such as teaching and sharply restricted in their capacity to act autonomously in trade, wives, when present in the paid workplace, found their remuneration subject to administration and control by their husbands. This dependence remained largely in place for a century. Although a 1931 law modifying the Civil Code and Code of Procedure permitted married women to administer income, goods, and immovables resulting from their own labour, it was only by laws in 1964 and 1969 and particularly after 1973 that Quebec women achieved equality in marriage.[7]

It is important to reiterate how pressures for codification and Civil law reform in the 1840s and 1850s changed in ideological direction from those of the pre-rebellion period. Before the rebellions, codification emanated from moderate nationalists striving to facilitate capitalist and professional activities with protection of the French language, the integrity of the Civil law system, and a hierarchical social system. Many nationalist reformers had difficulty disentangling the Civil law from seigneurialism. This was not surprising since changing property rights were at the core of the process; the first title of the Custom of Paris treated fiefs. This ambiguity disappeared with the collapse of the rebellions and Patriote ideals. In the 1840s and 1850s, codification was taken up by a broadening front of the political, capitalist, and bar élites who emphasized freedom of contract and a theoretical equality before the law over historic customary privileges. The insistence on bilingualism in the code was part of a changing institutional and social contract – positive for the anglophone minority and, for nationalists, the logical outcome of the humiliation of the conquest and 1837–8.

The idea of codification in the 1830s was linked to positive law and efforts to expand legislative power over the judiciary. This dynamic changed after 1840. As bourgeois democracy was instituted, politics remained a highly volatile and partisan arena for conflict resolution – witness the pistol duels between political opponents, the mob's torching of the Parliament Buildings in Montreal (1849), and troops firing on the crowd in the Gavazzi riots (1853). Political leaders like LaFontaine, Morin, and Cartier exhausted health, family life, and colleagues over issues like the clergy reserves, separate schools, the choice of a capital, and the nature of a new federal structure.

In contrast to executive and legislative instability, the bench or judicial commissions offered an attractive means of providing authoritative doctrine in the confusion of state formation. Deeply 'property-conscious,' that is, sensitive to ownership and the changing nature of property, judges emphasized principles of natural law and contract to justify fundamental decisions concerning the place of labour, debtors, women, squatters, or aliens in society. In their economic and social perspective, the judges could, in an American context, be characterized as Marshall men. But, unlike those of their American or French peers, their concepts of natural law and of the rights of property were unchecked by values expressed in the French Declaration of the Rights of Man or the American Bill of Rights.[8]

It is not surprising then, that in both seigneurial and Civil law reform, the Lower Canadian political leadership turned to judges. Indeed, the codification commissioners represented a particularly happy marriage of two of nineteenth-century society's more insular and bourgeois institutions: bench and university. For its part, the legislature, an increasingly important source of official authority and even sovereignty in bourgeois ideology, was involved seriously in only the preliminary stage and final approval stage of the process. Nor was a serious attempt made to encourage a wider diffusion of the draft codes or to solicit reaction from lawyers, notaries, or their professional associations. Although the commentaries of judges was sought for the Codification Act, the chief justice rebuffed this initiative. Most judges followed his lead in pleading overwork as an excuse for not commenting on commission reports.

Indeed, the very leadership that had fought for responsible government believed in a balanced constitution in which the bench was a conservative force. From their perspective, the legislature was not a 'suitable arena' for codification; it should be entrusted instead to judges removed from parliamentary partisanship.[9] The result was, as codifier René-Édouard Caron described it, a seigneurial law – and the same could be said for the Civil Code – that passed without 'any commotion.'[10]

The reduction of legal pluralism and the structuring of a legal bureaucracy were inherent to the modernization and uniformization of law across Quebec. The new structure included registry offices, judicial districts, courthouses, prisons, resident judges, and emerging local bars. Legal pillars of Quebec society for the century after Confederation, these institutions were central to the professionalization of the Quebec bar and to harmonization of the province's legal culture. Their importance in the larger sphere of Quebec's evolving capitalism lies in their role in creating a uniform framework of credit and property relations, in giving punch to contractual relations in the countryside, and in implementing regional court organizations for the efficient regulation of civil disputes.

Nor was this implementation of bourgeois law, and the Civil Code in particular, somehow foreign to a larger process that included the spread of parliamentary democracy, the thwarting of traditional French

Canadian nationalism, the decline of seigneurial institutions, the reform of property and registry law, the confirmation of the liberal state, and the establishment of civic bilingualism. These changes were accompanied by the settling into power in an emerging bourgeois and capitalist state of the legal professions, the church, and the francophone political élite. The marginalization of the Papineau group after the Rebellions of 1837–8, the subsequent ordinances of the Special Council, the extension of registry law across Lower Canada, the dismantling of seigneurialism, and the naming of Day as a codifier provide clear evidence of changing class and ethnic relations.

Attorney General Cartier and codifiers Morin and Caron were members of a new political élite, which captured power in the Union period. Profoundly conservative in political, social, and family relations, this indigenous élite was committed to an expanded freedom for property, labour, and capital. These attitudes led to new alliances with anglophone leaders, a process symbolized by the power-sharing of Cartier and Macdonald and, in the legal realm, by the central role in codification entrusted to Charles Dewey Day.

In codification, the political and bar élite received important support from their professional, business, and ecclesiastical peers. They were also able, given the obscurity of the law reform process, to implement codification without provoking strong public reaction. This contrasts sharply with that happened in the United States and Germany where codification was strongly contested by professional, legislative, and interest groups.

Codification served then as an important means of reducing antagonisms among various elements of the élite and of its insulation from popular pressure. As a political phenomena, the code was effectively engineered. Although nationalist elements had been removed from the codification movement by the Rebellions of 1837–8, thus breaking the tie between the French language and a national legal system, the code was regularly presented as a French, customary, and nationalist defence. In the words of a commission secretary, it would permit Quebec to enter Confederation 'without undergoing disturbing alterations in her laws and institutions.'[11] At the same time, it reassured the powerful anglophone minority by granting them linguistic equality in Quebec's legal culture. This equality had important ideological implications. As the most important codifier, Charles Dewey Day defended his constituency effectively, writing important titles, imposing his legal ideology across commission *Reports*, and, when necesseary, submitting a minority report. When commission secretary McCord reported that Civil law was 'rescued from antiquity and chaos' and rendered 'accessible and intelligible to all classes of the people whose rights and property they control,' he touched base with thinly veiled and historic attitudes of the British Community to French religious, land, and legal institutions.

In its final provisions, the code contained another provision reassuring to the minority. For while it abrogated laws in force at the coming into effect of the code, article 2613 also provided important protection against any retroactive effect on transactions or other matters formulated under laws predating 1866. Even more far-reaching – and its significance has been underlined by John Brierley – the code presumed, in his words, 'the continuance of the prior law save when it is otherwise provided.'[12] Included in this 'pool of historical sources' were decrees, customs, and judgments that had diverse roots in France, England, and North America.

Just months before Confederation, the code imposed a simple, written, organized, revised, unified, and universal civil law across what in 1867 became the province of Quebec. At the core of the process was the central position given in the code to the law of Obligations; this ensured dominance of the social relations of exchange over custom and feudalism, of contract law over property law, of what Thomas McCord called the 'free exercise of man's dominion over property.'[13]

But the code was much more than a simple application of universal principles of contract. It carefully confirmed old law concerning family matters such as patriarchal power, marriage, the civil status of the Catholic clergy, and the role of local notables such as the notary. This confirmation helped ensure acceptance of the code by lay and clerical authorities. And alongside this buttressing of family relations, the Civil Code had further moral piers; the principles of natural law, of individual responsibility, and of developmental capitalism were not at all incompatible with the ideology of either the Church of England or the Church of Rome.[14] In the same period, the state's conversion of the revenues of the great clerical seigneuries and fiefs into capitalist forms ensured a physical place at the head table for religious institutions.

Codification was closely linked to the evolution of the institutions of the law school and bar associations. The former took shape within McGill and Laval universities while the latter emerged as a corporate institution that protected and regulated practitioners. Lower Canada's two law faculties presided carefully over the codification process, with the dean of Laval's law school and the chancellor of McGill representing a majority on the Codification Commission. In the struggle between the teaching of the law as a trade learned by apprenticeship versus its study as a university discipline, law faculties understood codification's empirical and scientific qualities: 'The enactment of these Codes as law,' the McGill Faculty of Law announced in 1868, 'will lighten much the labours of professors and students, who need no longer view the study of the profession as a vast and ill-digested whole, wanting coherency and certainty.'[15] With codification, the emergence of law faculties, and the regionalization of the court system, the bar was given the physical and ideological means to expand and professionalize. While Cartier translated legal reform for the legal profession in terms of expanding opportunity for legal work and patronage, commission secretary McCord saw codification as a 'great additional means of legal education, from which may be expected a higher standard of professional excellence.'[16] Political conservatives, worried by the potential excesses of parliamentary democracy in a world of Jacksonian democracy and the revolutions of 1848, were assured that the code would act 'as a conservatory barrier against the continual inroads of fragmentary legislation.'[17]

Parallel to construction of this social 'conservatory barrier,' the code with its emphasis on contract and the larger law of Obligations opened Lower Canadian society to expanding capitalist activity. The commercial community moved from the particular bailiwick of merchant law, from creative legal instruments that subverted the intention of the custom, and from monopoly of bench and executive, to a post-rebellion environment where their economic values penetrated more widely across society. Despite the fears of some that their privileges would be swept away by bourgeois democracy, their power was entrenched in bar, bench, and legal faculty. Supporting allies in the francophone professional and political élite like Cartier, Morin, and Caron, they contributed to the preparation of a code that gave a central place to contract, to freedom of the individual, and to equality in contract. In the early and mid-nineteenth century, as written instruments supplemented oral, handshake, book accounts, and other customary arrangements in the community, dispute-settlement mechanisms changed. Arrangements that had been tempered by reputation, family, and community values now depended on paper. Nowhere was this change clearer than in the declining significance of the physical and often public act of delivery (*tradition*) against the increasing stature of the written sales or transfer agreement. This transition diminished the importance of possession and custom in favour of paper and contract.

The code went hand in hand with a changing capitalism, which represented much more than a transformation of landed-property relations. The move away from pre-industrial forms of appropriating labour opened the way to industrial millers, to railway entrepreneurs, to new security for mortgages, and to the increasing purchase of labour as a commodity. While they relied heavily on custom to mould civil relations concerning the family, the codifiers also turned emphatically to Roman law, which emphasized the individual, the automony of the citizen, and the rights of private property. It was Pothier who reconciled these Roman concepts with Grotius and the natural law school and its strong insistence on consent in contract. He also showed the means of harmonizing Roman principles with Catholic morals.[18] Carefully constructed titles on separation of bed and board, on paternal authority, on domicile, on majority, and on the rights of married women in commerce allowed the framers of the Lower Canadian Civil Code to impose the weight of customary tradition on artisans and workers, aliens, and wives in commerce or other paid work.

All of this resulted in a code that was a carefully constructed legal, political, and social instrument. Attorney General Cartier caught the political construct of past and present perfectly in describing codification as a process in which 'neither the codifiers nor himself desired to disturb the past.' 'They only,' he told the assembly, 'sought to legislate for the future.'[19]

Chronology

Date	Historical Events	Legal Landscape	Careers of Codifiers and Attorney General	Codification
1529–34				Justinian Code, Digest, & Institutes
1539		Dumoulin, *Révision de la Coutume de Paris*		
1560				Estates General (France) demands codification and unification of law
1580				Custom of Paris is codified
1608	Quebec founded			
1628		Coke on Littleton		
1629				Code Michaud (France)
1648		First notaries practising in New France		
1663	Conseil souverain established			

Date	Historical Events	Legal Landscape	Careers of Codifiers and Attorney General	Codification
1664		Custom of Paris only one permitted in New France		
1667				Code of Civil Procedure (France)
1673				Merchant Code (France)
				Savary Code (France) [commercial procedure]
1681				Marine Ordinance (France)
1694		Domat, *Civil Law in its Natural Order*		
1711		Edicts of Marly on seigneurial tenure		
1714		Valin, *Commentaire sur l'ordonnance de la Marine*		
1734				General Code of Sweden and Finland
1748		Montesquieu, *Spirit of the Laws*		
1756				Codex Maximilianus (Bavarian Civil Code)
1760	Articles of Capitulation of Montreal			
1761		Pothier, *Obligations* 1761-65: Diderot's *Encyclopedia*		
1763	Quebec becomes British colony (Treaty of Paris)	Royal Proclamation attempts to imposes British law on Quebec		

Date	Historical Events	Legal Landscape	Careers of Codifiers and Attorney General	Codification
1764		English criminal law comes into effect; status of civil law uncertain		
1765		Blackstone's *Commentaries*		
1768				Francis Maseres' plan for civil code
1772		Cugnet, Juchereau, Pressard, *An Abstract of the Parts of the Custom of Paris received in Quebec*		
1774	Quebec Act (French Civil law and institutions restored; freedom of willing granted; freehold lands excluded from French law)	Marriott, *Plan of a Code of Laws for ... Quebec*		
1775		Cugnet, *Traité des ancienes loix, coutumes*		
1776	American Declaration of Independance			
1777		English rules of evidence to be used in commercial cases		
1789	Declaration of Rights of Man (France)	Perrault, *Le juge de paix*		

Date	Historical Events	Legal Landscape	Careers of Codifiers and Attorney General	Codification
1791	Constitutional Act divides Quebec into Upper and Lower Canada and institutes elected assemblies			
1800			Caron b. Sainte-Anne de Beaupré	
1804				Napoleonic Code promulgated
1806		Pothier's *Obligations* translated into English	Day b. Bennington, Vermont	Code of Civil Procedure (France)
		Perrault, *Dictionnaire portatif ... des ... règles du parlement du Bas-Canada*		
1807				Commercial Code (France)
1808			Morin b. Saint-Michel de Bellechasse	
1810				Penal Code (France)
1811		Pyke's Report of Cases		
1814		Perrault, *Questions et réponses sur le droit criminel du Bas-Canada*	Cartier b. Saint-Antoine sur Richelieu	
1821		Bell, *Commentaries on the Laws of Scotland*		
1822	Union Bill			
1823		Sheriff's sales facilitated		

Date	Historical Events	Legal Landscape	Careers of Codifiers and Attorney General	Codification
1824		Sewell, *Essay on the Juridical History of France*		Amendment of Louisiana Civil Code
1825	Canada Tenures Act			
1826			Caron admitted to bar	
1827			Day admitted to bar	
1828			Morin admitted to bar	
1828		Advocates' Library established in Montreal		
1830		Registry offices granted to five counties in Eastern Townships		
1831				John Neilson & Elzéar Bédard call for codification
1832	British American Land Company chartered	Des Rivières Beaubien, *Traité sur les lois*; Perrault, *Code rural*; Stair, *The Institutions of the Law of Scotland*		
1834		Stuart's *Reports of Cases*	Morin edits Ninety-Two Resolutions	
1835			Cartier admitted to bar	
1837–8	Lower Canadian Rebellions		Morin and Cartier charged with treason	
1838	Durham arrives in Canada		Cartier sends loyalty oath to crown; Day prosecutes Patriotes	

Date	Historical Events	Legal Landscape	Careers of Codifiers and Attorney General	Codification
1840	Special Council Ordinances (1840-1)	Dismantling of seigneurialism begins on Seminary of Montreal lands	Day named solicitor general	
1841	Union Act reunites Upper and Lower Canada	N.B. Doucet publishes Custom of Paris in English; registry ordinance establishes registry offices across Lower Canada; Montreal Bar Association criticizes Civil law system		Commission established to compile statutes and ordinances of Lower Canada
1842			Day to bench	
1843		McGill College begins giving law courses	Caron speaker of Legislative Council	Publication of Tables Relative to the Acts and Ordinances of Lower Canada
1845	Montreal Building Society established (home mortgages)			
1846		Convention to discuss law reform est. in New York state		*Revue de législation et de jurisprudence* calls for codification
1847		Chamber of Notaries incorporated		
1848	Responsible government		Morin, speaker of assembly	New York Code of Procedure adopted
1849	Burning of Parliament in Montreal; abolition of Navigation Acts	Lower Canadian bar incorporated; system of Superior Courts established across Lower Canada;	Cartier elected to Assembly	

Date	Historical Events	Legal Landscape	Careers of Codifiers and Attorney General	Codification
1849		Imprisonment for debt in Lower Canada abolished; withdrawal of vote from women in Lower Canada		
1850				Introduction of Badgley's proposed Criminal Code; *Lower Canada Reports* established
1851–7	Railway boom links Montreal to Portland, Boston, & Toronto			
1851	Great Exhibition	Bibaud begins teaching law at Jesuit College	Morin, co-premier	
1852		Crémazie, *Manuel des notions utiles sur ... le droit civil*	Cartier, director of Grand Trunk Railway	
1853		McGill's Faculty of Law established; professor of Roman law named	LaFontaine becomes chief justice; Caron to bench; Day named principal of McGill	
1854		Seigneurial Act dismantles seigneurialism; Laval's faculty of law established; *Law Reporter* founded	Morin named first dean of Laval law faculty	
1855		Seigneurial Court established; *retrait lignager* abolished	Morin to bench	

Date	Historical Events	Legal Landscape	Careers of Codifiers and Attorney General	Codification
1856			Cartier becomes attorney general	
1857	Civil Divorce Courts established in England	Judicial decentralization bill passed; laws governing land to be uniform across Lower Canada; *Lower Canada Jurist* established		Act to establish Codification Commission
1858			Cartier accepts principle of federation	
1859	Opening of Victoria Bridge	Bibaud, *Commentaires sur les lois du Bas-Canada*		Codification Commission named and begins meeting
1861		Consolidated Statutes of Lower Canada come into effect; Henry Maine publishes *Ancient Law*		General Commercial Code (first of German codes) is promulgated
1862				Ramsay dismissed as commission secretary, replaced by Thomas McCord
1863				Ramsay, *Notes sur la Coutume de Paris*
1864	Charlottetown & Quebec Conferences on federation		Day named chancellor of McGill	Publication of *Digest of all the Reports*; last meetings of commission
1865			Morin dies; Day, honorary doctorate of law from Laval	Civil Code passed
1866				Civil Code into effect

Date	Historical Events	Legal Landscape	Careers of Codifiers and Attorney General	Codification
1867	Confederation			Code of Civil Procedure into effect.
1870				*Code des curés* published
1873			Cartier dies; Caron named lieutenant governor; Day on Pacific Railway Commission	
1875		Supreme Court of Canada established		
1876			Caron dies	
1884			Day dies	
1892				Canadian Criminal Code promulgated

Abbreviations

AJQM	Archives judiciaires du Québec, Montréal
ANQM	Archives nationales du Québec, Montréal
ASQ	Archives du Séminaire de Québec
ASSH	Archives du Séminaire de Saint-Hyacinthe
ASSM	Archives du Séminaire de Saint-Sulpice, Montréal
CC	Civil Code
DCB	*Dictionary of Canadian Biography*
Minutes	Minutes of the Codification Commission, Archives du Séminaire de Québec
NA	National Archives of Canada
Notes générales	Archives du Séminaire de Québec, Collection Caron, Notes générales

Notes

PREFACE

1 Arthur Lower, *Canadians in the Making* (Toronto: Longmans, Green & Co. 1958), 122; Castel, *Civil Law System*, 543
2 David Bercuson and Barry Cooper, *Deconfederation: Canada without Quebec* (Toronto: Key Porter 1991), 9
3 Whitman, *Legacy of Roman Law*, XI
4 Raymond Williams, *The Country and the City* (New York: Oxford 1973), 7
5 Brierley, 'Renewal of Quebec's Distinct Legal Culture,' 484

EPIGRAPHS

1 *Lower Canada Reports, Décisions des tribunaux du Bas-Canada: Seignioral Questions*, vol. IV, 65e
2 Cited in Arnaud, *Essai d'analyse structurale*, 220.

1 THE LEGAL LANDSCAPE

1 Cited in Tunc, 'Grand Outlines of the Code,' 436.
2 Montesquieu, *Spirit of the Laws*, 289
3 Portalis, *Discours, rapports et travaux inédits*, 4
4 For what codes contain historically, see J.-É.-M. Portalis's 'Discours préliminaire,' in Fenet, *Naissance du code civil*, 35–90.

5 Elizabeth Arthur, 'Francis Maseres,' *DCB*, VI, 494; see also Kolish, *Changements dans le droit privé*, 32–7.

6 For larger treatment of periodization in Quebec history, see John A. Dickinson and Young, 'Periodization in Quebec History: A Reevaluation,' *Quebec Studies* (1991) 12, 1–10.

7 See Le Barreau de Montréal, 'Minutes of the Advocates' Library,' 1828, p. 18. For the contents of law libraries, see Cameron Nish, *François-Étienne Cugnet*, 149; Veilleux, *Les gens de justice*, 447–93; Lamonde et Olivier, *Les bibliothèques personnelles*.

8 See, for example, Suzanne Zeller, *Inventing Canada: Early Victorian Science and the Idea of a Transcontinental Nation* (Toronto: University of Toronto Press 1987).

9 Kolish, 'Changements dans le droit privé,' 570, fixes the roots of codification in the pre-rebellion period while John Brierley, in 'Quebec's Civil Law Codification,' 530, dates the formal origins of codification from 1846. Gradualism in the political arena is taken up effectively by Buckner, *Transition to Responsible Government*, 6.

10 Yves Zoltvany ('Esquisse de la Coutume de Paris,' 383) is a strong proponent of a 'golden age' arguing that the Custom of Paris served to tighten family links, to retard the development of capitalism in the St Lawrence Valley, to ensure that French Canada remained egalitarian in its approach to immovable property, and to reinforce traditional paternal and religious values. Murray Greenwood, *Legacies of Fear*, shows the elements in this dialectic in the period from the French Revolution to the Napoleonic Wars. The view of Confederation as a dividing line between a golden age and exploitation can be seen in Jean-Pierre Charbonneau and Gilbert Paquette, *L'Option* (Montréal: Les Éditions de l'Homme 1978), 185, and in Victor Morin, 'L'anglicisation de notre droit civil' (novembre 1937), 40, no. 4 *La Revue du Notariat*, 145–55.

11 Brierley, 'Quebec's "Common Laws",' 123; see also Howes, 'From Polyjurality to Monojurality,' and Kasirer, 'Canada's Criminal Law Codification Viewed and Reviewed.'

12 'William Hey,' *DCB*, IV, 349

13 Kolish, 'Changements dans le droit privé,' 81; Frost, 'Early Days,' 150; Greenwood, *Legacies of Fear*, 4

14 For the use of urban seigneuries, see Louise Dechêne, 'La rente du faubourg Saint-Roch.' The abuse of seigneurial niceties by anglophone seigneurs in Berthier and Longueuil is described by Greenwood, *Legacies of Fear*, 16–17. For the frustration with sheriff sales, see Kolish, 'Le Conseil législatif,' and Normand and Hudon, 'Le contrôle des hypothèques secrètes,' 176.

15 An Act to provide for the Extinction of Feudal and Seignioral Rights and Burthens on Lands held à Titre de Fief and à Titre de Cens, in the Province of Lower Canada ... [Canada Tenures Act] (1825) United Kingdom, 6 Geo. IV, c. 59

16 Renée Balibar, 'L'action révolutionnaire des lettrés dans la simplification démocratique de la langue française,' in *La révolution*, ed. Vovelle, I, 89

17 Ibid., 96

18 Friedman, *History of American Law*, 295; Atiyah, *Rise and Fall*, 400–1

19 A. Colin and H. Capitant, *Traité de droit civil* (Paris: Dalloz 1957), cited in Arnaud, *Les origines doctrinales*, 171–2; Marty and Raynaud, *Droit Civil*, vol. 1, 7; Baudouin, *Les obligations*, 19

20 McGill University Archives, Torrance and Morris law firm, 'Authorities 5,' p. 179, p. 109

21 John L. Tobias, 'Protection, Civilization, Assimilation: An Outline History of Canada's Indian Policy,' in J.R. Miller, *Sweet Promises: A Reader on Indian-White Relations in Canada* (Toronto: University of Toronto Press 1991), 130; see also Daniel Francis, *A History of the Native Peoples of Quebec, 1760–1867* (Ottawa: Indian Affairs and Northern Development 1983), 36.

22 For an expression of concern over the rights of wives, see Bonner, *Essay*.

23 For instrumentalism in the United States, see Horwitz, *Transformation of American Law*, 16–20.

24 Fenet, *Naissance du code civil*, 38

25 *Le Courrier de Saint-Hyacinthe*, 3 February, 1 September 1865

26 Lorimier, *La bibliothèque du code civil*, I, 3, 8. For Montigny's social approach, see his 'Du mariage et du divorce,' 289–367; also see Loranger's *Commentaire*, especially the foreword to vol. 2.

27 McCord, *Civil Code*, iii

28 *Shaping Canada's Future*, federal government proposals on national unity (1991), in *Globe and Mail*, 10 January 1992

2 ATTITUDES TO CODIFICATION BEFORE THE REBELLIONS

1 Great Britain, *Report from Select Committee*, 151

2 *La Minerve*, 10 February 1831, reproduced in Ouellet, *Papineau*, 38

3 For the Custom of Paris, see Dickinson, *Law in New France* and Zoltvany, 'Esquisse.' Before 1664, there was confusion over which custom applied in New France. Since appeals from *prévôté* courts in Quebec went to the Parlement of Rouen, the Custom of Normandy was a significant influence (Cairns, *1808 Digest*, 117). For codification and the Custom of Paris, see Robinson, Fergus, and Gordon, *Introduction to European Legal History*, 338–9.

4 Doucet, *Fundamental Principles*, 272, 228. In his 1841 publication of the text and translation of the Custom of Paris, Doucet notes that articles 46, 48, 85, 86, 91, 95, 111, 112, 122, 163, 173, 174, 193, 219, 238, 347, 350, 351, 352, part of 353, as well as Title Twelve (265–71) were never applied in New France.

5 For the tightening of seigneurialism over time, see Dechêne, 'L'évolution du régime seigneurial,' 147; Dépatie, 'La seigneurie de l'île Jésus au XVIIIe siècle,' in Dépatie, Dessureault, et Lalancette, *Contributions*, 43, 78.

6 See the description of seigneurial inheritance, in Harris, *Seigneurial System*, 46–50.

7 Dechêne, *Habitants and Merchants*, 244; Desjardins, 'La Coutume de Paris,' 331–9. Using dowries, bequests, and particularly donations *inter vivos*, peasants regularly disregarded the customary principle of equality in favour of family strategies that favoured their comfort in old age, as well as settling the maximum number of sons on farms. While Allan Greer emphasizes the 'genuine solidarity' and 'democratic' succession practices of New France, Dépatie shows sharp discrimination against female heirs on Île Jésus, 1720–75, and Lavallée shows families in La Prairie in the mid-eighteenth century using marriages to reassemble land divided by the Custom. Writing of a later period, Gérard Bouchard illustrates how 'donations' in the Saguenay served as a means by which parents protected themselves from their children and family strife. (Greer, *Peasant, Lord and Merchant*, 74, for the inheritance practices of two seigneurial families, see 71–2; Dépatie, 'La transmission du patrimoine,' 187, 189; Lavallée, *La Prairie en Nouvelle-France*, 157; Bouchard, 'Donation entre vifs,' 448).

   Merchants were just as creative in dividing their property. While well-known Varennes merchant F.-A Bailly apparently adhered to customary practice in dividing his estate among his wife and seven children, merchant Jacques Leber bequeathed much of his fortune to a grandson leaving only a usufruct to his prodigal son. (Michel, 'Un marchand rural', 219; Dechêne, *Habitants and Merchants*, 245).

8 Great Britain, *Report from Select Committee*, 139. For examples of the influence of Roman law, see Dickinson, *Law in New France*, 4.

9 See, for example, Dumoulin's commentary, *Révision de la coutume de Paris* (1539) and Ferrière's *Nouveau commentaire sur la coutume de la prévôté et vicomté de Paris*.

10 David Parker, 'Sovereignty,' 41. Controversy arose over the legality of edicts, such as that of the Merchant and Marine codes, laws unregistered by the Conseil souverain in New France but that were, in John Brierley's analysis, 'statements of law.' Brierley, 'Quebec's Civil Law Codification', 548.

11 René-Édouard Caron, *Notes générales*, pp. 5–6.

12 Imbert, *Histoire du droit privé*, 57

13 McGill University, Rare Books Room, Stephen Sewell, 'Law Books,' MS235, vol. 2

14 Article 35, Ferrière, *Nouveau commentaire*, 95; Cugnet, in his 'Traité des fiefs,' 29, in *Traité des anciennes loix*, confirms that these laws applied in Canada.

15 Doucet, *Fundamental Principles*, 264; this power over the wife had a parallel in parental authority over children with majority being reached only at age twenty-five. For a comparison of customary and Roman treatment of married women's property laws, see Imbert, *Histoire du droit privé*, 59–60; for Roman law concerning women, see G.E.M. Ste Croix, *Class Struggle*, 101–3, and particularly Jane F. Gardner, *Women in Roman Law and Society* (Bloomington and Indianapolis: Indiana University Press 1991).

16 Dépatie, 'La transmission du patrimoine,' 187; for a broad discussion of women in pre-industrial society, see Hanawalt, *Women and Work*.

17 Conquest historiography is summarized in Cameron Nish, *The French Canadians, 1759–66: Conquered? Half-Conquered? Liberated?* (Toronto: Copp Clark 1966); Kolish, 'Impact of Change'; Greenwood, *Legacies of Fear*, 8.

18 Nicholas, *French Law of Contract*, 4

19 *Fuller v. Grand Trunk* (1865), 1 *Lower Canada Law Journal* 68; this judgment, based on English and American law, was confirmed in *Bourdeau v. Grand Trunk* (1866), 1 *Lower Canada Law Journal* 186–7. American courts themselves turned increasingly to Pothier. While federal courts cited Blackstone almost 800 times and Lord Coke 340 times in the pre-1900 period, Pothier was cited in 234 cases. Rogers, 'Scots Law,' 209–10.

20 See A.-N. Morin's statement to assembly, 28 June 1844, Canada, *Debates of the Legislative Assembly*, 527; Stuart, *Reports of Cases*, 72; for the confusion caused by differences in prescription under the Custom of Paris (actions had to be brought within one year) and English law (six years), see *Morrogh v. Munn*, 19 April 1811, in Stuart, *Reports of Cases*, 44; see also *Herald v. Skinner* (1810), *Hunt v. Bruce et al.* (1810), and *Pozer v. Meiklejohn* (1810), all in *Pyke's Reports of Cases*, 3–5, 8–19; for a description of this eclecticism in Lower Canadian commercial law, see Michel Morin, 'La perception,' 17.

21 See, for example, the testimony of Simon McGillivray in Great Britain, *Report from the Select Committtee*, 101.

22 Little, *Ethno-Cultural Transition*, 8, 13, 21

23 Brierley, 'Co-existence of Legal Systems,' 280

24 Great Britain, *Report from the Select Committee*, testimony of Samuel Gale, 18–19

25 *British Colonist* and St Francis *Gazette*, 28 February 1828; J.I. Little, 'The Short Life of a Local Protest Movement,' 49

26 Lower Canada, *Journals of the House of Assembly*, 'Petition of Grievances from the County of Missisquoi,' 20 February 1830

27 Testimony of Viger in Great Britain, *Report from the Select Committee*, 149; Lower Canada, *Journals of the House of Assembly*, 13 March 1826. Ellice is cited in Kolish, 'Changements,' 511; Cuvillier in Great Britain, *Report from the Select Committee*, 67.

28 Great Britain, *Report from the Select Committee*, 83

29 'An Act for rendering valid conveyances of lands and other immoveable property held in free and common socage within the Province of Lower Canada ...,' *Statutes of Lower Canada* (1831) 9 & 10 Geo. IV, c. 77; Brierley, 'Co-existence of Legal Systems,' 279; J.I. Little, *Crofters and Habitants: Settler Society, Economy and Culture in a Quebec Township, 1848–1881* (Montreal and Kingston 1991), 58; *Refour v. Sénécal* (1854), 4 *Lower Canada Reports* 412

30 Greenwood, *Legacies of Fear*, 177–86

31 See the discussion of this shift in Robinson, Fergus, and Gordon, *Introduction to European Legal History*, 466; Kolish, 'Some Aspects of Civil Litigation,' 359.

32 Sewell, *Orders and Rules of Practice in the Court of King's Bench* (1809); *Rules and Orders of Practice in the Provincial Court of Appeals* (1811); *An Essay on the Juridical History of France* (1824)

33 Murray Greenwood and James H. Lambert, 'Jonathan Sewell,' *DBC*, VII, 791

34 Cited in Kolish, 'Changements,' 335.

35 McGill University, Rare Books Room, Jonathan Sewell collection, Sewell to James Craig, 1810.

36 J.H. Stewart Reid, Kenneth McNaught, and Harry S. Crowe, *A Source Book of Canadian History* (Toronto: Longmans, Green and Company 1959), 72

37 *Pyke's Report*, 11–19; for other examples of important Sewell judgments, see pages 2, 7, 11, 59; for the biography of Pozer, see Louise Dechêne, 'George Pozer,' *DCB*, VII, 706–9.

38 Veilleux, *Les gens de justice*, 485–6

39 Stuart, *Reports*

40 Greenwood and Lambert, 'Jonathan Sewell,' 789

41 Sewell, *Essay on the Juridical History of France*, 480, 490, 498

42 Buckner, *Transition to Responsible Government*, 115

43 Great Britain, *Report from Select Committee*, 239

44 Ouellet, *Papineau*, 25

45 Great Britain, *Report from Select Committee*, 82

46 See, for example, the testimony of Edward Ellice and Augustin Cuvillier in Great Britain, *Report from Select Committee*, 56, 167.

47 Lower Canada, *Journals of the House of Assembly*, 3 December 1828, 68
48 Great Britain, *Report from Select Comittee*, 26, 267; an 1821 petition from Quebec City made many of the same demands. Lower Canada, *Journals of the House of Assembly*, 19 January 1821.
49 See his marginal notes at p. 28 in his copy of Daniel Chipman, *An Essay on the Law of Contracts for the Payment of Specifick Articles* (Middlebury, Vt: 1822), in the McCord Museum, J.S. McCord Collection.
50 Samuel Gale testimony, Great Britain, *Report from the Select Committee*, 259
51 Lower Canada, *Journals of the Legislative Council*, 27 February 1821, 225
52 Great Britain, *Report from Select Committee*, 86
53 Petot, *Histoire: La Famille*, 437–48; Crémazie, *Report*, 2. The significance of this changing relationship between law and local community can be seen effectively in Mann's *Neighbours and Strangers*, a study of seventeenth- and eighteenth-century Connecticut, 9.
54 Normand et Hudon, 'Le contrôle des hypothèques secrètes,' 174; see also article 101 of the Custom of Paris, in Doucet, *Fundamental Principles*, 236.
55 Kolish, 'Le Conseil législatif,' 220
56 Kolish, 'Changements,' 650
57 *Canadian Courant*, 12 February 1831, cited in Eric Whan, 'Stating the Case: Law Reporting in Lower Canada/Quebec, 1811–1891' (unpublished undergraduate paper, McGill University 1993), 16.
58 Morin, *Lettre à l'honorable Edward Bowen*; Lower Canada, *Journals of the House of Assembly*, 11 March 1826, 234
59 See Sylvio Normand, 'Un thème dominant.'
60 Ouellet, *Papineau*, 69
61 *La Minerve*, 10 February 1831, reproduced in Ouellet, *Papineau*, 38–42
62 Gérard Parizeau, *La vie studieuse*, 35
63 Linteau et Robert. 'Land Ownership and Society,' 28; Gérard Parizeau, *La vie studieuse*, 93; a copy of the inventory to Viger's library is held in the NA, MG24, B6, vol. 10; see also Alan M. Stewart, 'Settling an 18th Century Faubourg.'
64 Biographer Gérard Parizeau notes that Viger often quoted directly from Montesquieu, *La vie studieuse*, 277.
65 Viger, *Avis au Canada, à l'occasion de la crise importante actuelle ...* (1798); *Prospectus pour ... Dictionnaire de la jurisprudence civile du Bas Canada* (1812); see also Galarneau, *La France*, 294–6.
66 Viger, *Considerations*, 27–8; for a biography of Viger see Fernand Ouellet and André Lefort, 'Denis-Benjamin Viger,' *DCB*, IX, 807–17.
67 Great Britain, *Report from Select Committee*, 156
68 Ibid., 151

69 Ibid., 157
70 Claude Galarneau, 'Perrault,' *DCB*, VII, 690
71 Perrault, *Manuel pratique de l'école élémentaire française* (1829); *Code rural à l'usage des habitants tant anciens que nouveaux du Bas-Canada concernant leurs devoirs religieux et civils, d'après les loix en force dans le pays* (1832); for France's Rural Code, see Whitman, *Legacy*, 180.
72 Perrault, *Code rural à l'usage des habitants*, 1
73 Veilleux, *Les gens de justice*, 708; James H. Lambert, 'Vallières de Saint-Réal,' *DCB*, VII, 877. Stuart was a member of the Canadian party until 1834 when he broke with Papineau.
74 Amury Girod, *Notes diverses sur le Bas-Canada* (Saint-Hyacinthe 1835), 29, cited in Veilleux, *Les gens de justice*, 30.
75 Kolish, 'Some Aspects of Civil Litigation,' 351; Greer, *Peasant, Lord and Merchant*, 94
76 Great Britain, *Report from Select Committee*, 97
77 *Canadian Courant*, 12 February 1831
78 *Vindicator*, 25 March 1831, quoted in Kolish, 'Changements,' 570
79 Claude Baribeau, 'Denis-Benjamin Papineau,' *DCB*, VIII, 678
80 Ibid.; Baribeau, *La seigneurie de la Petite-Nation*, 143
81 Lower Canada, *Journals of the Legislative Council*, App. F (1836), 'Report of the Special Comittee respecting state of law relating … to incumbrances upon Real Estate …'
82 Ibid.
83 Ibid.
84 Philippe Pothier, 'Toussaint Pothier,' *DCB*, VII, 702–4
85 Gilles Paquet et Jean-Pierre Wallot, 'Le système financier bas-canadien au tournant du XIXe siècle' (septembre 1983), 58, no. 3 *L'Actualité économique*, 498
86 Alan Stewart, 'Settling an 18th Century Faubourg,' 129
87 'Mémoire de Toussaint Pothier à l'égard de la situation politique du Canada' (1829) published in *Rapport sur les Archives canadiennes* (1913), 92–103; for Pothier's social attitudes see Ouellet, 'Toussaint Pothier,' where it is noted (152) that Pothier and Viger were involved in a dispute over a succession.
88 Toussaint Pothier petition to Assembly of Lower Canada, 1836, quoted in Kolish, 'Changements,' 668
89 Jean-Paul Bernard, *Assemblées publiques, résolutions et déclarations de 1837–38* (Montréal: VLB, 1988), 181, 182, cited in Normand et Hudon, 'Le contrôle des hypothèques secrètes,' 179
90 Cited in Jean-Paul Bernard, *Assemblées publiques*, 243, 254
91 Fernand Ouellet, *Papineau*, 83

3 THE POLITICAL WILL TO CODIFY, 1838–57

1 James, Viscount of Stair, *The Institutions of the Law of Scotland* ([1684]; Edinburgh: Bell and Bradfute 1832), I, 14

2 (May 1846), 1, no. 8 *Revue de législation et de jurisprudence*, 339

3 Eörsi, *Comparative Civil (Private) Law*, 147

4 The bilingualism of the Civil Code, as with all legislation of Parliament or the legislature of Quebec, and of the Quebec legal system was confirmed by section 133 of the British North America Act.

5 For this process in Upper Canada, see Curtis, *Building the Educational State*.

6 Ibid., 52–4

7 'An Ordinance to prescribe and regulate the Registering of Titles to Lands ... and of Incumbrances on the same ...,' *Statutes of Canada* (1841), 4 Vict., c. 30. The ordinance did define five privileged creditors – co-heirs and partners, architects, builders, workmen, and creditors who had lent money to pay workmen – but each of these privileged creditors (with the exception of vendors) had to register their claims. Normand and Hudon, 'Le contrôle des hypothèques secrètes,' 196 [trans.]; for contemporary criticism of registration, see Bonner, *Essay on the Registry Laws*; Evelyn Kolish has analysed the effects of registration, see 'Changements,' 'Le Conseil législatif,' and 'Sir James Stuart,' *DCB*, VIII, 842–5.

8 'An Act to repeal an Ordinance ... concerning Bankrupts ... and to make provision for the same ...,' *Statutes of Canada* (1842) 7 Vict., c. 10. 'An Act to continue and amend the Bankrupt Laws ...' (1846) 9 Vict., c. 30

9 'An Act to amend the law regulating Inland Bills of Exchange and Promissory Notes ...,' *Statutes of Canada* (1849) 12 Vict., c. 22

10 'An Act to abolish Imprisonment for Debt ...,' *Statutes of Canada* (1849) 12 Vict., c. 42

11 'An Act ... relating to Masters and Servants in the Country parts of Lower Canada,' *Statutes of Canada* (1849) 12 Vict., c. 55

12 'An Act for the Organization of the Notarial Profession in that part of the Province called Lower Canada,' *Statutes of Canada* (1847) 10–11 Vict. c. 321; 'An Act to incorporate the Bar of Lower Canada,' *Statutes of Canada* (1849) 12 Vict., c. 46

13 'An Act to make better provision for the establishment of Municipal Authorities in Lower Canada,' *Statutes of Canada* (1847) 10–11 Vict., c. 7; 'An Act to amend the Municipal Law of Lower Canada,' *Statutes of Canada* (1850) 13–14 Vict., c. 34

14 'An Act for the Abolition of Feudal Rights and Duties in Lower Canada,' *Statutes of Canada* (1854) 18 Vict., c. 3

15 'An Act for settling the Law concerning Lands held in Free and Common Socage, in Lower Canada,' *Statutes of Canada* (1857) 20 Vict., c. 45

16 'An Act to Amend the Judicature Acts of Lower Canada,' *Statutes of Canada* (1857) 20 Vict., c. 44

17 LaFontaine, *Analyse de l'ordonnance*; *Statutes of Canada* (1843) 7 Vict., c. 21

18 *The Report of the Earl of Durham* (London: Methuen 1902), 81

19 See Macdonald's speech in *Debates of the Legislative Assembly of United Canada* (1846), 960. 'The words of the law,' Bentham insisted, 'ought to be weighed like diamonds ... In works of art, the perfection of art consists in its concealment: in a code of laws ... the perfection of science will be attained, when its efforts are not perceived, and its results are characterized by noble simplicity.' Mary Mack, *Jeremy Bentham: An Odyssey of Ideas* (London: Heinemann 1962), 159.

20 The resolutions were opposed by a rump of five anglophone lawyers that included William Badgely.

21 Barreau de Montréal, Chamber of the Association of the Bar, *Report* (1842), 13

22 Jacques Boucher, 'Nicolas-Benjamin Doucet,' *DCB*, VIII, 232

23 Doucet, *Fundamental Principles*, 9

24 Canada, *Debates of the Legislative Assembly of United Canada*, 15 June 1847, 847

25 Doucet, *Fundamental Principles*, 7

26 Stephen N. Subrin, 'David Dudley Field,' 318; for the debate in 1831, see *Canadian Courant*, 12 February 1831; Canada, *Tables Relative to the Acts and Ordinances of Lower Canada.*

27 Anon., 'La Codification des statuts,' 187, 189

28 Canada, *Tables Relative to the Acts and Ordinances of Lower Canada*, 6

29 Ibid., IX

30 *Statutes of Canada* (1849) 12 Vict., c. 46, s. XXVI

31 Macdonald, 'National Law Programme at McGill,' 232

32 Cited in ibid., 229

33 Robertson, *Digest*; Ramsay, *Digested Index*

34 Anon., *The Examiner: A Monthly review of Legislation and Jurisprudence* (Quebec), no. 1, January 1861

35 (May 1846), 1, no. 8 *Revue de législation et de jurisprudence*, 338

36 Ibid., 339

37 Ibid., 341

38 *Simard v. Jenkins*, 20 March 1854, Sup. C. of Montreal, McGill University, Faculty of Law Library, Canadiana Rare Books Room, 'Law Intelligence'

39 *Abbott v. the Montreal and Bytown Railway Company* (1856), 1 *Lower Canada Jurist*

40 Harris, 'Of Poverty and Helplessness in Petite Nation'; Sweeny, *Les relations ville/campagne*; Noël, *Christie Seigneuries*; Dechêne, 'La rente du faubourg Saint-Roch,' 571; Robert, 'Un seigneur entrepreneur, Barthélemy Joliette.' For a broader discussion of capitalism and feudalism, see R.S. Neale, *Writing Marxist History: British Society and Culture since 1700* (Oxford: Basil Blackwell 1985), 75–6.

41 Baker, 'Law Practice and Statecraft,' 59; Castel, *Civil Law System*, 16

42 Denis Gravel, *Monographie du moulin Fleming à ville de LaSalle* (LaSalle: Société historique Cavelier-de-LaSalle 1990); Young, *In its Corporate Capacity*, 41–2

43 McCord Museum, McCord Papers, #0232, Superior of seminary to Thomas McCord, 16 August 1816

44 Young, *In its Corporate Capacity*, 41–2; Baker, 'Law Practice and Statecraft,' 62

45 'An Ordinance to incorporate the Ecclesiastics of the Seminary of Saint-Sulpice ...,' no. 164, 8 June 1840, printed in *Copy of Ordinances passed by the Governor and Special Council of Lower Canada* (1841) 3–4 Vict.

46 Tom Johnson, 'In a Manner of Speaking,' 639

47 Doucet, *Fundamental Principles*, intro.

48 Pamela Miller, Brian Young, Donald Fyson, Donald Wright, and Moira T. McCaffrey, *The McCord Family: A Passionate Vision / La famille McCord: une vision passionnée* (Montreal: McCord Museum of Canadian History 1992), 39. The third commissioner was a lawyer and Montreal police inspector, George Vanfelson.

49 Cited in Tom Johnson, 'In a Manner of Speaking,' 664, 639.

50 Cited in ibid., 664.

51 Similar arguments were evident in the debate over usury. See *Debates of the Legislative Assembly of United Canada*, 1846, 957–67; for American comparisons see Horwitz, *Transformation of American Law*, 160–210.

52 *Lower Canada Reports; Décisions des tribunaux du Bas-Canada: Seigniorial Questions*, 65e

53 *Debates of the Legislative Assembly of United Canada*, 25 June 1850, 813

54 *Debates of the Legislative Assembly of United Canada*, 19 August 1851, 1472

55 *Lower Canada Reports; ... Seigniorial Questions*, vol. 4, 23a–24a. See also LaFontaine's speeches, Canada, *Debates of the Legislative Assembly of United Canada*, 25 June 1850, 810; 19 August 1851, 1472; and Jacques Monet, 'Louis-Hippolyte La Fontaine,' *DCB*, IX, 451.

56 *Lower Canada Reports; ... Seigniorial Questions* 2a. For Denis-Benjamin Viger's defence of seigneurialism, see Ouellet, *Éléments d'histoire sociale*, 305–15.

57 *Debates of the Legislative Assembly of United Canada*, 25 June 1850, 818–19

58 Ibid., 28 June 1847, 527; 16 July 1847, 1080

59 Ibid., 16 July 1847, 1080
60 Viger in ibid., 19 August 1851, 1471–72; see also Ouellet, *Éléments d'histoire sociale*, 315. The significance of settling the land question with landowners before codification is treated by Gyula Eörsi, *Comparative Civil (Private) Law*, 121; for the Rhenish example of changing attitudes to customary rights to collect firewood and its influence on Marx, see Pierre Lascoumes and Hartwig Zander, *Marx: du 'vol du bois' à la critique du droit. Karl Marx à la 'Gazette rhénane' naissance d'une méthode* (Paris: P.U.F. 1984).
61 Canada, *Debates of the Legislative Assembly of United Canada*, 14 August 1851, 1451
62 'An Act for the Abolition of Feudal Rights and Duties in Lower Canada,' *Statutes of Canada* (1854) 18 Vict., c. 3. For contemporary comparisons of French and English free tenure, see the testimony of Denis-Benjamin Viger and James Charles Grant in Great Britain, *Report from Select Committee*, 145, 198; see also Brierley, 'Co-existence of Legal Systems,' 286.
63 Little, 'Lewis Thomas Drummond,' *DCB*, XI 282–3. Jean-Pierre Wallot, in *Un Québec qui bougeait*, 236, reaches the same conclusion, describing it as 'the wish of the bourgeoisie, not of the people,' while Fernand Ouellet describes it as 'the victory of capitalism over an economic structure based on agriculture' in *Éléments d'histoire sociale*, 315. See also the manœuvring of the Torrance and Morris law firm with the end of seigneurialism in Baker, 'Law Practice and Statecraft,' 62–3. For the slow process of disassembly on the Seminary of Montreal's seigneuries, see my *Cartier*, 104.
64 'An Act for settling the Law concerning Lands held in Free and Common Socage, in Lower Canada,' *Statutes of Canada* (1857) 20 Vict., c. 45
65 *Civil Code of Lower Canada*, ii–iii
66 Livingston's penal code became a model for American codes.
67 Canada, *Debates of the Legislative Assembly of United Canada*, 28 June 1847, 525; 1 March 1849, 1057
68 Ibid., 15 May 1855, 3442
69 Bernard, *Les Rouges*, 93; Pierre Poulin, 'Jean Chabot,' *DCB*, VIII, 138
70 Canada, *Debates of the Legislative Assembly of United Canada*, 20 March 1855; Drummond loved to chide his Upper Canadian colleagues for their zenophobic attitude towards Civil law. Twice in 1850 he noted that each time reform was attempted in Upper Canada – regulating the medical profession or the rights of married women – they came up with 'almost an exact transcript' of Lower Canadian practice: 'It is a remarkable fact, that every attempt which had been made since the beginning of the Session to effect reform in the laws of Upper Canada – had a direct tendency to assimilate them to that system which had been frequently stigmatized as obsolete,

antiquated and barbarous – he alluded to the civil law as it exists in Lower Canada (ibid., 1850, 1198).

71 *Catalogue de la bibliothèque de feu l'hon. Sir G. E. Cartier* (Montreal 1873)

72 This interpretation should be compared to that of Cooper, 'Political Ideas of George-Etienne Cartier,' 286–94. For the 565 volumes on French law and 248 volumes on English law in LaFontaine's library, see *Catalogue de la bibliothèque de feu Sir. L. H. La Fontaine* (Montréal: Eusèbe Sénécal 1864). Chief Justice Jonathan Sewell had 1476 volumes in his library of which 1120 were on law, politics, or public administration. F. Murray Greenwood and James H. Lambert, 'Jonathan Sewell,' *DCB*, VII, 790.

73 J. Tassé, *Discours de Sir Georges Cartier* (Montreal 1893), 13 July 1866, 495

74 See Jean Hamelin's biography of Médéric Lanctot in the *DCB* X, 420–6.

75 Canada, *Debates of the Legislative Assembly of United Canada*, 25 June 1850, 816

76 For the role of patronage in the attorney general's office, see Romney, *Mr. Attorney*, 188–92; for Cartier's exercise of patronage, see my *Cartier*, 70–2. For the relationship of this 'pervasiveness of patronage' to fundamental changes in class structure, see Gordon Stewart, *Origins of Canadian Politics*, 57. See also Buckner, *Transition to Responsible Government*, especially chap. 8. This interpretation of the importance of conservatism in the legal ideology of mid-nineteenth–century Lower Canada should be compared to Jean-Marie Fecteau's emphasis on liberalism as the dominant ideology of the state in *L'émergence de l'idéal coopératif*, 13, and his *Un nouvel ordre des choses*.

77 For a full treatment of Cartier's career, see my 1981 biography, *George-Étienne Cartier* and my more recent 'Dimensions of a Law Practice.'

4 THE CODIFIERS

1 Cited in Stewart, *Origins of Canadian Politics*, 106.

2 ASSM, 'Draft for Codification Commission,' mfm 1, comments on 1152

3 LaFontaine's 565 volumes of law books in French and 248 volumes in English included classics like Ferrière, 8 volumes of Pothier, 17 volumes of Guyot, 36 volumes of Merlin, 15 volumes of Fenet, 15 volumes of Touillier, 5 volumes of Pardessus, and the Custom of Normandy (*Catalogue de la bibliothèque de feu Sir. L.H. LaFontaine*). For Cartier's letter to LaFontaine, 23 November 1857, and LaFontaine's refusal, see *Le Courrier de Saint-Hyacinthe*, 3 February 1865. See also Brierley, 'Quebec's Civil Law Codification,' 581.

4 Jean-Charles Falardeau describes this group, 'the second generation after the conquest,' as particularly affected by the turn-of-the-century 'ecology, social structures, and mentality'; 'Étienne Parent,' *DCB*, X, 584.

5   Cook, *American Codification Movement*, 166

6   Christina Cameron, *Charles Baillairgé: Architect and Engineer* (Kingston and Montreal: McGill-Queen's University Press 1989), 65

7   Béchard, *L'honorable A.N. Morin*, 6–7; *Le Courrier de Saint-Hyacinthe* in its obituary, 29 July 1865, notes that Morin was born a twin; James Lambert, 'Thomas Maguire,' *DCB*, VIII, 592.

8   Morin, *Lettre à l'honorable Edward Bowen*, 13

9   Jean-Marie Lebel, 'Ludger Duvernay,' *DCB*, VIII, 259–60; Monet, *Last Cannon Shot*, 124

10   *Le Courrier de Saint-Hyacinthe*, 29 July 1865; J.-L. Roy, *Édouard-Raymond Fabre: libraire et patriote canadien (1799–1854)* (Montréal: HMH 1974), 122.

11   ASSH, Collection Morin, AFG5, dossier #36, Attorney-General Charles Richard Odgen to Morin, 27 October 1839; Morin to Ogden, 28 October 1839; dossier #45, 'Biographie de Augustin-Norbert Morin'

12   Béchard, *L'honorable A.N. Morin*, 92–3.

13   Ibid., 60; (1865), 1 *Lower Canada Law Journal* 71

14   Monet, *Last Cannon Shot*, 196, 241; Béchard, *L'honorable A.N. Morin*, 170

15   Monet, *Last Cannon Shot*, 45

16   His detailed plans included the production of cheap library furniture. ASSH, AFG5, Collection Morin, #18, 'Catalogue; librairies; liste de livres à acheter, bibliothèques à organiser.'

17   Stewart, *Origins of Canadian Politics*, 106

18   Paradis, 'Augustin-Norbert Morin,' 172; Lower Canada, Legislative Assembly, 'First Report of the Standing Committee on Lands and Seigniorial Rights' (1836); see also Johnson, 'In a Manner of Speaking,' 639.

19   ASSH, AFG5, Collection Morin, #27, 'Enquête sur les enfants trouvés pour les hospices agricoles'; #15, Seigniorial Documents, Joseph Comte to Morin, 13 November 1854

20   ASSH, AFG5, Collection Morin, #17, Morin to Macdonald, 20 March 1855; for his response to Catholic criticism, see his letter to Abbé François Pilote cited in Paradis, 'Augustin-Norbert Morin,' 424–5.

21   His papers include handwritten notes prepared for Laurentian colonists outlining how to tie fly lines and the importance of dressing in sober and shaded colours. ASSH, AFG5, Collection Morin, #14, 'Notes sur la pêche et la chasse'; Paradis, 'Augustin-Norbert Morin,' 332; Veilleux, *Les gens de justice*, 506

22   ASSH, AFG5, Collection Morin, #21 'Marché avec Jacques Lessard,' 6 March 1840; in his marriage contract of 1843 he guaranteed his wife's dower by mortgaging six of his lots in Abercrombie, including a house, barn, and sawmill. ASSH, AFG5, Collection Morin, #32, 'Extrait de l'acte de mariage de

A.N. Morin et Adèle Raymond, 1843'; for documentation of his grants as minister, see #47.2, 'clipping.'

23 Paradis, 'Augustin-Norbert Morin,' *DCB*, IX, 571; ASSH, AFG5, Collection Morin, #30, 'Testament, 1855, Volontés de A.N. Morin en faveur de son épouse, 1857.'

24 ASSH, AFG5, Collection Morin, #30, 'Testament, 1855, Volontés de A.N. Morin en faveur de son épouse, 1857'

25 Young, 'John Alfred Poor,' *DCB*, X, 591

26 Monet, *Last Cannon Shot*, 381, 387

27 ASSH, AFG5, Collection Morin, #30, 'Testament, 1855, Volontés de A.N. Morin en faveur de son épouse, 1857'

28 Ibid.

29 For judges' salaries, see Doughty, *Elgin-Grey Papers*, 390; ASSH, AFG5, Collection Morin, #18, 'Catalogue; libraires; liste de livres ...' ASSH, AFG5, Collection Morin, #30, 'Testament, 1855, Volontés de A.N. Morin en faveur de son épouse, 1857'

30 ASSH, AFG5, Collection Morin, 36.145, 'A.N. Morin et C. Delagrave: Formation d'une société entre ces deux avocats'; Louis-Philippe Audet, 'Cyrille Delagrave,' *DBC*, X 217; Andrée Désilets, *Hector-Louis Langevin: un père de la Confédération canadienne* (Québec: Les presses de l'Université Laval 1969), 20

31 Béchard, *L'honorable A.N. Morin*, 38–9

32 ASSH, AFG5, #35, 'Leçon de Droit,' n.d.

33 Philippe Sylvain, 'Louis-Jacques Casault,' *DCB*, IX, 119; Paradis, 'Augustin-Norbert Morin,' 385, 398

34 Philippe Sylvain, 'Louis-Jacques Casault,' *DCB*, IX, 119

35 See, for example, the financial statement he made to his wife. ASSH, AFG5, Collection Morin, #30, 'Testament, 1855, Volontés de A.N. Morin en faveur de son épouse, 1857.'

36 Paradis, 'Augustin-Norbert Morin,' 420; Veilleux, *Les gens de justice*, 631

37 ASSH, AFG5, Collection Morin, #11, 'Essai d'un catalogue bibliographique de droit, surtout allemand'

38 An average of 49 per cent of the books in the libraries of Lower Canadian judges and lawyers, 1850–9, were on law, compared to 19 per cent on science. Even after his major law book purchases in 1855, Morin still had twice as many titles in agronomy as law. Veilleux, *Les gens de justice*, 459; ASSH, 'Séminaire administration financière,' Section A, Serie M, tiroir 14, dossier 1.4.

39 ASSH, AFG5, Collection Morin, #18, 'Catalogue; libraires, liste de livres à acheter ...'

40 ASSH, AFG5, Collection Morin, #39.49, Morin to Cartier, 2 February 1858

41 Yvan Lamonde, *La philosophie et son enseignement au Québec (1665–1920)* (Montréal: Hurtubise HMH 1980); Bonenfant, 'René-Edouard Caron,' *DCB*, X, 131–6.

42 Bonenfant, 'René-Edouard Caron,' *DCB*, X, 136; Veilleux, *Les gens de justice*, 340

43 Monet, *Last Cannon Shot*, 59, 101, 360

44 Anon., *Mère Mallet, 1805–71, et l'Institut des Sœurs de la Charité* (Québec: Sœurs de la Charité 1939), 204; Bonenfant, 'René-Edouard Caron,' *DCB*, X, 135

45 Monet, *Last Cannon Shot*, 59; Marcel Bellavance and Pierre Dufour, 'Charles-Félix Cazeau,' *DCB*, XI, 170–1.

46 Veilleux, *Les gens de justice*, 509, 512, 518, 550

47 Marc Desjardins, 'Joseph-François Deblois,' *DCB*, VIII, 206–7

48 *Le Courrier de Saint-Hyacinthe*, 3 February 1865. Caron's personal wealth is not known, but Veilleux, *Les gens de justice*, 720, uses inventories after death to determine the wealth of five Quebec City judges. These ranged from a low of £1679 to Jonathan Sewell's high of £8512. With his villa, urban properties, and lucrative practice, Caron was presumably near the top of this range.

49 Jean-Marie Lebel, 'Louis de Gonzague Baillargé,' *DCB*, XII, 46

50 Monet, *Last Cannon Shot*, 233; B. Young, *Promoters and Politicians: The North-Shore Railways in the History of Quebec, 1854–85* (Toronto: University of Toronto Press 1978), 67

51 Caron, *Notes générales*, 20

52 *Lower Canada Reports: Seignioral Questions*, II, 1d–64d

53 Ibid., 33d, 42d, 63d

54 Andrée Désilets, *Hector Langevin*, 173; (August 1867), III *Canada Law Journal*, 41

55 André Morel and Yvan Lamonde, 'François-Maximilien Bibaud,' *DCB*, XI, 70–2; R.St.J. Macdonald, 'Maximilien Bibaud,' 721–43

56 Morel and Lamonde, 'François-Maximilien Bibaud,' *DCB*, XI, 71

57 R.St.J. Macdonald, 'Maximilien Bibaud,' 725; see also David Howes description of Bibaud's program, 'Origin and Demise of Legal Education,' 132–7.

58 Bibaud, *Commentaries*, 276–7.

59 Morel and Lamonde, 'François-Maximilien Bibaud,' *DCB*, XI, 70; *La Minerve*, 19 May, 2 June, 1 July, 5 July 1851

60 *La Minerve*, 5 July 1851

61 Cited in Kolish, 'Changements,' 621.

62 Bibaud, *Commentaries*, 372; see also Normand and Hudon, 'Le contrôle des hypothèques secrètes,' 197, and particularly Normand, 'La codification de 1866,' 50.

63 R.A. Macdonald, 'The National Law Programme at McGill,' 227

64 ASQ, PVU.147; for Day's biography, see Carman Miller, 'Charles Dewey Day,' *DCB*, XI, 237–9.

65 Donald MacKay, *The Square Mile: Merchant Princes of Montreal* (Vancouver: Douglas & McIntyre 1987), 32; Anson A. Gard, *Pioneers of the Upper Ottawa and the Humors of the Valley* (Ottawa: Emerson Press 1907), 45–7; Archives nationales du Québec à Hull, Fonds Conroy, 07HP154, vol. 1, dossier 1, affadavit Charles Symmis, 1 June 1857; Canada, *Journals of the Legislative Assembly*, 15, no. 8 (1857), app. 50, Petiton of I.H. Day, 23 February 1830.

66 Day's father paid Gale a £25 fee at the signing of the apprenticeship contract and another £25 after two years. NA, RG 4, B8, vol. 23, reel H-1416, 'Commissions of Advocates and Notaries.' Gale was one of the biggest landowners in the parish of Montreal, commuting land worth £12,000 by 1845. He also owned 10,000 acres of land in the Eastern Townships. *Report on the Affairs of British North American from the Earl of Durham*, app. B., 61.

67 Miller, 'Charles Dewey Day,' *DCB*, XI, 238; R.W. Mackay, *Montreal Street Directory*, 1842–3, 149

68 C.W. Colby, 'Judge Day,' (April 1904), 3, no. 2 *McGill University Magazine*, 14; 'Report of the Royal Commission on the Pacific Railway,' in Canada, House of Commons, *Journals*, 1873, VII, app. 1.

69 Day's first wife was Barbara Lyon. Lorne Ste Croix, 'Benjamin Holmes,' *DCB*, IX, 396. *Montreal Directory*, 1844–5; 1845–6; C.W. Colby, 'Judge Day' (April 1904), 3, no. 2 *McGill University Magazine*, 16. The value of Day's propertyholdings is unknown, and he does not appear on the commutation roles for Montreal properties. He did own a corner lot at St Antoine and Seigneurs streets (McCord Museum, Phillips Collection). In 1833, apparently as part of a court case, his father signed over to him the family's property on the Aylmer Road in Hull. Canada, *Journals of the Legislative Assembly*, 15, no. 8 (1857), app. 50, 'Transport,' 12 December 1833. Judges' salaries are reported in Doughty, *Elgin-Grey Papers*, 390. For his social activity, see the J.S. McCord diaries, McCord Museum, #0414, 2 January 1860.

70 Miller, 'Charles Dewey Day,' *DCB*, XI, 237; for his service as a lieutenant, see Elinor Senior, *Redcoats and Patriotes: The Rebellions in Lower Canada, 1837–38* (Ottawa: Canada's Wings 1985), app.

71 Greenwood, 'Chartrand Murder Trial,' 151; Michel de Lorimier, 'Chevalier de Lorimier,' *DCB*, VII, 514

72 Canada, *Debates of the Legislative Assembly of United Canada*, 20 July 1841, 355, 357; the Common School Act's importance is emphasized in J. George Hodgins, *Documentary History of Education in Upper Canada* (Toronto 1897),

IV, 43, and in Curtis, *Building the Educational State*, 52–4; Monet, *Last Cannon Shot*, 85–6.

73 Monet, *Last Cannon Shot*, 197; Canada, *Debates of the Legislative Assembly of United Canada*, 5 May 1846, 1185

74 Buchanan, *Bench and Bar*, 128; Miller, 'Charles Dewey Day,' *DCB*, XI, 238

75 Barreau de Montréal, 'Minutes of the Advocates' Library'

76 R.A. Macdonald, 'National Law Programme,' 221; Baker, 'Law Practice and Statecraft,' 53

77 Cited in R.A. Macdonald, 'National Law Programme,' 228.

78 Buckner, *Transition to Responsible Government*; Stewart, *Origins of Canadian Politics*; Roy, *Les juges de la province de Québec*, 53

79 Cartier remarked on Day's weakness in French but went on to say that it improved greatly while he was on the bench. *Le Courrier de Saint-Hyacinthe*, 3 February 1865.

80 Day's biography in the *DCB*, inquiries at the McGill Law Faculty and at the university's archives, and a letter from Day's grandaughter in the McCord Museum of Canadian History (#5341) all agree that there are no extant Day papers. Thomas McCord, who served as secretary of the Codification Commission, had a law library of 3000 volumes including the complete works of Pothier, Demolombe, Duranton, Toullier, Troplong, and Pardessus. Judge T.K. Ramsay, who also served the commission, had 1477 items in his library, including 452 law volumes. Lamonde and Olivier, *Les bibliothèques personnelles au Québec*. While no accession list for his books can be found at McGill, books with Day's stencil are listed in Baker et al., *Sources in the Law Library of McGill University*, 143, 158, 162, 174, 225, 256.

81 Baker, 'Law Practice and Statecraft,' 65

82 For legal formalism, see Atiyah, *Rise and Fall of Freedom of Contract*, 389, and Horwitz, *Transformation of American Law*, 253–66. The similarity of Day's judgments to those of his Upper Canadian peers, such as John Beverley Robinson, can be seen in George and Sworden, 'Courts and the Development of Trade,' 270.

83 McGill University, Faculty of Law, Canadiana Rare Books Room, 'Law Intelligence,' 249, *Aitken v. Montreal Insurance Company*, n.d.

84 *Ravary v. Grand Trunk Railway* (1857), I *Lower Canada Jurist* 282; for similarities between Day's judgments and those in American jurisdictions, see Christopher Tomlins, *Law, Labor, and Ideology*, or his article, 'A Mysterious Power: Industrial Accidents and the Legal Contruction of Employment relations in Massachussetts' (1988), 6, no. 2 *Law and History Review*, 375–438.

85 *Cuvillier v. Munro* (1854), 4 *Lower Canada Reports* 154

86 *Whitney v. Brewster* (1852), 3 *Lower Canada Reports* 433; *Stewart v. McEdward* (1854), 4 *Lower Canada Reports* 422–4

87 *Boulanget v. Doutre* (1854), 4 *Lower Canada Reports* 170

88 McGill University, Faculty of Law, 'Law Intelligence,' *Kennedy v. Smith*, 28 February 1854; for Day's interpretation of a hiring contract, see *Lennan v. the St. Lawrence and Atlantic Railroad* (1853), 4 *Lower Canada Reports* 91.

89 *Syme et al. v. Heward* (1856), 1 *Lower Canadian Jurist* 39

90 *Bernier v. Beauchemin* (1858), 2 *Lower Canada Jurist* 289

91 *Lower Canada Reports: Seignioral Questions*, vol. 4, 4e

92 Ibid., 65e

93 *Monk v. Morris* (1852), 3 *Lower Canada Reports* 38 (Sup. Ct. of Montreal, #2407)

94 *Lower Canada Reports: Seignioral Questions*, vol. 4, 64e; for the changing seigneurial economy in the countryside and peasant attitudes to land, see SergeCourville,'Lemarchédes''subsistences.''L'   exempledelaplainede Montréal au début des anneés 1830: une perspective géographique' (1988), 42, 2 *Revue d'histoire de l'Amérique française*, 193–239.

95 *Boston v. L'Eriger dit Laplante* (1854), 4 *Lower Canada Reports* 409

5 POLITICS OF THE CODIFICATION COMMISSION, 1857–66

1 Ritchie, *Codification*, 4

2 Quoted in Morel, 'La codification,' 43

3 *Rules for the Government of the Rural Police*, 1

4 For the relationship of rural protest in New York and law reform and codification in that state, see Subrin, 'David Dudley Field and the Field Code,' 319–20; Winter, letter to commission, 27 July 1842, 'Report of the Commissioners on the Administration of Justice in the Inferior District of Gaspé.' Canada, *Appendix to the Third Volume of the Journal of the Legislative Assembly*, app. G (1843). For popular resistance in the countryside, see Nelson, '"Guerre des Éteignoirs,"' 68, 158, 170–5.

5 Lucien Brault, *Aylmer d'Hier / of Yesterday* (Aylmer: Institut d'histoire de l'Outaouais 1981), 88

6 'An Act to Amend the Judicature Acts of Lower Canada,' *Statutes of Canada* (1857) 20 Vict., c. 44; J. Tassé, *Discours de Sir Georges Cartier* (Montreal 1893), 17 April 1857, 123. Griswold, "Divorce," 97; E.P. Thompson prefers the term 'class theatre,' *Whigs and Hunters*, 261; the stipulation that they reside in their districts concerned judges. Judge John Samuel McCord expressed apprehension about having to leave his Montreal estate to live in the Bedford District: 'Walked around the garden for an hour,' he confided to his diary, 'resting at each seat, and thinking over our probable separation from

our beautiful garden, on the putting into effect of the New Judicature Act.' McCord Museum, McCord Papers, J.S. McCord diary, #0414, 3 October 1857.

7 Little, 'Short Life of a Local Protest Movement,' 60–1

8 J.C. Bonenfant, *French Canadians*, 9

9 *Stuart v. Bowman* (1851), 2 *Lower Canada Reports* 369, and reversed in appeal (Q.B.) (1853), 3 *Lower Canada Reports* 309–416; *Wilcox v. Wilcox* (1857), 2 *Lower Canada Jurist* 1. Brierley, 'Co-existence of Legal Systems in Quebec,' 284

10 *Statutes of Canada* (1857) 20 Vict., c. 45. See the importance given to this act by John Brierley in 'Co-existence of Legal Systems in Quebec,' 285–7.

11 'An Act to provide for the Codification of the Laws of Lower Canada relative to Civil matters and Procedure,' *Statutes of Canada* (1857) 20 Vict., c. 43, 182

12 Tassé, *Discours de Cartier*, 8 March 1857

13 *Civil Code: Codifiers' Report, Legislative Proceedings*, 18 August 1865

14 Morin to Abbé François Pilote, Collège de Sainte-Anne-de-la Pocatière, 2 January 1865, cited in Paradis, *Augustin-Norbert Morin*, 424–5.

15 Atias, *Le droit civil* (Paris: P.U.F. 1984), 14

16 'An Act to Provide for the Codification of the Laws of Lower Canada relative to Civil matters and Procedure,' *Statutes of Canada* (1857) 20 Vict., c. 43, 182, 185

17 The formal ethnic equality of the Codification Act's secretariat had its parallel in the Montreal bar's resolution that in the appointment of Lower Canadian judges 'the division ought to be equal between the French and British members of the profession.' Barreau de Montréal, 'Minutes of the Bar of Lower Canada: Section of the District of Montreal,' 11 March 1856.

18 Quebec *Morning Chronicle*, 1 February 1865

19 Translation of speech in assembly, 16 May 1860, cited in Tassé, *Discours de Cartier*, 251–2.

20 John, *Politics and the Law*, 38

21 Newmyer, *Supreme Court Justice Joseph Story*, 279

22 In France, for example, the Civil Code (1804) was followed by the Code of Civil Procedure (1806), the Commercial Code (1807), the Code of Criminal Procedure (1808), and the Penal Code (1810).

23 'An Act to provide for the Codification of the Laws of Lower Canada relative to Civil matters and Procedure,' *Statutes of Canada* (1857) 20 Vict., c. 43

24 *Notes générales*, 25; ASSH, AFG5, #39.45, Morin to Cartier, 2 February 1858

25 Brierley, 'Quebec's Civil Law Codification,' 543

26 Eörsi, *Comparative Civil (Private) Law*, 190

27 'An Act to Provide for the Codification of the Laws of Lower Canada relative to Civil matters and Procedure,' *Statutes of Canada* (1857) 20 Vict., c. 43, 183

28 John, *Politics and the Law*, 9, 37, 28–9, 146–55

29 Cook, *American Codification Movement*, 123, 134–5, 140, 158–9, 172, 179–80, 196

30 Newmyer, *Supreme Court Justice Joseph Story*, 277–80; Cook, *American Codification Movement*, 145, 194; Subrin, 'David Dudley Field and the Field Code,' 323; for labour's criticism of codes, see Tomlins, *Law, Labor, and Ideology*, 107.

31 Tassé, *Discours de Cartier*, 27 April 1857, 130

32 For evidence that there was no Lower Canadian consensus on these political attitudes, see the Rouge manifesto to the electors of Terrebonne (1851) calling for the popular election of the Legislative Council, judges of the peace, militia officers, and mayors. ASSH, AFG5, Collection Morin, #36.113, 'Electeurs du Comté de Terrebonne.'

33 For the first commission, see Lower Canada, *Journals of the Assembly*, app. EEE (1 March 1836); the second is reported in Canada, *Journals of the Assembly*, app. F (4 October 1843). For discussion of the two commissions, see Johnson, 'In a Manner of Speaking'.

34 Toronto *Globe*, 22 April 1857

35 Canada, *Journals of the Legislative Assembly of United Canada*, 26 May 1857, 515

36 Toronto *Globe*, 27 February 1857

37 Ibid., 2 March, 22 April 1857

38 Ibid., 22 April 1857

39 Canada, *Journals of the Legislative Assembly of United Canada*, 2 April 1857; Toronto *Globe*, 22 April 1857

40 Toronto *Globe*, 22 April 1857

41 Canada, *Journals of the Assembly of United Canada*, 23 April 1857, 254

42 Ibid.

43 NA, RG 4, c. 1, vol. 567, no. 2618 (1864), Provincial Secretary C. Alleyn, Circular to the Judges of the Court of Queen's Bench and Superior Court, 13 December 1861; P. Winter to Provincial Secretary, 26 December 1862

44 Ibid., P. Winter to Provincial Secretary, 26 December 1862

45 Ibid., Mondelet to Provincial Secretary, 29 December 1862

46 Barreau de Montréal, 'Minutes of the Advocates' Library,' 20 October 1830, 12 December 1833; 'Minutes of the Bar of Lower Canada. Section of the District of Montreal,' 20 April 1857

47 McCord Museum, Cartier Papers, 'Minutes of Montreal Bar Association meeting,' 21 March 1857; *Courrier de Saint-Hyacinthe*, 14 April 1857; Young, *George-Étienne Cartier*, 66

48 Morel, 'La codification,' 37–8; Young, *George-Étienne Cartier*, 15

49 Ritchie, *Codification of the Laws of Lower Canada*, 4

50 McGill University Archives, Torrance and Morris law firm, Torrance Letter-books, #8, p. 88, F. Torrance to Caron, 15 November 1864

51 Members of this committee were the *bâtonnier* of the bar Toussaint-Antoine-Rodolphe Laflamme, H. Stuart, Robert McKay, Joseph Doutre, François Pominville, Alexander Cross, Gédéon Ouimet, Cyrille Archambault, T. Ritchie, P.R. Lafrenaye, Andrew Robertson, F.W. Torrance, George Stephens, and Francis Cassidy. Barreau de Montréal, 'The Bar of Lower Canada: Section of the District of Montreal,' 2 May 1864, 69.

52 The members of the committee on civil procedure were Thomas Ritchie, Andrew Robertson, Gonzalve Doutre, Louis-Amable Jetté, and Strachan Bethune: (August 1866) 2, no. 2 *Lower Canada Law Journal*, 25–8.

53 Two McGill graduates later published critiques of the codes: Désiré Girouard, 'Considérations sur les lois civiles du mariage' (1868), and Gonzalve Doutre, 'Les lois de la procédure civile' (1869).

54 Co-author of his paper was his partner Alexander Morris who had clerked with John A. Macdonald. Baker, 'Law Practice and Statecraft,' 67, 60; McGill University Archives, Torrance and Morris law firm, Letterbooks #8, Torrance to Cartier, 19 September 1865. Later prime minister, J.J.C. Abbott was himself a holder of a McGill bachelor of civil law and was author of *The Insolvency Act of 1864, with notes together with the rules of practice and the tariff of fees for Lower Canada* (Quebec 1864).

55 Jean-Pierre Chalifoux, 'Andrew Robertson,' *DCB*, X, 620

56 For codification as a means of controlling the legal profession, see Subrin, 'David Dudley Field and the Field Code,' 319; Baker, 'Law Practice and Statecraft,' 66.

57 Cited in R.A. Macdonald, 'National Law Programme,' 227 (trans.).

58 (January 1866) 1, no. 3 *Lower Canada Law Journal*, 74; Baker, 'Law Practice and Statecraft,' 89; Ritchie, Codification of the Laws of Lower Canada,' 4–5

59 Bibaud, *Corrigé du code civil*, 9–10

60 *Le Courrier de Saint-Hyacinthe*, 1 September 1865

61 Ibid., 3 February, 1 September 1865

62 Holcome, *Wives and Property,* 98–9; for a description of divorce legislation, see Snell, *In the Shadow of the Law*, 49.

63 *Second Report*, 191; *Notes générales*, 55

64 B.-A. Testard de Montigny, 'Du mariage et du divorce,' 359

65 *Parliamentary Debates on the Subject of Confederation* (Quebec 1865), 192

66 *Connolly v. Woolrich* was finally settled out of court. Backhouse, *Petticoats and Prejudice*, 20, 33–4.

67 See Dorion's speech in *Le Courrier de Saint-Hyacinthe*, 10 March 1865, and Joseph Cauchon's on 21 March.

68 *Le Courrier de Saint-Hyacinthe*, 21 March 1865; the Supreme Court Bill of 1875 would revive fears of the central court's power over Quebec's Civil and provincial laws and lead to attempts to restrict the Supreme Court's jurisdiction to matters under the jurisdiction of the federal Parliament. Snell and Vaughan, *Supreme Court of Canada*, 8–9; see also 'La Cour Suprême et le Barreau de Montréal,' (janvier 1881), 2, no. 12 *La Thémis*, 353–66.

69 Canada, *Journals of the Legislative Assembly of United Canada*, 24 (1865), 49, 3 February 1865; McCord, *Civil Code of Lower Canada*, vii. Members of the committee were Cartier, Solicitor General Langevin, Charles Alleyn, John Rose, Antoine-Aimé Dorion, Joseph Cauchon, Lucius Seth Huntington, Maurice Laframboise, François Évanturel, Christopher Dunkin, Louis Archambault, William Webb, – Geoffrion, – Dufresne (Montcalm), Paul Denis, George Irvine, Henri-Gustave Joly, Antoine-Charles Taschereau, – Harwood, and Louis-Charles Boucher de Niverville. Geoffrion, Archambault, and Dufresne were notaries.

70 Cartier reported to the assembly that the committee had 'adopted [this part of the text] without amendment' while Dorion complained that the committee had never even read the code. Canada, *Journals of the Legislative Assembly of United Canada*, 13 March 1865, 196; *Civil Code: Codifiers' Report, Legislative Proceedings*, Dorion in assembly, 25 August 1865; see also McCord, *Civil Code of Lower Canada*, vii.

71 *Civil Code: Codifiers' Report, Legislative Proceedings*

72 *Le Courrier de Saint-Hyacinthe*, 29 August 1865

73 Petition of the Quebec City Board of Trade, 20 February 1865, *Civil Code: Codifiers' Report, Legislative Proceedings*

74 *Le Courrier de Saint-Hyacinthe*, 29 August, 1 September 1865

75 Ibid., 1 September 1865. The bill was passed in the assembly without a division being recorded in the *Journals*, 31 August, 1 September 1865, 132, 138. Brierley, 'Quebec's Civil Law Codification,' 571, notes that no changes were made. 'An Act Respecting the Civil Code of Lower Canada,' *Statutes of Canada* (1865) 29 Vict., c. 41.

76 *Notes générales*, 82; two decades later in Exchange Bank and others v. the Queen, the Judicial Committee of the Privy Council confirmed the subordinate role of procedure. While noting that 'the two codes should be construed together,' it held that when there was overlap between principles in the two codes, it was the code of procedure which should be modified. 'Exchange Bank and others versus the Queen (1886),' *Gazette*, 5 March 1886,

clipping in McGill University Archives, Judge T.K. Ramsay, 'Newspaper Clippings,' 47.

77 The members of the select committee on procedure were Cartier, Thomas D'Arcy McGee, Charles Alleyn, John Rose, A.-A. Dorion, Joseph Cauchon, Lucius Seth Huntington, Hector Langevin, J.J.C. Abbott, Maurice Laframboise, – Remillard, Christopher Dunkin, Louis Archambault, Wiliam Webb, – Geoffrion, – Dufresne (Montcalm), Paul Denis, George Irvine, Henri-Gustave Joly, Antoine-Charles Taschereau, – Harwood, Louis-Charles Boucher de Niverville, and – Huot. *Civil Code: Codifiers' Report, Legislative Proceedings.*

78 Ibid.; 'An Act respecting the Code of Civil Procedure of Lower Canada,' *Statutes of Canada* (1866) 29 & 30 Vict., c. 25; Brisson, *La formation d'un droit mixte*, 147

79 Brisson, *La formation d'un droit mixte*, 158, 157. See also Gonzalve Doutre's criticisms in 'Les lois de la procédure civile.'

80 See my *In Its Corporate Capacity*, 120.

81 See, for example, Morin's correspondance with Abbé François Pilote in Morel, 'La codification, 42, and the letters of Vicar-General Edmond Langevin to Hector Langevin (Archives nationales du Québec à Québec, Chapais Collection, Box 32, Edmond Langevin to Hector Langevin, various dates, 1865). Cartier's brother-in-law, Édouard-Charles Fabre, as canon of the cathedral in Montreal was close to Bourget; Morin's brother-in-law, Joseph-Sabin Raymond, was superior of the Séminaire de Saint-Hyacinthe; Langevin's brother Edmond was vicar-general in Quebec and another brother, Jean, was superior of the École normale in Quebec.

82 Morin to Abbé François Pilote, Collège de Sainte-Anne-de-la-Pocatière, 2 January 1865, cited in Paradis, *Augustin-Norbert Morin*, 424–5.

83 *Second Report*, 'Special Report of Mr. Commissioner Day,' 238; *Second Report*, 153; Article 34 cc; for the effects of civil death, see Article 35–8 cc.

84 Petot, *Histoire du droit privé français: La famille*, 439

85 For evidence of common law marriages, see Morgan et al. and Gauvreau (March 1867) *Lower Canada Law Journal*, 247–9.

86 *Second Report*, 181; *Second Report*, 'Special Report of Mr. Commissioner Day,' 239; Article 128 cc states that 'Marriage must be solemnized openly, by a competent officer recognized by law.'

87 Lefebvre de Bellefeuille, 'Code civil du Bas-Canada. Législation sur le mariage' and 'La nouvelle législation du Bas-Canada'. Closely linked to Bishop Bourget, Lefebvre de Bellefeuille became secretary of the papal Zouaves.

88 René Hardy, *Les Zouaves. Une stratégie du clergé québécois au XIXe siècle* (Montréal: Boréal Express 1980), 242; Sylvain and Voisine, *Histoire du catholicisme québécois*, 369

89 Hardy, *Les Zouaves*, 242–3
90 Cited in Bonenfant, 'Thomas-Jean-Jacques Loranger,' *DCB*, X, 530.
91 Jean-Jacques Lefebvre, 'Joseph-Ubalde Beaudry,' *DCB*, X, 37–8; *DCB*, XI, 103, 250; Hardy, *Les Zouaves*, 243–4
92 Quoted in Morel, 'La codification,' 43.

6 THE COMMISSION AT WORK

1 Jean Domat, *Civil Law in its Natural Order*, cited in Goyard-Fabre, 'Montesquieu entre Domat et Portalis,' 719 (trans.)
2 *First Report*, 10
3 For a detailed treatment of articles of the code, see John Cairns's doctoral thesis, 'The 1808 Digest of Orleans and 1866 Civil Code of Lower Canada,' and his treatment of labour in 'Employment in the Civil Code'; for successions, see Morel, *Les limites de la liberté testamentaire*.
4 Friedman, *History of American Law*, 406
5 Staves, *Married Women's Separate Property*, 4
6 *Statutes of Canada* (1857) 20 Vict., c. 73; for the exclusion of feudalism from the Napoleonic Code, see Arnaud, *Les origines doctrinales du code civil français*, 163; the larger significance of this change in property is treated in Macpherson, *Property*, 1–4.
7 *Third Report*, 367
8 Article 406 CC
9 McCord, *Civil Code of Lower Canada*, iii
10 McCord Museum, Cartier Collection, Cartier to Caron, 5 January 1859; ASSH, AFG5, Collection Morin, #39.49, Morin to Cartier, 2 February 1859; *Le Courrier de Saint-Hyacinthe*, 3 February 1865
11 *Le Courrier de Saint-Hyacinthe*, 3 February 1865
12 Jean-Jacques Lefebvre, 'Joseph-Ubalde Beaudry,' *DCB*, X, 37; McCord, *Civil Code of Lower Canada*, viii, names him as drafter of these sections of the code.
13 Jean-Charles Bonenfant, 'Louis-Siméon Morin,' *DCB*, X, 533; although Bonenfant states that Morin had been attorney general, McCord, *Civil Code of Lower Canada*, vi, describes him as solicitor general.
14 Jean-Charles Bonenfant, 'Thomas Kennedy Ramsay,' *DCB*, XI, 721–2; it is not clear if Ramsay was connected to the family of George Ramsay, Earl of Dalhousie and governor of Canada. Ramsay, *Notes sur la coutume de Paris*, ii.
15 Ramsay, *Notes sur la coutume de Paris* (1863); *A Digested Index to the Reported Cases in Lower Canada* (1865); *Government Commissions of Inquiry* (1863)

16 Lamonde and Olivier, *Les bibliothèques personnelles au Québec*, 65. With 164 books or pamphlets on agriculture and gardening (almost 10 percent of his library), he shared Morin's interest in horticulture.

17 Minutes, 230, Étienne Parent to R.E. Caron, 25 October 1862; Ramsay, *Government Commissions of Inquiry*, 17; for evidence of his contentiousness, see his attempt as crown attorney to impeach the well-known reformer and judge, Lewis Thomas Drummond, (27 August 1866), 3 *Lower Canada Law Journal*, 75; (December 1866) 121; (July 1868) 53; Jean-Charles Bonenfant, 'Thomas Kennedy Ramsay,' *DCB*, XI, 721–2; (June 1867), 3 *Lower Canada Law Journal*, 267–8. A volume of newspaper clippings of his trials can be found in the McGill University Archives.

18 McCord, *Civil Code of Lower Canada*. This extremely useful volume includes a synopsis of the changes, authorities used by the codifiers, condordances with the Napoleonic Code and the Code de Commerce, relevant articles for professionals such as notaries and doctors, and an index. At his death, McCord had an impressive library of 3000 volumes including the complete works of Pothier, Touillier, Troplong, Pardessus (Lamonde and Olivier, *Les bibliothèques personnelles au Québec*, 58).

19 As well as Morin's illness, commission minutes note that Day was absent in England until May. Minutes, 27 October 1859.

20 Caron's 108-page *Notes générales* are of great importance in understanding the commission's first months of work in 1859. The original is in the ASQ, but John Brierley has deposited a typed copy in the McGill Law Library. For the office space and library, see 73–7, 106–7.

21 Day, Beaudry, and Ramsay borrowed Story on sales, Montgomery Throop on verbal agreements, and Walter Fell on mercantile guarantees. Baker, 'Law Practice and Statecraft,' 60.

22 *Notes générales*, 14; Minutes, 6 November 1862, note that Thomas McCord was paid $1200 a year and presumably other commission secretaries were paid the same.

23 Minutes, 27 October 1859

24 Robertson, *Digest of Reports*; McCord, *Civil Code of Lower Canada*, vi; see also John Brierley's comments in 'Quebec's Civil Law Codification,' 583.

25 ASSH, AFG5, Collection Morin, #39.49, Morin to Cartier, 2 February 1858

26 *Notes générales*, 20. Brierley, 'Quebec's Civil Law Codification,' 584, suggests that the choice of Day for Obligations was made at the meeting of 10 June.

27 'An Act to Provide for Codification,' *Statutes of Canada* (1857) 20 Vict., c. 43; McCord, *Civil Code of Lower Canada*, vi

28 *First Report*, 6

29 Ibid., article 254

30 See, for example, Day's resistance to his two colleagues' amendment on the prescription of bills of exchange, *Third Report*, 437. Morin's notes on the issue are in ASSH, AFG5, Collection Morin, #2, 'Titre de Prescription.'

31 Paradis, *Augustin-Norbert Morin*, 420

32 *Notes générales*, 107. Two of the volumes borrowed by Day – Greenleaf on *Evidence* and Story on *Contracts* – appear as authorities in the *First Report*, 103, 117. In June 1863 Ramsay borrowed Mackenzie's *Roman Law* from the library of Torrance and Morris. Uncatalogued volume of library loans, p. 15, in McGill University Archives, Torrance and Morris law firm.

33 Minutes, various dates. Absences were noted in the commission minutes and the commissioners and secretaries were assiduous in their attendance. Day missed several meetings in September 1862, and Ramsay was absent for an extended period in 1861.

34 *Notes générales*, 'Document A: Plan à suivre dans la codification'; using the Codification Commission records, Day's workbooks on Obligations can be compared to later workbooks. ASQ, Collection Caron, Cahiers de Travail, vol. 764, p. 779.

35 Brierley, 'Quebec's Civil Law Codification,' 556

36 Day's worksheets show his handwriting in some of the 'Present Law' columns; other are in a secretary's hand. Compare, for example, pages 32 and 37. On Morin's worksheets for Prescription, 'Present Law' was apparently filled in by a secretary with Morin's corrections appearing in red. ASQ, Collection Caron, Cahiers de Travail, vol. 764; ASSH, AFG5, Collection Morin, #2, 'Titre de Prescription.'

37 Cited in Cairns, 'Employment in the Civil Code of Lower Canada,' 680.

38 *Sixth Report*, 14, 165

39 *Sixth Report*, 8; see the debate in *Fourth Report*, 28, 30, and the full discussion in Cairns, 'Employment in the Civil Code of Lower Canada,' 692.

40 ASQ, Collection Caron, Cahiers de Travail, vol. 764, p. 39. Charles-Bonaventure-Marie Toullier (1752–1835) is best known for his commentaries on the Napoleonic Code: *Le Droit civil français suivant l'ordre du Code Napoléon*.

41 For the amendments, see *Civil Code: Codifiers' Report, Legislative Proceedings*, Schedule: Resolutions 3–71; McCord, *Civil Code of Lower Canada*, iii–xxxii.

42 McCord, *Civil Code of Lower Canada*, ii

43 Ibid., viii

44 ASQ, Codification Commission, vol. 779, 83; for other of Day's objections, see *Third Report*, 423, 437; *Fifth Report*, 177.

45 *Notes générales*, 14; Minutes, 27 October 1859. Also see Brierley on this question, 'Quebec's Civil Law Codification,' 537; this logic of bilingualism in

the law was apparently not shared by T.K. Ramsay, the commission's English-language secretary. Publishing his *Notes sur la coutume de Paris* entirely in French in 1863, he explained that 'the amalgamation of two modern languages in the same work poses serious inconveniences' (ii).

46 *Second Report*, 143; ASQ, Day, 'Draft for the Codification Commission' (1860), 45

47 McCord, *Civil Code of Lower Canada*, ix. Although Brierley, 'Quebec's Civil Law Codification,' 535–6, expresses surprise that the codifiers apparently did not make greater use of Doucet's 1841 translation of the Custom of Paris or of translations of works by Pothier and Domat, it seems likely that both Day and Ramsay (the latter was responsible for much of the early translation) were very familiar with American and English translated terms. Day, for example, borrowed a translation of the Louisiana Code from the commission's library (*Notes générales*, 106). See also the titles they apparently consulted in the Torrance and Morris law library (Baker, 'Law Practice and Statecraft,' 63).

48 *Second Report*, 181; *Second Report*, 'Special Report of Mr. Commissioner Day,' 239; *Third Report*, 363; McCord, *Civil Code of Lower Canada*, 56

49 *Notes générales*, 18 (trans.); see also Brierley, 'Quebec's Civil Law Codification,' 546.

50 *Second Report*, 141

51 Brierley points out that the codifiers did not consider oral custom, although it may have still existed as a source of Lower Canadian law, 'Quebec's Civil Law Codification,' 552–3.

52 *First Report*, 242, 244, 245, 250, 251, 254, 265

53 *Sixth Report*, 30; see articles 2580, 2582, 2584, and *Seventh Report*, 256, for fire insurance articles citing Lower Canadian cases.

54 *First Report*, articles 154, 184, 226; for Story's importance in partnerships, see *Sixth Report*, 32; for the New York civil code draft, see *Seventh Report*, 240; for Kent, see *Seventh Report*, 252.

55 *Seventh Report*, 240, 256, 258

56 Robinson et al., *Introduction to European Legal History*, 435; Imbert, *Histoire du droit privé*, 68

57 Carbonnier, *Droit Civil 4: Les Obligations*, 14

58 Pothier, *Treatise on the Contract of Sale*, vi, ix

59 Ourliac, *Histoire du droit privé français*, 335

60 Walter Johnson, 'Legal Education in the Province of Quebec,' 456

61 Civil Code, articles 115–85, 237–41, 242–5; for the reaction of revolutionary jurists to Pothier's definition of paternity and illegitimacy, see Jacques Mulliez, 'Révolutionnaires, nouveaux pères? Forcément nouveaux pères! Le

droit révolutionnaire de la paternité,' in Vovelle, *La révolution et l'ordre juridique privé*, vol. 1, 372–98.

62 Pothier, *Treatise on Obligations*, 34

63 McGill Law Library, Codification Commission mfm, #1, 10; for relevant parts of the civil code and the reliance on Pothier as authority, see articles 177, 986.

64 *Second Report*, 165; articles 79, 80, 83 CC; for the confusion of domicile in France before Pothier, see Ourliac, *Histoire du droit privé français*, 201.

65 For elements of the complexity of this transition, see, for example, Peter Bischoff, 'Des forges du Saint-Maurice aux fonderies de Montréal: mobilité géographique, solidarité communautaire et action syndicale des mouleurs, 1829–1881' (1989), 43 *Revue d'histoire de l'Amérique française*, 3–30; Joanne Burgess, 'The Growth of a Craft Labour Force: Montréal Leather Artisans, 1815–31' (1988) *Historical Papers/Communications historiques*, 48–62; Laing Hogg, *Legal Rights*; Gilles Lauzon, *Habitat ouvrier et révolution industrielle: le cas du village St-Augustin* (Montréal: Regroupement des chercheurs-chercheures en histoire des travailleurs et travaileuses du Québec 1989); Poutanen, 'For the Benefit of the Master'; Sweeny, *Les relations ville/campagne*.

66 Cairns, 'Employment in the Civil Code of Lower Canada'; the employer's use of criminal law is treated in Laing Hogg, *Legal Rights*. For the Napoleonic Code's failure to treat industrial phenomena, see Arnaud, *Les origines doctrinales du code civil français*, 175.

67 Cairns, *The 1808 Digest of Orleans and 1866 Civil Code of Lower Canada*, 574.

68 McGill Law Library, Codification commission, mfm #1, Day draft for Obligations, 55. In the published *First Report*, 32, Day's text appeared in slightly revised form: 'Every code of laws, however complete, necessarily presupposes the obligation of certain primary and fundamental principles which must underlie and sustain all positive legislation; and no care or foresight can secure such comprehensiveness and precision as to render unnecessary processes of reasoning and inference based upon these, and upon the experience and knowledge which lie outside of the expressed law.' John Brierley, 'The Renewal of Quebec's Distinct Legal Culture,' 497, has noted the great similarity between Day's statement and that of Portalis in his 'Discours Préliminaire.' Day's separation of law from the expression of larger questions of principles also closely echoed Montesquieu's admonition on 'the Natural means of changing the mores and manners of a nation.' The lawmaker, Montesquieu insisted, must only 'reform by laws what is established by laws': 'it is a very bad policy to change by laws what should be changed by manners.' Montesquieu, *Spirit of the Laws*, 315.

69 Compare Pothier, *Obligations*, 3, articles 1101–7 in the *French Civil Code*, and articles 982–3 CC.
70 *First Report*, 10
71 *First Report*, 10, 32
72 *Second Report*, 143; McCord, *Civil Code of Lower Canada*, 1–6
73 *Fifth Report*, 151
74 The commissioners noted that the Napoleonic Code had a section under irregular successions that dealt with the 'Rights of Natural Children.' 'Natural children, under our actual law, which the Commissioners have no intention of changing, having no heritable rights, the section of the Code which applies to them specially, had to be omitted.'
75 *Fifth Report*, 155
76 Article 768 CC

7 THE PERSISTENCE OF CUSTOMARY LAW: MARRIED WOMEN AS TRADERS

1 McCord, *Civil Code of Lower Canada*, 160
2 NA, Macdonald Papers, MG26, no. 70, vol. 200–3, no. 85862–3, Cartier to Macdonald, 6 March 1869
3 Virginia Woolf, *A Room of One's Own* (Harmondsworth: Penguin 1974), 38–9
4 Greenwood, *Legacies of Fear*, 5, 6, 8–11, 254
5 For a discussion of the patriarchal relations of production in capitalist society, see Marjorie Griffin Cohen, *Women's Work, Markets, and Economic Development in Nineteenth-Century Ontario* (Toronto: University of Toronto Press 1988), 42–5.
6 Doige, *Montreal Street Directory*, 1819; ANQM, Mondelet, #1151, 25 August 1814; Doucet, #7559, 15 May 1820
7 AJQM, Special Sessions, 25 January 1830
8 AJQM, Court of Special Sessions, 25 September 1832
9 ANQM, Court of Special Sessions, 30 January 1846
10 Backhouse, 'Nineteenth-Century Canadian Prostitution Law,' 391
11 Picard, *Les femmes et le vote*, 66
12 Ibid., 73
13 Ibid., 58, 61
14 Kolish, 'Imprisonment for Debt in Lower Canada,' 615
15 *Statutes of Canada* (1849) 12 Vict., c. 42
16 *Statutes of Canada* (1843) 7 Vict., c. 53; Ellen James, *John Ostell, Architect, Surveyor* (Montreal: McCord Museum 1985), 54; for the activity of bourgeois women in the Montreal Lying-in Hospital, see Rhona Richman Kenneally,

'The Montreal Maternity Hospital, 1843–1926: Evolution of a Hospital' (Unpublished MA thesis, McGill University 1983).

17 *Statutes of Canada* (1864) 27 & 28 Vict., c. 18

18 For an example of a wife granted separation from bed and board and who, thirteen years later, sought court permission to end the separation, see ANQM, Banc du roi, no. 1209, 13 April 1829, Marie-Françoise Desautels v. Michel David.

19 Article 223, Custom of Paris, in Doucet, *Fundamental Principles*, 264

20 Bradbury et al., *Property and Marriage*, 8, 14–15, note that by the 1840s only 12 per cent of Roman Catholic couples and 7 per cent of Protestant couples made formal marriage contracts; Bradbury, *Working Families*, 50.

21 Dickinson, *Law in New France*, 15

22 Harvey, '"To Love, Honour and Obey"'; Backhouse, 'Nineteenth-Century Canadian Prostitution Law'; Bradbury, *Working Families:* Backhouse, *Petticoats and Prejudice*, 9–39

23 NA, RG 4, C1, vol. 567, dossier 2618 (1864), Dominique Mondelet to É. Parent, Assistant Secretary, 29 December 1862 (trans.)

24 McGill University Archives, Torrance and Morris law firm, 'Mr. Justice Torrance Notebook, Points of Procedure etc.,' 81; AJQM, Circuit Court, Montreal, Leduc v. Doré, November 1874

25 McGill University Archives, Torrance and Morris law firm, Authorities 5, 1860; this was regulated by provisions of the act (1865) 29 Vict., c. 17 (repeated in article 1265 of the CC) permitting a husband to insure his life for the benefit of his wife and children.

26 McGill University Archives, Torrance and Morris law firm, Authorities 1864, 156, International Life Association Company v. Mrs. C.F. Hill, 1865

27 Atiyah, *Rise and Fall*, 400

28 For American rationalization of republicanism and inequality to women, see Berthoff, 'Conventional Mentality,' 754; for feminists and codification, see Rabkin, 'Origins of Law Reform'; see also Lebsock, *Free Women of Petersburg;* Salmon, *Women and the Law of Property;* Grossberg, *Governing the Hearth*.

29 Cambacérès, *Projet de Code Civil;* for inequality of wives under the Napoleonic Code, see articles 213, 214, 298, and Arnaud, *Essai d'analyse structurale du code civil français*, 73; Halperin, *L'impossible code civil*, 63, 122, 125, 288–9.

30 Shanley, *Feminism, Marriage, and the Law*, 11

31 Staves, *Married Women's Separate Property*, 230

32 *Statutes of Canada* (1841) 4 Vict., c. 30

33 *Dame Rachel Boudria et Mathew McLean* (4 March 1862), 6 *Lower Canada Jurist* 65

34 Bonner, *Essay on the Registry Laws*, 24

35 See, for example, the legal opinion sought by the Montreal Permanent Building Society on the mortgage application of Alexander Colquehouse, 6 May 1862, McGill University Archives, Torrance and Morris law firm, Authorities 3, p. 95, or Letters, p. 22, Torrance and Morris to Montreal Permanent Building Society, 12 December 1859. For a short history of building societies, see Robert Sweeny, *A Guide to the History and Records of Montreal Businesses before 1847* (Montreal: Montreal Business History Project 1978), 171–3. For difficulties with registry in the 1840s, see Normand and Hudon, 'Le contrôle des hypothèques secrètes,' 185.

36 *Statutes of Canada* (1843) 7 Vict., c. 10, s. 79

37 McGill University Archives, Torrance and Morris law firm, Letters, 5, Torrance & Morris to Nolney S. Fulham, Ludlow, Vermont, 16 September 1859

38 For the law as a masculine profession, see Grossberg, 'Institutionalizing Masculinity.' The origins of feminist influence is described in Collectif Clio, *L'histoire des femmes au Québec depuis quatre siècles* (Montréal: Les quinze 1982), 230–1.

39 Gérald Bernier and Robert Boily, *Le Québec en chiffres de 1850 à nos jours* (Montréal, Association canadienne-française pour l'avancement des sciences 1986), 46

40 Sylvain and Voisine, *Histoire du catholicisme québécois*, II, 98–9

41 ASSM, arm. 3, vol. 37, 13 May 1871

42 Young, 'Édouard-Charles Fabre,' *DCB*, XII, 300–5

43 *Laviolette et Martin* (1856), 2 *Lower Canada Jurist* 61–7

44 *Caissé v. Hervieux* (1856), 6 *Lower Canada Reports* 73–6 (Sup. C. of Montreal); writing on judicial laxity towards wife-beating, Backhouse, *Petticoats and Prejudice*, 176, describes Day's decision as 'remarkable.'

45 *Guernon v. Lauzon* (20 May 1854), 1, no. 2 *Law Reporter* 71 (Sup. C. of Montreal, no. 2002)

46 Pothier, *Treatise on Obligations*, 34

47 McGill Law Library, Codification Commission mfm, #1, 10; for relevant parts of the civil code and the reliance on Pothier as authority, see articles 177, 986

48 Grossberg, *Governing the Hearth*, 26; *Fifth Report*, 211; for an example of secretary Ramsay's emphasis on parental authority, see *Regina v. Mondelet* (1877) cited in unidentified clipping in Judge Ramsay's 'Newspaper Clippings,' 25–6.

49 *Second Report*, 165, 191; articles 79, 80, 83, 185 CC

50 *Fifth Report*, 211; marriage as a form of partnership is raised again in 227.

51 *Fifth Report*, 213

52 Articles 186–217 CC; see F.W. Torrance's comments of custody under old law and under the Civil Code, McGill University Archives, Torrance and Morris law firm, Authorities 1864, p. 133, *L'Esperance v. Thompson*, 27 June 1864.

53 Articles 844, 851 CC

54 Taschereau, 'Les petits commerçants,' 31

55 Article 229, Custom of Paris, in Doucet, *Fundamental Principles*. Husbands and wives (article 280) could also grant usufructure of their half of the community to a surviving spouse. Immovable property given to one of the spouses with the stipulation that it was *propre* did not fall into the community (article 246).

56 Heleieth I.B. Saffioti, *Women in Class Society* (New York and London: Monthly Review Press 1978), 41

57 In the Sainte-Anne suburb of Montreal, Bradbury, *Working Families*, 198, found about 20 per cent of widows with a declared 1861 census occupation trading, keeping a shop, or running a boarding-house. This figure does not include the important number of female traders in sewing trades. Marta Danylewcyz in *Taking the Veil*, 52, reports that, in the 1870s, over a third of Montreal women were still spinsters at age forty.

58 AJQM, Court of Queens Bench, February and April 1843

59 *Census of 1831*

60 Ibid.

61 Archives de la Ville de Montréal, Census of 1842. For examples of female traders as heads of families in which there no males or only young unmarried males, see Widow McConnell, trader in the Saint-Laurent suburb; Widow Albeck, grocer in the Saint-Laurent suburb; Widow Hamelin, tavern-keeper in the Saint-Laurent suburb; Widow Burns, trader on Wellington Street; Miss McLean, milliner in Saint-Laurent ward (in her household of twelve, ten were declared to be married women over forty-five); Miss Ferguson, milliner on Craig Street; Widow Fournier, trader on Saint-Joseph Street; Widow Leighton, trader in Queens suburb; and Miss Macindoe, milliner on Grey Nuns Street. There are also many households in which female traders were heads and in which younger married males (presumably sons or sons-in-law) resided, for example, that of Widow Currin, grocer on Bleury Street.

62 The term 'trader' is itself an important legal category affecting the laws applied to particular disputes, jury composition, the obligation to register marriage contracts, etc. The assembly's definition of a 'trader' included merchants, brokers, bankers, insurers, builders, carpenters, shipwrights, keepers of inns, taverns, hotels or coffeehouses, millers, lumberers, ship-owners, and all other persons who lived by 'buying or selling, or by buying or letting for hire, or by the workmanship of goods or commodities' (*Statutes of Canada* (1843) 7 Vict., c. 10).

63 Common law recognized longstanding local practices among which were the trading practices of London. By the custom of London, a married

woman could trade independently of her husband with the legal rights of a feme sole trader. J. Johnson, *The Laws Respecting Women* (London 1777), 174. For feme sole trader laws in the colonies of Pennsylvania, South Carolina, and Massachussetts, see Salmon, *Women and the Law of Property*, 44–53.

64 Langelier, *Cours de droit civil*, vol. 1, 319

65 See also Bidaud, *Commentaires sur les lois*, 431.

66 Pothier, *Oeuvres de Pothier*, VII, 9

67 Bidaud, *Commentaires sur les lois*, 431; Des Rivières Beaubien, *Traité sur les lois civiles*, 48

68 Jacques Monet and Gerald J.J. Tulchinsky, 'Augustin Cuvillier,' *DCB*, VII, 224

69 *Canadian Courant and Montreal Advertiser*, 24 April, 6, 27 May, 7 October 1811, 13 April 1812; ANQM, Doucet, no. 7768, 19 July 1820, 'Protest,' *M.C. Cuvillier v. J. Scott*; no. 7786, 22 July 1820, 'Protest,' *J. Scott and Co. v. M.C. Cuvillier*

70 AJQM, Superior Court, no. 713, 1866, Ontario Bank v Marie V.L. Duchesnay, marchande publique

8 'WITTINGLY AND WILLINGLY': THE LAW OF OBLIGATIONS

1 Domat, *Civil Law*, 165

2 El-Gammal, *L'adaptation du contrat*, 6 (trans.)

3 McCord, *Civil Code of Lower Canada*, vi

4 See, for example, Brierley, 'Quebec's Civil Law Codification,' 540–1.

5 The contrast between customary and Roman law is effectively drawn by Ourliac, *Histoire du droit privé français*, 66, 357; not all historians agree on the centrality of capitalist principles in Roman law. James Whitman, for example, in *Legacy of Roman Law*, 216, 230–1, accuses Theodor Mommsen of a 'materialist' selection from Roman history, overemphasizing its qualities as a bourgeois, individualist, and commercial capitalist society.

6 For this process in France, see Halperin, *L'impossible code civil*, 287–96; for England, Atiyah, *Rise and Fall*; and for Germany and what Anton Menger called 'a victory of the commercial spirit over the propertied order, of the law of trade over the law of property,' see John, *Politics and the Law*, 118; contract-clause jurisprudence in the United States is treated in Hovenkamp, *Enterprise and American Law*, 20–35.

7 *First Report*, 6

8 McCord, *Civil Code*, ii–iii

9 An obligation is a 'juridical relationship between two or more persons, by virtue of which one of them, the *debtor*, is held towards another, the *creditor*, to perform a certain prestation which may consist in giving, in

doing or in not doing something,' Robert P. Kouri et al., *Private Law Dictionary and Bilingual Lexicons*, 296; see also the definitions given by Carbonnier, *Droit Civil 4*, 15 and Baudouin, *Les Obligations*, 8–9. For the nature of Roman law, see the treatment of Cicero in G.E.M. de Ste Croix, *Class Struggle*, 328, 426; for the source of obligation in Roman law, see Stephen Neff, 'Decline and Emergence: Roman Law and the Transition from Antiquity to Feudalism' (1984) 5 *Journal of Legal History*, 91, and Arnaud, *Les origines doctrinales*, 131.

10 G. Lepointe and R. Monier, *Les obligations en droit romain et dans l'ancien droit français* (Paris: Librairie du recueil Sirey 1954), 448–53; Imbert, *Histoire du droit privé*, 9–14; Olivier-Martin, *Histoire du droit français*, 120–3; Robinson et al., *Introduction to European Legal History*, 72, 191; Ourliac, *Histoire du droit privé français*, 152

11 Ourliac, *Histoire du droit privé français*, 244

12 Olivier-Martin, *Histoire du droit français*, 354, 427; Imbert, *Histoire du droit privé*, 57; Ourliac, *Histoire du droit privé français*, 167

13 Arnaud, *Les origines doctrinales*, 69. 'Covenants being voluntary agreements which are formed by the consent of the parties concerned,' Domat wrote, 'they ought to be made with knowledge and freedom,' *Civil Law*, 165.

14 Atiyah, *Rise and Fall*, 351

15 Pothier, *Treatise on Obligations*, no. 85–7, pp. 57–8; this should be compared with the Civil Code articles 'On the effect of contracts,' articles 1022–3.

16 Ibid., 76

17 Ibid., 1–2; Carbonnier, *Droit Civil 4*, 16

18 John, *Politics and the Law*, 36

19 Zoltvany, in 'Esquisse de la Coutume de Paris,' 365, asserts that the custom 'regulated the recovery of debts' as well as family organization, succession, and land tenure.

20 Dickinson, 'La justice seigneuriale en Nouvelle-France,' 335; *Justice et justiciables*, 123

21 Lise St-George, 'Commerce, crédit et transactions foncières,' 332; Christian Dessureault makes the same observation for Lac-des-Deux-Montagnes, 'La Seigneurie du Lac-des-Deux-Montagnes,' in Dépatie et al., *Contributions*, 206.

22 Michel, 'Un marchand rural en Nouvelle-France,' 240 (trans.)

23 See, for example, Noël, *Christie Seigneuries*, 25.

24 Greer, *Peasant, Lord and Merchant*, 24

25 See my *In Its Corporate Capacity*, 26, and Dessureault, 'L'Egalitarianisme paysan,' 206.

26 Michel, 'Un marchand rural en Nouvelle-France,' 261 (trans.)

27 Kolish, 'Le Conseil législatif,' 219–20; for the Ordinance of 1667, see Arnaud, *Les origines doctrinales du Code Civil français*, 173.

28 St-Georges, 'Commerce, crédit et transactions foncières,' 339–40; Evelyn Kolish, in 'Changements,' 350, relates the rise in litigation to the increase in the British population, noting that 61 per cent of litigants in the Superior Court session of 1825 were British in origin. Employment contracts also seem to have been subject to increasingly strict written conditions. See, for example, 'The Act for regulating persons who hire or engage to perform voyages to the Indian Country or to Winter there,' *Provincial Statutes of Lower Canada* (1796) 30 Geo. III, c. 10.

29 Sweeny, *Les relations ville/campagne*, ci; Noël, *Christie Seigneuries*, 61; Baribeau, *La seigneurie de la Petite-Nation*, 138; Young, *In its Corporate Capacity*, 28

30 Françoise Noël, 'La gestion des seigneuries de Gabriel Christie dans la vallée du Richelieu (1760–1845)' (1987) 40, 4 *Revue d'histoire de l'Amérique française*, 580 n42; *Christie Seigneuries*, 59; Ouellet, *Lower Canada*, 146–7; for the Edicts of Marly, see Y.F. Zoltvany, ed., *The French Tradition in America* (New York: Harper & Row 1969), 90–3.

31 (1854), IV *Lower Canada Reports* 410

32 ANQM, Lower Canada Court of Appeal, Banc du Roi, 1828–29, No. 224, *Bazile Garand et al. et Louis Morin*

33 McGill University, Faculty of Law, Canadiana Rare Books Room, 'Law Intelligence,' Sup Ct of Montreal, *Kennedy v. Smith*, 28 February 1854.

34 Hilda Neatby, *The Administration of Justice under the Quebec Act* (Minneapolis: University of Minnesota Press 1937), 16–17, 155–60

35 McCord Museum, Arthur Davidson papers, #8448, purchases from Whieldon and Waller, 1780; G.P. Browne, 'Arthur Davidson,' *DCB*, V, 224–7

36 McCord Museum, McCord Collection, #1443, Arthur Davidson to Joseph Butterworth, 2 November 1799. See also the book orders of Torrance and Morris including Pothier on partnerships, McGill University Archives, Torrance and Morris law firm, Torrance and Morris to –, 17 November 1862, 19.

37 Frederick Pollock and Frederic William Maitland, *The History of English Law* (Cambridge: Cambridge University Press 1985), 184; see also Atiyah, *Rise and Fall*, 102–3.

38 Arnaud, *Les origines doctrinales*, 173; see also Lepointe and Monier, *Les obligations en droit romain et dans l'ancien droit français*, 485–8.

39 Des Rivières Beaubien *Traité sur les lois civiles*, 9; for his brief treatment of obligations and contract, see 98.

40 Crémazie, *Manuel des notions utiles*, 43, 52

41 Bibaud, *Commentaires sur les lois*, 222

42 Baker, 'Law Practice and Statecraft,' 56; McGill University Archives, Torrance and Morris law firm, Torrance, 'The Roman Law: A Lecture' (1854), 13, 25

43 Baker, 'Law Practice and Statecraft,' 62, 63, 60; *Civil Code: Codifiers' Report. Legislative Proceedings,* Cartier in Legislative Assembly, 1 September 1865

44 Ritchie, *Codification of the Laws of Lower Canada,* 5

45 Articles 983, 984 CC

46 ASQ, Caron Collection, Microfilm #1, 35

47 Ibid., 'Draft for Codification Commission,' microfilm #1, Day, Worksheets for Obligations, 36, 55. Day's thinking here closely parallels that of Hugo Grotius (1583–1645). See, for example, A.P. d'Entrèves, *Natural Law: An Introduction to Legal Philosophy* (London: Hutchinson University Library 1961), 53.

48 Atiyah, *Rise and Fall,* 294, 400

49 Articles 996, 997 CC

50 Friedman, *History of American Law,* 28

51 *First Report,* 30

52 Article 1206 CC; ASQ, Collection Caron, vol. 817, 'Livre des minutes,' 15 January 1861

53 Article 2278 CC; see also ASQ, Collection Caron, vol. 817, 'Livre des minutes,' 351.

54 ASQ, Collection Caron, Day draft of 'Obligations,' 61

55 *First Report,* 18; see also McCord's synopsis in *Civil Code of Lower Canada,* viii.

56 *First Report,* 18

57 Article 1025 CC

58 Articles 777, 795, 1596 CC; article 1472 concerning sales made special provision for the transfer of registered vessels; in the sale of debts, the sale was perfected by completion of the title if signed before notary (i.e. 'authentic') but, if the sale was done by private signature, delivery had to occur (article 1570). For changing American views of delivery, see Horwitz, *Transformation,* 160–210.

59 W.W. Buckland, *A Text-Book of Roman Law from Augustus to Justinian* (Cambridge: Cambridge University Press 1921), 228; Guyot, *Répertoire universel et raisonné de jurisprudence,* vol. 17, 221.

60 *Bonacina v. Seed* (1853), 3 *Lower Canada Reports* 446–53

61 See Stuart, *Reports,* 357–64, *Vankoughnet and Maitland et al.* (1829).

62 (1852), 2 *Lower Canada Reports* 257–72

63 *Bowen v. Ayer* (18 November 1836), II *Revue de législation et de jurisprudence* 106–7

64 Alan Stewart, 'Settling an 18th Century Faubourg,' 172

65 *Bowen v. Ayer* (18 November 1836), II *Revue de législation et de jurisprudence* 102–19

66 *Stuart v. Ives* (1851), I *Lower Canada Reports* 203

9 CONCLUSION

1 *Civil Code: Codifiers' Report. Legislative Proceedings*, Cartier in Legislative Assembly, 1 September 1865

2 Cited in New York *Review of Books*, 10 June 1993

3 David Bercuson and Barry Cooper, *Deconfederation: Canada without Quebec* (Toronto: Key Porter 1991), 7; Mordecai Richler, 'A Reporter at Large,' *New Yorker*, 23 September 1991, p. 46, revives the cliché of Quebec women as 'sows.'

4 Bercuson and Cooper, *Deconfederation*, 7

5 Cited in James W. Ely, Jr, *The Guardian of Every Other Right: A Constitutional History of Property Rights* (New York and Oxford: Oxford University Press 1992), 6

6 See, for example, John, 'Peculiarities of the German State,' and Arnaud, *Essai d'analyse structurale du code civil français.*

7 'Loi modifiant le Code civil et le Code de procédure civile, relativement aux droits civils de la femme,' *Statutes of Quebec* (1931) 21 Geo. V, c. 101; Ann Robinson, 'Féminisme, droit et philosophie ou la condition des femmes en droit québecois' (September 1991), XVIII, no. 1 *Humanities Association of Canada Bulletin*, 23–5

8 Edward G. White, *The Marshall Court and Cultural Change, 1815–1835* (New York and Oxford: Oxford University Press 1992), 2

9 (May 1846), 1, no. 8 *Revue de législation et de jurisprudence*. For an American counterpart, see Grossberg, *Governing the Hearth*, 16.

10 *Lower Canada Reports: Seigniorial Questions* (1856), 2d

11 McCord, *Civil Code of Lower Canada*, ii

12 Brierley, 'Quebec's "Common Laws" (Droits communs),' 118

13 McCord, *Civil Code of Lower Canada*, iii

14 A.P. d'Entrèves, *Natural Law: An Introduction to Legal Philosophy*, 93; for the attitudes of the Catholic hierarchy, see William Ryan, *The Clergy and Economic Growth in Quebec (1896–1914)* (Québec: Les presses de l'Université Laval 1966).

15 Quoted in R.A. Macdonald, 'National Law Programme,' 19.

16 McCord, *Civil Code of Lower Canada*, xiii

17 Ibid.

18 Arnaud, *Les origines doctrinales du code civil français*, 207; Olivier-Martin, *Histoire du droit français*, 76

19 *Civil Code: Codifiers' Report. Legislative Proceedings*, Cartier in Legislative Assembly, 1 September 1865

Essay on Sources

The bibliography lists the more important works cited in the notes. The most significant source for students of Lower Canadian codification are the commission's seven reports and supplementary report published between 1861 and 1864. Materials surrounding the legislative debate have been collected in *Civil Code: Codifiers' Report, Legislative Proceedings* (1865).

It is far from coincidental that the major collections of codification papers, of nineteenth-century law libraries, and of private papers concerning codification are housed in the archives of three institutions – the Séminaire de Québec (the founder of Université Laval), McGill University, and the Séminaire de Saint-Hyacinthe. As well as being central to the educational and professional careers of the three codifiers, these institutions played a larger role in fostering the legal, ecclesiastical, and political élite.

The most useful primary source is the partial record of the Codification Commission found in the Collection Caron, Archives du Séminaire de Québec (a microfilm copy of the collection is deposited in the Law Library of McGill University). This collection of fifty-three volumes includes the minute books and many codification workbooks, in particular those of Charles Dewey Day.

The Archives du Séminaire de Saint-Hyacinthe contains the collection of codifier Augustin-Norbert Morin. This includes sixteen of his codification notebooks (AFG5 #1–9). However, because of Morin's fragile health during much of the codification period, most are simply copies prepared by the clerks of reports by his colleagues Caron and Day. Of the sections Morin was responsible for, 'Of Gifts inter vivos & by Will' and 'Of Prescription,' only the latter (AFG5 #2) is Morin's working copy and includes his notes and certain of his worksheets. The Morin

Collection also contains considerable material on Morin's career, finances, and personal life. Of particular importance for his legal ideology are his 'Leçon de droit' (#35) and his two handwritten volumes of trial notes, 'Notes sur des causes' (#10). Also of interest is his law library which can be examined – apparently intact – in the seminary's library. A catalogue of his library can be found in Séminaire Administration Financière, Section A, Série M, tiroir 14, dossier 1.4. The archives also contains a coloured photo of the Codification Commission (reproduced here at page 125), a duplicate of which is in the McGill Law Faculty.

The Canadiana Rare Books Room of the McGill Law Library has a rich collection of Lower Canadian legal history including all the major treatises and pamphlets concerning codification. Of help in working one's way through the Lower Canadian materials in the McGill Law Library is Baker et al., *Sources in the Law Library of McGill University*. As well as holding microfilm copies of the codification reports deposited in the Séminaire de Québec, the Law Library has all of the codification reports, as well as *Civil Code: Codifiers' Report: Legislative Proceedings*.

Several rich collections of lawyers' papers are held by the archives of the McCord Museum of Canadian History (Montreal). Of particular importance are the papers of Arthur Davidson and John Samuel McCord. The museum also has a small but important collection of the papers of George-Étienne Cartier which is useful for his legal career. In the McLennan Library of McGill University, the Lande Room and Rare Books and Special Collections have important pamphlet collections as well as the papers from important legal families such as the Sewells. The McGill University Archives has the important – and recently inventoried – papers of the Torrance and Morris law firm.

Until mid-century, law reporting in Lower Canada was sporadic and was contained in just five volumes: Pyke's seventy-seven–page *Cases Argued* (1810), Stuart's one-volume *Reports of Cases* (1834), and the three volumes of the *Revue de législation et de jurisprudence* (1846–8) – all available in the Canadiana Rare Books Room of the McGill Law Faculty. Professionalization of the bar and expansion of legal education in the universities increased pressure for the publication of law reports. In 1850 the government passed legislation enabling it to subsidize publication of court decisions in Lower Canada. A year later, publication of *Lower Canada Reports* in Quebec City was greeted by protests from the Montreal bar who complained of its irregular publication and its meager treatment of decisons in the District of Montreal. In 1854 T.K. Ramsay and L.S. Morin launched the Montreal-based *Law Reporter* and, when it failed within a year, the Montreal bar–backed publication of the *Lower Canada Jurist* (1857). Published in Montreal by John Lovell, four of the review's twelve editors taught law at McGill.

Given the gaps in law reporting during this period, newspapers are of great importance, particularly their legal columns. The McGill Law Faculty Canadiana Rare Books Room possesses a very useful bound volume of newspaper clippings entitled 'Law Intelligence.' For the political side of codification, the speeches of Cartier collected in *Discours de Cartier* and edited by Joseph Tassé (Montreal 1893) are of great value.

For an introduction to Canadian legal history, one cannot do better than David Flaherty's 'Writing Canadian Legal History' in volume 1 of *Essays in the History of Canadian Law* (1981). My own 'Law in the Round' (1986) also surveys Canadian legal history, particularly from the standpoint of the integration of legal and social history. A broad – and still the best – survey of the literature of Quebec legal history is Vince Masciotra's 'Quebec's Legal Historiography' included in a special 1987 issue (32, no. 3) of the *McGill Law Journal* devoted to the study of Quebec legal history; this issue includes important articles on the mid-nineteenth century by Jean-Marie Fecteau, Evelyn Kolish, Tom Johnson, and others.

For the context of codification in Europe, see the very readable *Introduction to European Legal History* (1985) by O.F. Robinson, T.D. Fergus, and W.M. Gordon. The literature on French civil law is massive and a good place to begin is Jean Imbert's slim volume, *Histoire du droit privé* (1950). The more adventurous should read J. Brissaud's *Manuel d'histoire du droit privé* (1898). Starting places for the Custom of Paris include Claude de Ferrière, *Nouveau commentaire sur la coutume de la prévôté et vicomté de Paris* (1742) and Fr. Olivier-Martin's *Histoire de la coutume de la prévôté et vicomté de Paris* (1972); for applicable elements of the Custom in Canada, see François-Joseph Cugnet, *An Abstract of Those Parts of the Viscomty and Prevostship of Paris, Which Was Received in the Province of Quebec in the Time of the French Government* (1773). André-Jean Arnaud's *Les origines doctrinales de code civil français* (1969) shows the Napoleonic Code as a compromise of customary and Roman law.

For the ideology of the Napoleonic Code, one should plunge directly into the preparatory work of the codifiers themselves. This is readily available in an edited version (1989) of Pierre-Antoine Fenet's longer collection. The relationship between French codification and the bourgeois revolution is effectively shown in André-Jean Arnaud's *Essai d'analyse structurale du code civil français* (1973).

The contribution of Roman law to both the Napoleonic and Lower Canadian civil codes, strongly emphasized in this work, can be seen in G. Lepointe and R. Monier's *Les obligations en droit romain et dans l'ancien droit français* (Paris 1954) and Charles Eisenmann, H. Batiffol, and M. Villey, *Les origines doctrinales du code civil français* (Paris: Pichon et Durand-Auzias 1967). The form of Roman law, obligations, and tradition are traced in W.W. Buckland's *A Text-Book of Roman Law from Augustus to Justinian* (Cambridge: Cambridge University Press 1921). A thoughtful treatment of the effect of Roman law can be found in James Q. Whitman, *The Legacy of Roman Law in the German Romantic Era*. The classic on the law of Obligations is Pothier's *Obligations*, available in English as *A Treatise on Obligations*. For Obligations since codification, see Jean Carbonnier's *Droit Civil*, vol. 4: *Les obligations* (1956) for France, and Jean-Louis Baudouin's *Les obligations* (1993) for Quebec.

Given the importance of law in Marxist thought, it is not surprising that Marxist history on comparative European law interprets codification as part of the process of *embourgeoisement*. Gyula Eörsi's *Comparative Civil (Private) Law* (1979) is particularly fertile for the Lower Canadian example as he locates codification in relation to feudalism and the French Revolution. Michael John's *Politics and Law in Late Nineteenth-Century Germany: the Origins of the Civil Code* (1989) links codification to the process of nation-building and bureaucratization, and confirms the clear relationship of law, class, and nation. Also useful is Susan Staves' argument in *Married Women's Separate Property in England, 1660–1833* (1990) on the resolution of the contradiction between patriarchy and freedom of contract and her strong insistence that the non-specialist in legal history can vigorously enter the debate.

While Morton Horwitz's well-known work, *The Transformation of American Law, 1780–1860*, emphasizes commodity exchange and the relation of evolving contract law to the free market, Bruce Mann's *Neighbours and Stangers: Law and Community in Early Connecticut* (1987) pushes back the capturing of communal methods of dealing with dispute settlement by uniform and centralized nineteenth century methods to the eighteenth and seventeenth centuries. In *Governing the Hearth*, Michael Grossberg shows the transformation of American family law by the extension of private contract into areas such as matrimony. For American codification, R. Kent Newmyer's biography of Joseph Story (1985) shows the conservative New England jurist's ambiguity to the process, while Charles M. Cook's *American Codification Movement* (1981) gives a clear description of the process.

Hilda Neatby's *Administration of Justice under the Quebec Act* (1937) was sharply critical of the judicial system before 1774 ('no system but rather a confused growth of law and custom') and described that set up by the Quebec Act as 'deplorable' and 'not adapted to any colony with commercial interests, not even one that was entirely French' (90, 18). Neatby's work has been surpassed by Murray Greenwood's *Legacies of Fear* (1993). While emphasizing the inconsistency of Civil law for merchants in the post-conquest period, Greenwood effectively situates seigneurialism, religion, and family as central tenets of Lower Canada's pre-industrial legal system. For the background of Lower Canadian codification, the several works of Evelyn Kolish are essential, particularly *Nationalismes et conflits économiques: le débat sur le droit privé au Québec 1760–1840* (1994). Also important are the articles of Sylvio Normand, especially his 1990 article on secret hypothecs co-authored by Alain Hudon. Christine Veilleux's thesis, *Les gens de justice à Québec, 1760–1867* (1990) is useful for its sense of the material life and ideology of the legal profession in Quebec City in the codification period, while Richard Larue's 'Code Napoléon et codification des lois civiles au Bas-Canada' (1989) gives a strong Marxist interpretation to the process. The *Dictionary of Canadian Biography* includes many legal biographies including those of the three codifiers and Murray Greenwood's and James H. Lambert's important study of Jonathan Sewell. Two recent publications of the Montreal History Group provide important background to codification: D. Fyson, C. Coates, and K. Harvey, eds., *Class, Gender and the Law in Eighteenth- and Nineteenth-Century Quebec* (1993), and D. Fyson, *The Court Structure of Quebec and Lower Canada, 1764 to 1860* (1994).

Secondary material on codification in Quebec is dominated by the work of John Brierley whose 1968 article, 'Quebec's Civil Law Codification: Viewed and Reviewed,' not only interpreted the subject effectively but opened up the commission's papers to other researchers. His subsequent works – especially 'The Co-existence of Legal Systems in Quebec: "Free and Common Socage" in Canada's "pays de droit civil"' (1979), 'The English Language Tradition in Quebec Civil Law' (1987), and 'La notion de droit commun dans un système de droit mixte: le cas de la province de Québec' (1989) – have emphasized the close connections between mid-nineteenth century law reform and the language issue and poly-jurality. His recent article, 'The Renewal of Quebec's Distinct Legal Culture: the New Civil Code of Quebec' (1992), provides a clear and provocative description of the new Civil Code as 'free-standing' and 'autonomous' and the code of 'a new nation-state' (498–9). Also very much in the law-school tradition of legal history are André Morel's many works, several of which treat codification, and, more recently, John Cairns's 1980 PhD thesis, 'The 1808 Digest of Orleans and 1866 Civil Code of Lower Canada' and his subsequent work including an important examination of labour regulation in the code (1987). For the codification of procedure, see Jean-Maurice Brisson's *La formation d'un droit mixte: l'évolution de la procédure civile de 1774 à 1867* (1986).

Select Bibliography

Primary Sources

MANUSCRIPT SOURCES

Archives du Séminaire de Québec
    Collection Caron, manuscrits 764 à 817: 53 *Cahiers de travail* including the minute books and *Notes générales* of René-Édouard Caron (microfilm of the collection is held in the library of McGill University, Faculty of Law)
    Minutes of the Codification Commission
Archives du Séminaire de Saint-Hyacinthe, Saint-Hyacinthe
    AFG5 Collection Morin, Augustin-Norbert
    AFG5.1-.9 22 *cahiers sur la codification* (Prescription; propriété; donations et testaments; vente; loan, deposit, contrainte par corps, pledge; mandate; partnership)
    AFG.34 'Leçon de droit'
    AFG.35 Correspondance de A.-N. Morin, 182 lettres
    Dossiers divers relatif à A.-N. Morin
    'Bibliothèque de Augustin-Norbert Morin'
Archives nationales du Québec à Montréal
    Appeal Case Dockets, various dates
    Plumatif, Superior Court of Montreal, 1849
    Register, Court of Appeals of Quebec/Lower Canada, 1782–1829
Le Barreau de Montréal
    'Minutes of the Advocates' Library,' 27 March 1828 – 21 June 1855

'The Bar of Lower Canada. Section of the District of Montreal,' vol. 2, 28 July
1849 – 22 April 1861; vol. 3, 1 May 1861 – 16 December 1894
McCord Museum of Canadian History, Montreal
George-Étienne Cartier Collection
Arthur Davidson Collection
John Samuel McCord Collection
McGill University Archives
Judge Andrew Stuart, 7 volumes including 'Notebook' (October 1843)
Torrance and Morris law firm, books and registers
Judge Frederick Torrance papers, 13 volumes
Judge T.K. Ramsay, 'Newpaper Clippings,' 1 volume
McGill University Libraries
Rare Books Room, McLennan Library
William Badgley Minute Book
Jonathan Sewell papers, 'Report on sedition in Montreal,' 1796
Stephen Sewell 'Law Books,' 5 volumes
John G. Thompson, 'Compendium of Legal ... 1810–1855'
Faculty of Law Library, Canadiana Rare Books Room
Cases in Appeal, folio
'Law Intelligence' (reported for the Montreal *Herald* and Montreal *Gazette*),
folio
National Archives of Canada, Ottawa
MG 24, 19, vol. 4, Hill Collection, J.M. Christie Papers: Correspondence, 1839–41
RG 4, B8, vol. 23, reel H-1416, 'Commissions of Advocates and Notaries'
RG 4, B37, vol. 1, Rebellion Records: Affadavits re: Trials for Treason, 1837–8
RG 4, C1, vol. 567, dossier 2618 (1864), 'Rapport des commissaires pour la
codification des lois du Bas Canada'

Government Documents

GREAT BRITAIN
Report from the Select Committee on the Civil Government of Canada. House of
Commons, 22 July 1828. Available in the British Parliamentary Papers. Irish
University Press Series of Colonies: Canada, 1.
Report on the Affairs of British North America from the Earl of Durham. London
1839

LOWER CANADA
Journals of the Assembly. 'First Report of the Standing Committee on Lands and
Seigniorial Rights.' App. EEE, 1 March 1836
Journal of the Legislative Council, 1821

Journals of the Legislative Council. App. F (1836). 'Report of Special Committee respecting state of law relating ... to incumbrances upon Real Estate in this Province'

PROVINCE OF CANADA
Appendix to the Third Volume of the Journals of the Legislative Assembly of the Province of Quebec
    App. F (1843). 'Report of the Commissioners appointed to inquire into the state of the laws and other circumstances connected with the Seigneurial Tenure ...'
    App. G (1843). 'Report of the Commissioners on the Administration of Justice in the Inferior District of Gaspé'
Civil Code of Lower Canada. Quebec
  First Report. October 1861
  Second Report. May 1862
  Third Report. December 1862
  Fourth Report. February 1863
  Fifth Report. January 1864
  Sixth Report. July 1864
  Seventh Report. November 1864
  Supplementary Report. November 1864
Civil Code: Codifiers' Report, Legislative Proceedings. Quebec 1865
Debates of the Legislative Assembly of United Canada. Edited by Elizabeth Nish. 1841–54
Journals of the Legislative Assembly of the Province of Canada. 1857, 1865, 1866
Journals of the Special Council of Lower Canada. Quebec 1840
Ordinances Made and Passed by His Excellency the Governor General and Special Council. 6 vols. Quebec
Parliamentary Debates on Confederation of the British North American Provinces. Quebec 1865
Statutes of Canada. 1841–67
Tables relative to the Acts and Ordinances of Lower Canada. Kingston 1843

Legal Periodicals and Reports

Lower Canada Jurist: Collection de décisions du Bas-Canada. 1857–66
Lower Canada Law Journal. 1866–7
Lower Canada Reports/Décisions des tribunaux du Bas-Canada. 1851–6
Lower Canada Reports. Décisions des tribunaux du Bas-Canada. Seigniorial Questions. Quebec and Montreal 1856

Pyke's Reports of Cases Argued and Determined in the Court of the King's Bench for the District of Quebec. Montreal 1811

Revue de législation et de jurisprudence et collection de décisions des divers tribunaux du Bas-Canada. 3 vols. Montréal 1846–8

Stuart, George Okill. *Reports of Cases argued and determined in the Courts of Kings Bench and in the Provincial Court of Appeals with a few of the more important cases in the court of vice admiralty and on appeals from Lower Canada before the Lords of the Privy Council.* Quebec 1834

Pamphlets, Treatises, and Other Legal Sources

Anon. 'De la codification des lois du Canada.' (May 1846), 8 *Revue de législation et de jurisprudence* [Montréal] 337–41

Anon. 'La Codification des statuts du Bas-Canada.' (1879) *La Thémis* 185–91

Bellefeuille, Joseph-Édouard Lefebvre de. 'Code civil du Bas-Canada. Législation sur le mariage.' (1864, 1865) *La Revue canadienne*

– 'La nouvelle législation du Bas-Canada.' (1864) *La Revue canadienne*

Bibaud, François-Maximilien. *Commentaires sur les lois du Bas-Canada, ou Conférences de l'école de droit.* Montréal 1859

– *Corrigé du code civil avec un sommaire des lois nouvelles.* Pamphlet. n.d.

– 'Revue critique du code Badgley.' *La Minerve*, 19 mai, 2 juin, 1, 5 juillet 1851

Bonner, John. *An Essay on the Registry Laws of Lower Canada.* Quebec 1852

Civil Code of the State of Louisiana. New Orleans 1838

The Code Napoleon or the French Civil Code. Edited by George Spence. 1804; London 1827

Crémazie, Jacques. *Manuel des notions utiles sur les droits politiques, le droit civil, la loi criminelle et municipale, les lois rurales, etc.* Québec 1852

– *Report of J. Crémazie, Esquire: appointed by virtue of the act of the Fourth Victoria ...* Montréal 1846

Cugnet, François-Joseph. *An Abstract of Those Parts of the Viscomty and Prevostship of Paris, Which Was Received in the Province of Quebec in the Time of the French Government.* London 1773

– *Traité des anciennes loix de propriété en Canada, aujourd'huy province de Québec.* Québec 1775

Des Rivières Beaubien, Henry. *Traité sur les lois civiles du Bas-Canada.* Montréal 1832

Doucet, Nicolas-Benjamin. *Fundamental Principles of the Laws of Canada as they existed under the natives ...* Montreal 1841

Ferrière, Claude de. *Nouveau commentaire sur la coutume de la prévôté et vicomté de Paris.* 2 vols. Paris 1742

LaFontaine, L.-H. *Analyse de l'ordonnance du Conseil spécial sur les bureaux d'hypothèques.* Montréal 1842

Marriott, James. *Plan of a Code of Laws for the Province of Quebec reported by the Advocate General.* London 1774

Maseres, Francis. *A Collection of Several Commissions and Public Instruments Proceeding from His Majesty's Royal Authority, and other papers ...* London 1772

McCarthy, Justin. *Dictionnaire de l'ancien droit du Canada ou compilation des édits, déclarations royales, et arrêts du conseil d'état des roix de France concernant le Canada.* Québec 1809

Morin, A.-N. *Lettre à l'honorable Edward Bowen, écuyer, un des juges de la Cour du banc du Roi de sa Majesté pour le District de Québec.* Montréal 1825

Perrault, Joseph-François. *Code rural à l'usage des habitants tant anciens que nouveaux du Bas-Canada concernant leurs devoirs religieux et civils, d'après les loix en force dans le pays.* Québec 1832

– *Dictionnaire portatif et abrégé des loix et règles du parlement du Bas-Canada.* Québec 1806

– *Extraits ou précédents des arrêts tirés des régistres du conseil supérieur de Québec ...* Quebec 1824

– *Le juge de Paix et officier de paroisse, pour la province de Québec; Extrait de Richard Burn, chancellier du diocèse de Charlisle, et un des juges de paix de sa majesté, pour les comtés de Westmorland et Cumberland.* Montréal 1789

– *Questions et réponses sur le droit criminel du Bas-Canada dédiées aux étudiants en droit.* Québec 1814

Ramsay, T.K. *Digested Index to the Reported Cases in Lower Canada.* Quebec 1865

– *Government Commissions of Inquiry.* Montreal 1863

– *Notes sur la coutume de Paris indiquant les articles encore en force avec tout le texte de la coutume à l'exception des articles relatifs aux fiefs et censives ...* Montréal 1863

Report of the State Trials before a General Court Martial Held at Montreal in 1838–9: Exhibiting a Complete History of the Late Rebellion in Lower Canada. Montreal 1839

Ritchie, T.W. *Codification of the Laws of Lower Canada: Some Remarks on the Title 'Of Obligations' as Reported by the Commissioners.* Montreal 1863

Robertson, Andrew. *A Digest of All the Reports Published in Lower Canada to 1863.* Montreal 1864

Rubidge, F.P. *Specification for District Court Houses and Jails in Lower Canada.* Quebec 1860

Rules and Orders of Practice for the Court of King's Bench, District of Montreal, February term, 1811. (Amended and augmented till 20 June 1823) to which is added the rules and orders of practice in the provincial court of appeals. Montreal 1823

Rules for the Government of the Rural Police: Circular Memorandum for the Informa-tion and Guidance of the Inspecting Stipendiary Magistrate ... in the Montreal District. Montreal 1839

Sewell, Jonathan. *An Essay on the Juridical History of France, so far as It Relates to the Law of the Province ...* Quebec 1824. Reprinted in *Revue de législation et de jurisprudence ... des divers tribunaux du Bas-Canada.* Montreal 1846

Taylor, Hugh. *Manual of the Office, Duties, and Liabilities of a Justice of the Peace with Practical Forms, for the Use of Magistrates out of Session.* Montreal 1843

Torrance, Frederick William. *The Roman Law: A Lecture.* Montreal 1854. Col-lected in *Law Pamphlets* (Canadiana Rare Books Room, McGill University Libraries, Faculty of Law)

Viger, Denis-Benjamin. *Considérations sur les effets qu'ont produit en Canada, la conservation des établissements du pays, les mœurs, l'éducation, etc. de ces habi-tants.* Montréal 1809

– *Prospectus pour l'impression par souscription d'un dictionnaire de la jurisprudence civile du Bas-Canada.* 1812

– [Par un canadien]. *Analyse d'un entretien sur la conservation des établissements du Bas-Canada ... dans une lettre à un de ses amis.* Montréal 1826

Secondary Sources

Arnaud, André-Jean. *Essai d'analyse structurale du code civil français: la règle du jeu dans la paix bourgeoise.* Paris: Pichon et Durand-Auzias 1973

– *Les origines doctrinales du Code Civil français.* Paris: Pichon et Durand-Auzias 1969

Atiyah, P.A. *The Rise and Fall of Freedom of Contract.* Oxford: Oxford University Press 1979

Backhouse, Constance B. 'Nineteenth-Century Canadian Prostitution Law: Reflection of a Discriminating Society.' (1985), 18 *Histoire sociale/Social History,* 387–424

– *Petticoats and Prejudice: Women and Law in Nineteenth-Century Canada.* Tor-onto: Osgoode Society 1991

Baker, G. Blaine. 'Law Practice and Statecraft in Mid-Nineteenth-Century Mont-real: The Torrance-Morris Firm, 1848–1868.' In *Beyond the Law: Lawyers and Business in Canada 1830 to 1930,* edited by Carol Wilton, 45–91. Toronto: Osgoode Society 1990

Baker, G. Blaine, Kathleen E. Fisher, Vince Masciotra, and Brian Young. *Sources in the Law Library of McGill University for a Reconstruction of the Legal Culture of Quebec, 1760–1890.* Montreal: McGill Law School/Montreal Business His-tory Project 1987.

Baribeau, Claude. *La seigneurie de la Petite-Nation, 1801–1854: le rôle économique et social du seigneur.* Hull: Asticou 1983

Baudouin, Jean-Louis. *Les obligations.* Cowansville: Les éditions Yvon Blais 1993

Béchard, A. *L'honorable A.N. Morin.* Québec: *La Vérité* 1885

Bell, George Joseph. *Commentaries on the Laws of Scotland and on the Principles of Mercantile Jurisprudence.* Edinburgh: Archibald Constable and Co., 1821. 2 vol.

Bernard, Jean-Paul. *Les Rouges. libéralisme, nationalisme et anticléricalisme au milieu du XIXe siècle.* Montréal: Les presses de l'Université du Québec, 1971.

Berthoff, Rowland. 'Conventional Mentality: Free Blacks, Women, and Business Corporations as Unequal Persons, 1820–1870.' (1989), 76 *Journal of American History,* 753–84

Blackstone, William. *Commentaries on the Law of England.* London: Revised Apollo Press 1813

Bonenfant, J.C. *The French Canadians and the Birth of Confederation.* Centennial Commission Historical Booklet No. 10. Ottawa 1967

Bonner, John. *An Essay on the Registry Laws of Lower Canada.* Quebec: Lovell 1852

Bouchard, Gérard. 'Donation entre vifs et inégalités sociales au Saguenay. Sur la reproduction familiale en contexte de saturation de l'espace agraire.' (1993), 46 *Revue d'histoire de l'Amérique française,* 443–61

Bradbury, Bettina. *Working Families: Age, Gender, and Daily Survival in Industrializing Montreal.* Toronto: McClelland & Stewart 1993

Bradbury, Bettina, Peter Gossage, Evelyn Kolish, and Alan Stewart. 'Property and Marriage: The Law and the Practice in early Nineteenth Century Montreal.' (May 1993), 51 *Histoire sociale / Social History,* 9-93

Brierley, John E.C. 'The Co-existence of Legal Systems in Quebec: "Free and Common Socage" in Canada's "pays de droit civil."' (1979), 20 *Cahiers de Droit,* 277–87

– 'The English Language Tradition in Quebec Civil Law.' *L'actualité terminologique/Terminology Update,* 20, no. 6. Ottawa: Secretary of State of Canada 1987

– 'La notion de droit commun dans un système de droit mixte: le cas de la province de Québec.' In *La Formation du droit national dans les pays de droit mixte,* 104–18. Marseille: Presses universitaires d'Aix-Marseille 1989

– 'Quebec's Civil Law Codification: Viewed and Reviewed.' (1968), 14 *McGill Law Journal,* 521–89

– 'Quebec's "Common Laws" (Droits communs): How Many Are There?' *Mélanges Louis-Philippe Pigeon.* Montréal: Wilson & Lafleur 1989

– 'The Renewal of Quebec's Distinct Legal Culture: The new Civil Code of Québec.' (1992), 42 *University of Toronto Law Journal,* 484–503

Brisson, Jean-Maurice. *La formation d'un droit mixte: l'évolution de la procédure civile de 1774 à 1867*. Montréal: Thémis 1986

Buchanan, P. *The Bench and Bar of Lower Canada down to 1850*. Montreal: Burton's 1925

Buckner, Phillip A. *The Transition to Responsible Government: British Policy in British North America, 1815–1850*. Westport, Conn. 1985

Cairns, John W. 'The 1808 Digest of Orleans and 1866 Civil Code of Lower Canada: An Historical Study of Legal Change.' Unpublished PhD thesis, University of Edinburgh 1980

– 'Employment in the Civil Code of Lower Canada: Tradition and Political Economy in Legal Classification and Reform.' (July 1987), 32, no. 3 *McGill Law Journal*, 673–711

Cambacérès, Jean-Jacques Regis de. *Projet de Code Civil*. Paris: Chez Garnery An Cinquième

Carbonnier, Jean. *Droit Civil 4: Les obligations*. Paris: P.U.F. 1956

Castel, Jean-Gabriel. *The Civil Law System of the Province of Quebec: notes, cases, and materials*. Toronto: Butterworths 1962

Cook, Charles M. *The American Codification Movement: A Study of Antebellum Legal Reform*. Westport, Conn.: Greenwood Press 1981

Cooper, John I. 'The Political Ideas of George-Etienne Cartier.' *Canadian Historical Association Report*, 1942, 286–94

Curtis, Bruce. *Building the Educational State: Canada West, 1836–1871*. London: Althouse Press 1988

Curzon, L.B. *English Legal History*. Plymouth: Macdonald and Evans 1968

Danylewycz, Marta. *Taking the Veil: An Alternative to Marriage, Motherhood, and Spinsterhood in Quebec, 1840–1920*. Toronto: McClelland and Stewart 1987

Dechêne, Louise. 'L'évolution du régime seigneurial au Canada: le cas de Montréal aux XVIIe et XVIIIe siècles.' (mai-août 1971), 12, no. 2 *Recherches sociographiques*, 143–83

– *Habitants and Merchants in Seventeenth Century Montreal*. 1974; Kingston & Montreal: McGill-Queen's 1992

– 'La rente du faubourg Saint-Roch à Québec – 1750–1850.' (mars 1981) 34, no. 4 *Revue d'histoire de l'Amérique française*, 569–96

Dépatie, Sylvie. 'La transmission du patrimoine dans les terroirs en expansion: un exemple canadien au XVIIIe siècle.' (automne 1990), 44, no. 2 *Revue d'histoire de l'Amérique française*, 171–98

Dépatie, Sylvie, Christian Dessureault, et Mario Lalancette. *Contributions à l'étude du régime seigneurial canadien*. Montréal, Hurtubise HMH 1987

Desjardins, Pauline, 'La coutume de Paris et la transmission des terres – le rang de la Beauce à Calixa-Lavallée de 1730 à 1975.' (décembre 1980) 34, no. 3 *Revue d'histoire de l'Amérique française*, 331–39

Dessureault, Christian. 'L'égalitarisme paysan dans l'ancienne société rurale de la vallée du St. Laurent: éléments pour une ré-interprétation.' (hiver 1987), 40, no. 3 *Revue d'histoire de l'Amérique française*, 373–408

Dickinson, John A. *Justice et justiciables: la procédure civile à la prévôté de Québec, 1667–1759.* Québec: Presses de l'université Laval 1982

– 'La justice seigneuriale en Nouvelle-France: le cas de Notre-Dame-des-Anges.' (décembre 1974), 28, no. 3 *Revue d'histoire de l'Amérique française*, 323–46

– *Law in New France.* Winnipeg: University of Manitoba Canadian Legal History Project 1992

Dictionary of Canadian Biography/Dictionnaire biographique du Canada. Edited by George Brown, Marcel Trudel, et al. 13 vols to date. Toronto and Quebec: University of Toronto Press and Les Presses de l'université Laval 1964-

Domat, Jean. *Civil Law in its Natural Order.* 1694; Boston: Little, Brown and Co. 1861

Doughty, A.G., ed. *The Elgin-Grey Papers, 1846–52.* 4 vols. Ottawa: King's Printer 1937

Doutre, Gonzalve. 'Les lois de la procédure civile.' (1869), 6 *Revue canadienne*, 481-9

El-Gammal, Mostapha Mohamad. *L'adaptation du contrat aux circonstances économiques: étude comparée de droit civil français et de droit civil de la République arabe unie.* Paris: Pichon et Durand-Auzias 1967

Eörsi, Gyula. *Comparative Civil (Private) Law: Law Types, Law Groups, The Roads of Legal Development.* Budapest: Akadémiai Kiadó 1979

Fecteau, Jean-Marie. *L'émergence de l'idéal coopératif et l'état au Québec, 1850–1914.* Montréal: UQAM 1989

– *Un nouvel ordre des choses: la pauvreté, le crime, l'état au Québec, de la fin du XVIIIᵉ siècle à 1840.* Montréal: vlb 1989

Fenet, Pierre-Antoine. *Naissance du code civil An VIII–an XII – 1800–1804.* Edited by François Ewald. Paris: Flammarion 1989

Flaherty, David. *Essays in the History of Canadian Law.* 2 vols. Toronto: University of Toronto Press 1981, 1983

Friedman, Lawrence. *A History of American Law.* New York: Simon and Schuster 1985

Frost, Stanley B. 'The Early Days of Teaching at McGill.' (June 1985), 9, no. 2 *Dalhousie Law Journal*, 150–57

Galarneau, Claude. *La France devant l'opinion canadienne (1760–1815).* Québec: Les Presses de l'Université Laval 1970

George, Peter, and Philip Sworden. 'The Courts and the Development of Trade in Upper Canada, 1830–1860.' (Summer 1986), 60 *Business History Review*, 258–80

Girard, Philip. 'Themes and Variations in Early Canadian Legal Culture: Bearmish Murdoch and his "Epitome of the Laws of Nova Scotia."' (Spring 1993), 11, no. 1 *Law and History Review*, 101–44

Girouard, Désiré. *Considérations sur les lois civiles de mariage*. Montréal: Nouveau Monde 1868

Goyard-Fabre, Simone. 'Montesquieu entre Domat et Portalis.' (1990), 35, no. 4 *McGill Law Journal*, 715–45

Greenwood, Murray F. 'The Chartrand Murder Trial: Rebellion and Repression in Lower Canada, 1837–1839.' (1984), V *Criminal Justice History*, 129–59

– *From Higher Morality to Autonomous Will: The Transformation of Quebec's Civil Law, 1774–1866*. Winnipeg: University of Manitoba Canadian Legal History Project 1992

– 'The General Court Martial of 1838–39 in Lower Canada: An Abuse of Justice.' In *Canadian Perspectives on Law and Society: Issues in Legal History*, edited by Wesley Pue and Barry Wright, 249–90. Ottawa: Carleton University Press 1988

– *Legacies of Fear: Law and Politics in Quebec in the Era of the French Revolution*. Toronto: The Osgoode Society 1993

Greer, Allan. *Peasant, Lord and Merchant: Rural Society in Three Quebec Parishes 1740–1840*. Toronto: University of Toronto Press 1985

Griswold, Robert. 'Divorce and the Legal Redefinition of Victorian Manhood.' In Mark C. Carnes and Clyde Griffen, *Meanings for Manhood: Constructions of Masculinity in Victorian America*, 96–110. Chicago and London: University of Chicago Press 1990

Grossberg, Michael. *Governing the Hearth: Law and the Family in Nineteenth-Century America*. Chapel Hill: University of North Carolina Press 1985

– 'Institutionalizing Masculinity: The Law as a Masculine Profession.' In Mark C. Carnes and Clyde Griffen, *Meanings for Manhood: Constructions of Masculinity in Victorian America*, 133–51. Chicago: University of Chicago Press 1990

Guyot. *Répertoire universel et raisonné de jurisprudence civile, criminelle, canonique et bénéficiale* ... vol. 17. Paris 1785

Halperin, Jean-Louis. *L'impossible Code civil*. Paris: P.U.F. 1992

Hanawalt, Barbara, ed. *Women and Work in Preindustrial Europe*. Bloomington: Indiana University Press 1986

Harris, R. Cole. 'Of Poverty and Helplessness in Petite Nation.' In *Canadian History before Confederation: Essays and Interpretations*, edited by Jack Bumsted, 329–54. Georgetown: Irwin-Dorsey, 1979

– *The Seigneurial System in Early Canada*. Kingston and Montreal, McGill-Queen's University Press 1984

Harvey, Kathryn. '"To Love, Honour and Obey": Wife-battering in Working-Class Montreal, 1869–1879.' (October 1990), X, 2 *Urban History Review*, 128–40

Holcome, Lee. *Wives and Property: Reform of the Married Women's Property Law in Nineteenth-Century England*. Toronto: University of Toronto Press 1983

Horwitz, Morton J. *The Transformation of American Law 1780–1860*. Cambridge, Harvard University Press 1977

Hovenkamp, Herbert. *Enterprise and American Law, 1836–1937*. Cambridge: Harvard University Press 1991

Howes, David. 'From Polyjurality to Monojurality: The Transformation of Quebec Law, 1875–1929.' (1987), 32, no. 3 *McGill Law Journal*, 523–58

– 'The Origin and Demise of Legal Education in Quebec (or Hercules Bound).' (1989), 38 *University of New Brunswick Law Journal*, 127–49

Imbert, Jean. *Histoire du droit privé*. Paris: P.U.F. 1950

John, Michael. 'The Peculiarities of the German State: Bourgeois Law and Society in the Imperial Era.' (May 1988), 119 *Past and Present*, 105–31

– *Politics and the Law in Late Nineteenth-Century Germany: The Origins of the Civil Code*. Oxford: Clarendon Press 1989

Johnson, Tom. 'In a Manner of Speaking: Towards a Reconstitution of Property in Mid-Nineteenth Century Quebec.' (1987), 32, no. 3 *McGill Law Journal*, 636–72

Johnson, Walter. 'Legal Education in the Province of Quebec.' (October 1905), 10 *Canadian Law Review*, 451–7; (November 1905), 11 *Canadian Law Review*, 491–99

Kasirer, Nicholas. 'Canada's Criminal Law Codification Viewed and Reviewed.' (September 1990), 35, no. 4 *McGill Law Journal*, 841–79

Kolish, Evelyn. 'Changements dans le droit privé au Québec/Bas-Canada entre 1760 et 1840: attitudes et réactions des contemporains.' Unpublished PhD thesis, Université de Montréal 1980

– 'Le Conseil législatif et les bureaux d'enregistrement (1836).' (septembre 1981), 35, no. 2 *Revue d'histoire de l'Amérique française*, 217–30

– 'The Impact of Change in Legal Metropolis on the Development of Lower Canada's Legal System.' (1988), 3 *Canadian Journal of Law and Society*, 1–26

– 'Imprisonment for Debt in Lower Canada, 1791–1840.' (1987), 32, no. 3 *McGill Law Journal*, 559–601

– *Nationalismes et conflits économiques: Le débat sur le droit privé au Québec, 1760–1840*. Montréal: HMH 1994

– 'Some Aspects of Civil Litigation in Lower Canada, 1785–1825: Towards the Use of Court Records for Canadian Social History.' (1989), 70, no. 3 *Canadian Historical Review*, 337–65

Kouri, Robert P., et al. *Private Law Dictionary and Bilingual Lexicons*. 2nd ed. Cowansville: Les Éditions Yvon Blais 1991

Laing Hogg, Grace. 'The Legal Rights of Masters, Mistresses, and Domestic Servants in Montreal, 1816–29.' Unpublished MA thesis, McGill University 1990

Lamonde, Yvan, and Daniel Olivier. *Les bibliothèques personnelles au Québec*. Montréal: Bibliothèque nationale du Québec 1983

Langelier, F. *Cours de droit civil*, vol. 1. Montreal: Wilson and Lafleur 1905

Larue, Richard. 'Code Napoléon et codification des lois civiles au Bas-Canada: notes sur le problème de l'égalité.' In *Le Canada et la Révolution française*, edited by Pierre Boulle et Richard A. Lebrun, 147–61. Montréal: Interuniversity Centre for European Studies 1989

Lavallée, Louis. *La Prairie en Nouvelle-France, 1647–1760*. Montreal and Kingston: McGill-Queen's University Press 1992

Lebsock, Suzanne. *The Free Women of Petersburg: Status and Culture in a Southern Town, 1784–1860*. New York: Norton 1984

Linteau, Paul-André, and Jean-Claude Robert. 'Land Ownership and Society in Montreal: An Hypothesis.' In *The Canadian City: Essays in Urban History*, edited by G. Stelter and A. Artibise. Toronto: McClelland and Stewart 1977

Little, J.I. *Ethno-Cultural Transition and Regional Identity in the Eastern Townships of Quebec*. Ottawa: Canadian Historical Association 1989

– 'The Short Life of a Protest Movement: The Annexation Crisis of 1849–50 in the Eastern Townships.' (1992), new ser., 3 *Journal of the Canadian Historical Association/Revue de la société historique du Canada*, 45–67

Loranger, Thomas-Jean-Jacques. *Commentaire sur le code civil du Bas-Canada*. 2 vols. Montréal: A.E. Brassard 1873–9

Lorimier, Charles-Chamilly de. *La bibliothèque du code civil de la province de Québec*. Montréal: La Minerve 1871

McCord, Thomas. *The Civil Code of Lower Canada*. Montreal: Dawson 1867

Macdonald, R.St.J. 'Maximilien Bibaud, 1823–1887: The Pioneer Teacher of International Law in Canada.' (March 1988), 11, no. 2 *Dalhousie Law Journal*, 721–43

Macdonald, Roderick A. 'The National Law Programme at McGill: Origins, Establishment, Prospects.' (May 1990), 13, no. 1 *Dalhousie Law Journal*, 211–363

– 'Understanding Civil Law Scholarship in Quebec.' (1985), 23, no. 4 *Osgoode Hall Law Journal*, 573–608

Macpherson, C.B. *Property: Mainstream and Critical Positions*. Toronto: University of Toronto Press 1978

Mann, Bruce H. *Neighbors and Strangers: Law and Community in Early Connecticut*. Chapel Hill: University of North Carolina Press 1987

Marty, Gabriel, and Pierre Raynaud. *Droit civil: Les obligations*. vol. 1. Paris: Sirey 1988

Michel, Louis. 'Un marchand rural en Nouvelle-France – François-Augustin Bailly de Messein, 1709–1771.' (1979), 33, no. 2 *Revue d'histoire de l'Amérique française*, 215–62

Monet, Jacques. *The Last Cannon Shot: A Study of French-Canadian Nationalism, 1837–1850*. Toronto: University of Toronto Press 1969

Montesquieu, Charles Louis de Secondat. *The Spirit of the Laws*. 1748; Cambridge: Cambridge University Press 1989

Montigny, B.-A. Testard de. 'Du mariage et du divorce.' *La Thémis*, novembre 1879 – janvier 1880, 289–367

– *Histoire du droit canadien*. Montréal 1869

Morel, André. 'La codification devant l'opinion publique de l'époque.' In *Livre du centenaire du Code civil*, edited by Jacques Boucher et André Morel, 27–45. Montréal: Presses de l'Université de Montréal 1970

– *Les limites de la liberté testamentaire dans le droit civil de la province de Québec*. Paris: R. Pichon et R. Durand-Auzias 1960

– 'Réflexions sur la justice criminelle, au 18e siècle.' (1975), 29, no. 2 *Revue d'histoire de l'Amérique française*, 241–53

Morin, Michel. 'La perception de l'ancien droit et du nouveau droit français au Bas-Canada, 1774–1866.' In *Droit québécois et droit français: communauté, autonomie, concordance*, edited by Patrick Glenn, 1–41. Cowansville: Les Éditions Yvon Blais 1993

Neatby, Hilda. *The Administration of Justice under the Quebec Act*. Minneapolis: University of Minnesota Press 1937

Nelson, Wendie. 'The "Guerre des Éteignoirs": School Reform and Popular Resistance in Lower Canada, 1841–1850.' Unpublished MA thesis, Simon Fraser University 1989

Newmyer, R. Kent. *Supreme Court Justice Joseph Story: Statesman of the Old Republic*. Chapel Hill and London: University of North Carolina Press 1985

Nicholas, Barry. *French Law of Contract*. London: Butterworths 1982

Nish, Cameron. *François-Étienne Cugnet, entrepreneur et entreprises en Nouvelle-France*. Montréal: Fides 1975

Noël, Françoise. *The Christie Seigneuries. Estate Management and Settlement in the Upper Richelieu Valley, 1760–1854*. Montreal and Kingston: McGill-Queen's University Press 1992

Normand, Sylvio. 'La codification de 1866: contexte et impact.' In *Droit québécois et droit français: communauté, autonomie, concordance*, edited by Patrick Glenn, 43–62. Cowansville: Les Éditions Yvon Blais 1993

– 'Un thème dominant de la pensée juridique traditionnelle au Québec: la sauvegarde de l'intégrité du droit civil.' (July 1987), 32 *McGill Law Journal*, 559–601

Normand, Sylvio, and Alain Hudon. 'Le contrôle des hypothèques secrètes au XIXe siècle: ou la difficile conciliation de deux cultures juridiques et de deux communautés ethniques.' (1990), *Recueil de droit immobilier*, 171–201

Olivier-Martin, Fr. *Histoire du droit français des origines à la Révolution*. 1948; Paris: CNRS 1984

Ouellet, Fernand. *Éléments d'histoire sociale du Bas-Canada*. Montréal: HMH 1972
– *Lower Canada, 1791–1840: Social Change and Nationalism*. Toronto: McClelland and Stewart 1980
– *Papineau*. Québec: Les presses de l'université Laval 1970
– 'Toussaint Pothier et le problème des classes sociales (1829).' (1955), 61, no. 4 *Bulletin des recherches historiques*, 147–59
Ourliac, Paul. *Histoire du droit privé français de l'An mil au code civil*. Paris: Albin Michel 1985
Paradis, Jean-Marc. 'Augustin-Norbert Morin (1803–1865).' Unpublished PhD thesis, Université Laval 1989
Parizeau, Gérard. *La vie studieuse et obstinée de Denis-Benjamin Viger*. Montréal: Fides 1980
Parker, David. 'Sovereignty, Absolutism and the Function of Law in Seventeenth-Century France.' (February 1989), 122 *Past and Present*, 36–74
Petot, Pierre. *Histoire du droit privé français: La famille*. Paris: Éditions Loysel 1992
Picard, Nathalie. 'Les femmes et le vote au Bas-Canada de 1792 à 1849.' Unpublished MA thesis, Université de Montréal 1992
Portalis, Jean-Étienne-Marie. *Discours, rapports, et travaux inédits sur le code civil*. Paris: Joubert 1844
Pothier, Robert Joseph. *Oeuvres de Pothier*. vol. 13. Paris 1823
– *Treatise on the Contract of Sale*. Boston: Little and Brown 1839
– *A Treatise on Obligations Considered in a Moral and Legal View*. Newbern, N.C.: Martin and Ogden 1802
Poutanen, Mary-Anne. 'For the Benefit of the Master: The Montreal Needle Trades During the Transition 1820–1842.' Unpublished MA thesis, McGill University 1986
Rabkin, Peggy. 'The Origins of Law Reform: The Social Significance of the Nineteenth-Century Codification Movement and Its Contribution to the Passage of the Early Married Women's Property Acts.' (1974–5), 24 *Buffalo Law Review*, 683–760
Risk, R.C.B. 'The Last Golden Age: Property and the Allocation of Losses in Ontario in the Nineteenth Century.' (1977), 27 *University of Toronto Law Journal*, 199–239
Robert, Jean-Claude. 'Un seigneur entrepreneur, Barthélemy Joliette, et la fondation du village d'Industrie (Joliette).' (1972), 26, no. 3 *Revue d'histoire de l'Amérique française*, 375–96
Robinson, O.E., T.D. Fergus, and W.M. Gordon. *An Introduction to European Legal History*. Abingdon: Professional Books 1985

Rogers, C. Paul III. 'Scots Law in Post-Revolutionary and Nineteenth-Century America: The Neglected Jurisprudence.' (1990), 8, no. 2 *Law and History Review*, 205–36

Romney, Paul. *Mr. Attorney: The Attorney General for Ontario in Court, Cabinet, and Legislature 1791–1899*. Toronto: Osgoode Society 1986

Roy, Pierre-Georges. *Les juges de la province de Québec*. Québec: Rédempti Paradis 1933

Ste Croix, G.E.M. de. *The Class Struggle in the Ancient Greek World*. London: Duckworth 1981

St-George, Lise. 'Commerce, crédit et transactions foncières: pratiques de la communauté marchande du bourg de l'Assomption, 1748–1791.' (1986), 39, no. 3 *Revue d'histoire de l'Amérique franççaise*, 323–44

Salmon, Marylynn. *Women and the Law of Property in Early America*. Chapel Hill: University of North Carolina Press 1986

Shanley, Mary Lyndon. *Feminism, Marriage, and the Law in Victorian England*. Princeton: Princeton University Press 1989

Snell, James G. *In the Shadow of the Law: Divorce in Canada, 1900–1939*. Toronto: University of Toronto Press 1991

Snell, James G., and Frederick Vaughan. *The Supreme Court of Canada: History of the Institution*. Toronto: The Osgoode Society 1985

Stair, James, Viscount of. *The Institutions of the Law of Scotland deduced from its originals and collated with the civil, canon and feudal laws ...* Edinburgh: Bell and Bradfute 1832

Staves, Susan. *Married Women's Separate Property in England, 1660–1833*. Cambridge: Harvard University Press 1990

Stewart, Alan M. 'Settling an 18th Century Faubourg: Property and Family in the Saint-Laurent Suburb, 1735–1810.' Unpublished MA thesis, McGill University 1988

Stewart, Alan M., and Bettina Bradbury. 'Marriage Contracts as a Source for Historians.' In *Class, Gender and the Law in Eighteenth- and Nineteenth-Century Quebec*, edited by D. Fyson, C. Coates, and K. Harvey, 29–54. Montreal: Montreal History Group 1993

Stewart, Gordon. *The Origins of Canadian Politics*. Vancouver: University of British Columbia Press 1986

Subrin, Stephen N. 'David Dudley Field and the Field Code: A Historical Analysis of an Earlier Procedural Vision.' (1988), 6, no. 2 *Law and History Review*, 311–74

Sweeny, Robert. *Les relations ville/campagne: le cas du bois de chauffage*. Montreal: Montreal Business History Project 1988

Sylvain, Philippe, and Nive Voisine. *Histoire du catholicisme québécois*. vol. II: *Réveil et consolidation (1840–1898)*. Montréal: Boréal Express 1991

Taschereau, Sylvie. 'Les petits commerçants de l'alimentation et les milieux populaires montréalais, 1920–1940.' Unpublished PhD thesis, Université du Québec à Montréal 1992

Thompson, E.P. *Whigs and Hunters: The Origin of the Black Act*. Middlesex: Penguin 1975

Tomlins, Christopher L. *Law, Labor, and Ideology in the Early American Republic*. Cambridge: Cambridge University Press 1993

Tunc, André. 'The Grand Outlines of the Code.' In *The Code Napoleon and the Common-Law World*, edited by B. Schwartz. New York: NYU Press 1956

Veilleux, Christine. 'Les gens de justice à Québec, 1760–1867.' Unpublished PhD thesis, Université Laval 1990

Vovelle, Michel, ed. *La révolution et l'ordre juridique privé: rationalité ou scandale*. Actes du colloque d'Orléans, septembre 1986. 2 vols. Paris: P.U.F. 1988

Wallot, Jean-Pierre. *Un Québec qui bougeait: trame socio-politique au tournant du XIXe siècle*. Trois-Rivières: Boréal Express 1973

Whitman, James Q. *The Legacy of Roman Law in the German Romantic Era*. Princeton: Princeton University Press 1990

Young, Brian. 'The Business of Law in Missisquoi and the District of Bedford before 1861.' (1990), 20 *Proceedings of the Missisquoi Historical Society*, 10–24

– 'Dimensions of a Law Practice: Brokerage and Ideology in the Career of George-Etienne Cartier.' In *Beyond the Law: Lawyers and Business in Canada, 1830 to 1930*, edited by Carol Wilton, 92–111. Toronto: Osgoode Society 1990

– *George-Étienne Cartier: Montreal Bourgeois*. Kingston and Montreal: McGill-Queen's University Press 1981

– 'Getting around Legal Incapacity: The Legal Status of Married Women in Trade in Mid Nineteenth Century Lower Canada.' In *Canadian Papers in Business History*, 1–16. Victoria: University of Victoria 1989

– *In its Corporate Capacity: The Seminary of Montreal as a Business Institution, 1816–1876*. Kingston and Montreal: McGill-Queen's University Press 1986

– 'Law in the Round.' (Autumn 1986), *Acadiensis*, 155–165

Zoltvany, Yves. 'Esquisse de la Coutume de Paris.' (1971), 25, no. 3 *Revue d'histoire de l'Amérique française*, 365–84

Index

Picture Credits and Sources

British Museum: Thomas Rowlandson, 'The Contrast,' 1793 (DG8204, negative P5067460)

McCord Museum of Canadian History, Notman Photographic Archives: George-Étienne Cartier (7956–1, photo by W. Notman), François-Maximilien Bibaud (2572–1), Charles Dewey Day (15,318–1, photo by W. Notman), Codification Commission (MP1815[2], photograph by Livernois), Commission's Offices (17,501–Misc. 1, John Street, Quebec City, 1865), Legal Chambers (77380–II, Mr Cherrier's Office, 1885), Université Laval (MP1157–8, photographer unknown); Prints and Drawings: Seigneurial Court (M5524, by William Lockwood)

McGill University Law Library: *Code rural*, 1832

Musée de l'Amérique française: villa 'Clermont,' Sillery (painting by Joseph Légaré, photo by Patrick Altman, 1980)

National Archives of Canada: René-Édouard Caron (C49561, photo by W. Notman), Jonathan Sewell (C111156, painting by Théophile Hamel); Denis-Benjamin Viger (C6070, lithograph by C. Hamburger); Joseph-François Perrault (C21961, woodcut printed in *L'opinion publique*, 4 January 1872); 'Hanging the Patriotes at the Montreal Jail' (C13493, by Henri Julien); Sweetsburg (National Map Collection 14737)

Private Collections: District of Bedford Courthouse (author); Civil Code at Napoleon's Tomb (photo by Julien Leloup)

Archives du Séminaire de Saint-Hyacinthe: Justice Morin's Library; statuette of Augustin-Norbert Morin by Philippe Hébert

PUBLICATIONS OF THE OSGOODE SOCIETY
FOR CANADIAN LEGAL HISTORY